The Academic Pattern

The Academic Pattern

A Comparison between Researchers and
Non-Researchers, Men and Women

*Gunnar Boalt, University of Stockholm and
Southern Illinois University*

Herman Lantz, Southern Illinois University

Helena Herlin, University of Stockholm

Almqvist & Wiksell · Stockholm

Printed in Sweden by

Almqvist & Wiksell Informationsindustri AB

Uppsala 1973

Contents

PART ONE
by Herman Lantz

CHAPTER 1

The scientific role in the context of Swedish society

The study of the behavior of scientists in relation to the research process, including their productivity, and the relationship of sociological variables involved in research and productivity are emerging as an important area of study. Such investigations suggest the neglected, but significant, role which sociological variables play in scientific output. The stereotype of the scientist as one unaffected by interpersonal events is naive and oversimplified. Not only is he influenced by events around him, but he must work out patterns that enable him to deal with his scientific life and his interpersonal life (1). In dealing with the question of research and career in the context of Sweden it might be useful to think first in terms of some broad macroscopic factors that are involved.

The scientific role

First, Swedish society has a history in which science has a lengthy tradition (2). Science was accepted and established in the preindustrial period; with the advent of industrialization the prestige of the scientific role became even more institutionalized and imbued with significance. With regard to the present, the physical and natural sciences, including medical sciences, are well developed, and Swedish research in these areas is highly valued in Sweden and respected throughout the world. The "fall out" of such prestige has carried over into the social and behavioral sciences, as well.

A second point to be noted is that science and social planning are perhaps more interrelated in Sweden than in most western societies, although the extent of the relationship, and the amount of influence, might vary

from one scientific field to another. Thus, the scientific role would seem to carry considerable appeal for people in Sweden, and one finds that a significant number seek a career in science. For those who are successful, who achieve the appropriate degrees and attain a professorial rank, there are significant rewards. Not only at the prestige level in the abstract, but in practical ways as well. There are rewards, salary, opportunities for publishing and for membership in research councils. It is significant to note, however, that only a comparative few achieve this level for at least one major reason.

Structural blockage

We may have a situation in which Swedish science has not expanded at a rate sufficient to accommodate those who seek the scientific role (3). Thus, we may have a case in which one sector of the social structure values a professional role very highly, while another sector of the society does not, namely the support of scientific development has not kept pace with the number of people who are perhaps sufficiently competent and capable of fulfilling the scientific role. The result of the split between the high status of the scientific role and the limited number of commensurate openings has led to serious difficulties for those who have such aspirations. This development is aggravated still further by the fact that persons considered competent in the scientific role a decade or two ago when scientific skills were less readily available, now may be replaced by persons more competently trained. These numbers add to others, more recently trained, who cannot be accommodated.

While sociologists have developed analytic devices for explaining the consequences of blockage in the opportunity structure, these studies have almost always dealt with populations denied opportunity because of limited education, class, race, or religion. The case in Sweden is especially interesting since one is dealing with blocked opportunity for special reasons not related to conventional social discrimination, but related possibly to the size and needs of Swedish society. This kind of problem is noted in both Sweden and in the Soviet Union, societies in which poverty essentially has been eliminated. It does highlight another problem, however, namely the complexities of economic and social planning. Certainly, one can anticipate consequences in Sweden.

A first such consequence is noted in the major outlet for scientists, the university. Here some of the underlying tensions and competitiveness can

be brought into perspective. Observers of Swedish academic life seem to suggest that much of the interpersonal strife within academic departments is due to the discrepancy between career aspirations and available opportunities.

Such problems, difficult for men, may be especially difficult for Swedish female scientists. Swedish society has generally espoused an ideology of equality between the sexes, an ideology which presumably applied to the occupations and professions. Given a context in which opportunities for fulfillment of the scientific role are limited, women may, indeed, fare less well than men. Under such circumstances, one may ask, how are female scientists selected? What happens to those who are blocked in the opportunity structure and how do women deal with these problems? (4). We shall address ourselves to some of these matters in a subsequent chapter.

Scientist and technician

A second consequence of blockage might be manifest in what appears to be a high degree of technical competence which characterizes Swedish science. We must distinguish between the scientist and the technician. The scientist is identified not only by an awareness of method, including how data is dealt with and manipulated, but he is also one who is sufficiently liberated so that his creative energies can find expression. To be a scientist one needs a careful balance of technique, vision, and openness, all brought to bear on the conception of a problem, its execution and final resolution. Probably only a small percentage of people who claim to be functioning as scientists actually are. A far greater number function as technicians, in spite of advanced degrees. These are people, highly skilled, capable of utilizing quantitative techniques. They are processors of data rather than creators of data. As such, they are passive, both controlled and led by the data, but often unable to go beyond it. What frequently is covered under the norm of science, objectivity, for example, is more often a fear of "letting go". Although all scientists are in some sense technicians, not all technicians are scientists. Thus, it becomes necessary to think of people in terms of their capacity for scientific endeavor. A discussion of the technician in all branches of science would be a presumptuous undertaking in a manuscript of this kind. But the authors can speak with some confidence about the existence of a high degree of technical competence in Swedish social and

9

behavioral science. Such competence may well be a function of the re-allocation of basically scientific talent into functions involving technical competence. Such a development, if correct, could have several outcomes. It could serve to channel talent, that might be blocked, into socially productive technical roles necessary for science. As such, it could be an important factor in the development of science in Sweden. Nevertheless, there are difficulties. One notes, for example, that the subordination of the scientific role might be frustrating but tolerable if one were to believe that his or her efforts as a technician do have a significant relationship to the programs of social planning in the broader society. To what extent do Swedish social and behavioral technicians see their work as having an impact? This is a matter still to be understood and studied. If planning agencies in Sweden are like planning agencies in other societies, one could have serious doubts about the use which planning agencies make of contributions from the social and behavioral fields. On the other hand, it is important to note that to the extent persons see their work as having little bearing on what happens in society, they may come to feel alienated from their society and their work roles.

One wonders whether our comments directed to the role of the Swedish scientists and technicians may not have a broader relationship to Swedish society. Do we have a context here in which creative energy in other areas of life is in a constant process of accommodation? In this regard some facets of life in Sweden do begin to take on meaning. First, one is impressed with the orderliness of Swedish work roles and one is impressed by the way in which people in different positions go about their tasks. Each following his own role, each working for relatively small goals and small rewards. For many of these people one has the sense of a constricted role, doing little to offend, but with controlled anger and frustration, living an existence of safety at a very high price, the cost often being the suppression of creative energies.

Secondly, one is impressed by the fact that large sections of Swedish society are characterized by a pattern of controlling and managing feelings, this in spite of occasional social protests (5). One finds such patterns in personal and social dealings with Swedish people. Feelings do run deep, but there is a good deal of "holding back", of not revealing oneself to another. The sense of humor is kept under check and balance. Bodily weight appears to be managed and controlled. One suspects, for example, that bodily overweight is much less a problem in Sweden than in the U.S.

The creative element

Dramatically opposite, indeed side by side, are the Swedish creative contributions both in science and medicine, but more interesting may be the contributions to art, drama, and the film. Here one finds much that is avant garde. The modern, surrealist art of Sweden and the themes of the greats such as Ingmar Bergman reveal a very different trend. It is not simply a matter of creating new art forms which is of significance, but a sensitivity to the basic enduring problems of mankind which is also present. Note, for example, that the great American playwright, Eugene O'Neill, was well recognized and appreciated in Sweden long before he was in his own country. And that, perhaps his most important play, "Long Day's Journey into Night" was produced first in Stockholm. How does one explain a pattern of constriction and accommodation along with significant patterns of emancipation in art, drama, and interpersonal relationships?

A first reason is that one can find a condition of opposites within all social forms and social structures. And it is precisely this polarization which accounts for social change. Thus, in the Swedish case it could be argued that those creative and avant garde movements represent efforts to break out and transcend the constricted and accommodating aspects of life in Sweden.

A second major reason for these contradictory trends has specifically to do with the problems of a postindustrial society. Sweden, as the most affluent society in Europe, is beginning to experience some of the problems of the postindustrial age, an age where the basic material and sustenance needs are fulfilled but where a new priority of difficulties are experienced. Affluence is not synonomous with self-fulfillment. The satisfaction of the material necessities encompasses problems of existence and survival, while the problems of selffulfillment represent being and living. The problem of existence can be dealt with more readily than the problem of living. The problem of working out meaningful work and professional roles in a society which is affluent may take a long time and may never be solved. In between it is very possible that a lag will exist between work roles that are meaningful and satisfying in the personal sense and the goals and priorities which a society is capable of visualizing and implementing during any given period. Herein lies one of the basic sources of alienation in the postindustrial era (6). Moreover, such a lag may become more pronounced as a society prepares people for the possibility of meaningful work roles, but it is also unable to provide sufficient outlets for the development of such roles. Note that

11

the problem is not one of economic employment as such. The problem is rather one of believing that what one does is both personally and socially relevant. Thus, we can ask what do people seek once the basic problems of material necessity have been resolved. In the more global sense, search for meaning to one's life, personal fulfillment in one's professional role, and fulfillment as a person. This quest for the meaning of things has been thrust upon Sweden on a rather grand scale and neither Sweden nor any society is wholly prepared to deal with these matters. A problem of such magnitude is one many societies may face in the future. The inability to resolve these difficulties may well produce more personal and social pathology than we have had during earlier periods of industrialization. So long as people are concerned with basic economic problems and related problems of social security, then the reason for being becomes absorbed with these goals and energies. Once economic problems are resolved, the reason for being has to be found in another search. The ultimate purpose and goal of social welfare in Sweden, or elsewhere, is to make life more meaningful and significant, to enable the person to achieve goals of self-realization which could not readily be found so long as he was bogged down with material fears. In Sweden for the first time large masses of people can be sufficiently free to search for personally fulfilling goals and it is ironic that such success at the material level may usher in the most profound problems at the interpersonal level (7).

One significant search for meaning in Sweden is to be found in efforts to handle the basic problems of interpersonal relationships in new and different ways. One can, for example, examine the Swedish tendency to be different from many, not only in personal-social and sexual matters, but also in political and economic matters. Their responses may not be a mere accident, but may well be an integral part of their sympathy and appreciation for those people who wish to work out their problems and their lives in different ways, in ways that do not necessarily please all groups. For, indeed, this acceptance of differences in others also implies an acceptance of their right to be different.

Sex, marriage and the family

In regard to sex, a subject frequently misunderstood and distorted, one has to look for the larger meaning. It is important to note that in these relationships there is a quest for the most important components of

human experience, closeness, love, warmth, and mutual respect. While a superficial view suggests to some a pattern of promiscuity, anyone who has seriously studied Sweden recognizes that "love is not for anyone". Here we find an effort to locate meaning and purpose to life by transcending the conventional puritanical, and often hypocritical, ways of looking at sexual relationships. Yet there are always consequences to such boldness and creativity. If a society wishes to explore new patterns of sexual relationships, how may this be done? Does anyone really know, are there formulas to follow? (8) Thus, to chart new courses in these unexplored areas carried with it unintended effects, perhaps promiscuity among some sections of the population. On the other hand, do we not have such problems in almost every society? As societies become less concerned with the problem of economic security and turn to the man–woman relationship for meaning the possibilities for both greater destructiveness and constructiveness can emerge. And while there may be periods of consequences which are not conducive to constructive man–woman relationships, we must poise this question. Does the society relatively unencumbered by problems of economic security, a society in which the woman is less likely to be victimized as a result of her economic plight, offer a woman a better chance for a constructive relationship with a man, than more conventional societies? If one answers affirmatively, it could be argued that the more pronounced problems of promiscuity and pornography (whatever they are) may be only a transitional phenomena (9).

The family

Much of what we have said concerning the search for meaning and purpose is applicable to some aspects of family life in Sweden. The Swedish family is perhaps the best illustration of a family that to a large extent does not have to remain together for economic reasons. Thus, they are in the throes of the significant challenge of the postindustrial era. The need to find some meaning and purpose to human relationships within the family in a society that has increasingly less social and religious support for the institution itself creates many difficulties. Here the cumulative tensions generated by the broader society and the frustration in roles, often career roles, become manifest. A major problem for the family is one of enabling individuals to achieve a sense of integration so that they can lead both meaningful and productive lives. Yet the per-

sonal and emotional demands made upon family relationships are so enormous that few are capable of doing very much with them. There are difficulties for several reasons. First, we have already noted the problem of restricted career opportunities for women in a society which espouses equality. Secondly, and most important, is the fact that while marriage and the family carry with them burdens and difficulties, they also carry with them benefits. Thus, in the best kind of marital relationship the women could look forward to emotional support from husband and children. In a poor marriage, however, she can look forward to her husband's needs for emotional support, her own needs for emotional support, her children's needs for emotional support, all within a context of a marital system going through change. No family system has evolved at a point where it can absorb the frustration individuals feel on the outside while caring for the realization of individual personalities within the home.

A major question that societies like Sweden will have to deal with has to do with the purpose and function of the family; certainly the reasons for family life are not for simple sexual arrangements. Is the family to remain a relationship whose major function is one of care and socialization of children? Is the family to provide an opportunity for the fulfillment and self-realization of adult personalities. If the answer is largely the latter, then those functions of child-rearing may be taken over by outside agencies in combination with the family. If the functions include both the care for children and self-realization of personalities of children and adults, then the burdens on the stability of the unit will be formidable, indeed.

Emotional involvements

While there is a search for meaningful relationships both within a family context and outside, emotional involvement for the Swedish person is at best troublesome. First in the process of developing new and different relationships, the relationships one has can become extremely fragile and tenuous. For people who are uncertain about the future, the management of one's life becomes a necessity. Resources have to be maximized because you never know when they will disappear. One has to guard against overinvolvement with one person or group since this always carries with it imbalance in other spheres of life. Thus, the questions of loyalties can always constitute a problem. What is the price one must pay for loyalty? Often it may result in the loss of other resources.

14

A second reason why the emotional involvements is precarious is that there is always an ongoing emotional burden of managing the involvements one already has, while searching for still more because so few are really satisfying. Thus, there can be an ongoing pattern of using people for emotional support and reassurance, of rejecting people, and of searching for still more people. These activities may apply both within and outside the family. In all these pursuits the human relationship which has the greatest potential for human fullfillment remains the most fragile. It is both sought and also feared. As such, the human relationship is the most vulnerable to being ignored, and postponed at times, while at other times it is the most vulnerable to manipulation. These basic human problems involving the search for meaning both in one's self and through some relationship with others operate within some set of patterns, reactions, and consequences, but we are so inexperienced and so uninformed that it will probably take long periods of time before the mistakes and the human consequences and costs are fully understood.

Given the difficulties faced by Swedish society in the areas we have discussed one wonders about the response to these problems on the part of Swedish social and behavioral scientists. Have they responded with studies in these areas? In a separate section of the appendix of this book, a trend report and analysis about Swedish youth may be found.

Family and career

In the opening sections of this presentation we tried to deal with certain rather broad basic patterns which seem to characterize some contemporary sections of Swedish society. It is within this context that we might try to examine the relationship between one's career, one's research and a significant aspect of one's life, the family. As has been suggested earlier many aspects of Swedish society are goal oriented and orderly. At the personal and interpersonal level there is both a need and a desire for management, management of one's personal and social life, management of stresses and tensions. The ideal achievement would be maximum satisfaction of all goals, that is, fulfillment of one's ambitions, minimum stresses, and fulfillment in one's personal and social life. It could take the form of trying to achieve maximum rewards from the scientific role and maximum rewards from family roles as well. However, such achievement is seldom possible. Thus, compromises have to be made, one or the other, research or the family, may be neglected. The

15

individual faced with such problems is faced with a struggle and tries to maintain some sort of balance, yet the price in the form of tension may be so great that the balance becomes impossible to continue. Thus, either the role of scientist begins to suffer, less time devoted to it, less research, fewer publications, or it might be some aspect of the family role that suffers.

Generally speaking the more identified the individual is with a particular social structure the greater the conflict in giving up the rewards from that structure. If one thinks in a purely hypothetical sense of the scientist as an individual completely dedicated to his scientific role, then his relationships with others would be minimal, permanent involvement such as marriage would be uncommon. But we know that this is seldom the case. Thus, the task becomes one of inquiring how the scientist deals with interpersonal involvements to produce maximum rewards in the scientific role and maximum rewards in the role as husband and parent or wife and parent. Such a tenuous balance between different sectors of one's life would seem to place an unusual amount of stress and tension, tension consistently in need of outlets. The fact that the scientific role is generally accorded such high status in Sweden also suggests that whenever this role is minimized in favor of other roles the psychic costs in the form of tensions must be high. Under some circumstances when the pull toward conflicting roles, career and family, becomes too great there may be a temporary or even permanent rejection of either role and an escape into drink, sex, or other forms of narcotizing behavior. These tendencies, however, go beyond the scope of this presentation but are significant subjects for further study.

References

1. Jerry Gaston, "The Reward System in British Science," *Am. Soc. Rev.*, Vol. 35, No. 4, Aug. 1970, pp. 718–733. Gunnar Boalt, *The Sociology of Research,* Carbondale, Illinois: Southern Illinois University Press, 1969.
2. Joseph Ben-David, "Scientific Productivity and Academic Organization in 19th Century Medicine," pp. 39–61 in Norman Kaplan (Ed.), *Science and Society,* Chicago: Rand McNally, 1965.
3. Joseph Ben-David, "The Scientific Role: The Conditions of its Establishment in Europe," Minerva, 4, Autumn 1965, pp. 15–54.
4. Alva Myrdal and Viola Klein, *Women's Two Roles,* New York: Humanities Press.

5. Richard F. Tomasson, *Sweden: Prototype of Modern Society,* New York: Random House, 1970, p. 173. The book is a perceptive analysis of Swedish society.
6. Jacques Ellul, *The Political Illusion,* New York: Alfred A. Knopf, 1967.
7. Ernst Michanek, *For and Against the Welfare State: Swedish Experiences,* Stockholm: Forum, Swedish Institute, 1964.
8. Birgitta Linnér. *Sex and Society in Sweden,* New York: Pantheon, 1967.
9. Lars Ullerstam, *The Erotic Minorities,* New York: Grove Press, 1966.

PART TWO

by Gunnar Boalt

CHAPTER 2

Problem and material

This is a study of scientists, of their behavior in research, family, and society. These research fields have been largely ignored. Scientists seem to be too occupied with their research to have any interest left for the more general problem of the consequences: how does their occupation or preoccupation interact with their own acting outside the laboratory or department. They probably feel a bit resentful that their own research and behavior should be studied by a behavioral scientist, completely untrained in their field. We admit that researchers doing research on researchers tend to be a bit peculiar and frustrated. Frustration makes most researchers desperately anxious to pull all strings in their research method and to manipulate every person with some influence on their academic situation. A researcher must have considerable inside information to do so and his field of vision can hardly be larger than his area of personal experience. This is serious as it means that those with Swedish background cannot hope to generalize discussions of research behavior to other countries, not even to Scandinavia, and certainly not to the U.S.

Then, why write in English? If other studies are made, it should be possible to compare them and get a more general picture although far more complicated as the interaction between the researcher and the groups he belongs to should be easier to study in a comparatively small society where it is still possible to have personal contacts with a large part of the researchers and the academic administrators and where the groupnorms of the scientific community still may, as a matter of course, command respect.

The Swedish background

This section includes relevant cultural points. The first point would be the position of the researchers. Full professors are comparatively few, about 700 for nearly 100 000 students in a country of 8 million. They en-

joy high status as well as good pay. All full professors are paid the same amount, which may be one of the factors creating the Swedish conviction that every professor is an average professor. The associate professors with commissions are few, but the assistant professors again are more numerous and have a heavy load of teaching. Their pay is little below that of the professors, but they have considerably lower status. Until recently the full professors had a monopoly on the chairmanships in the departments, but still the posts of university president, vice president, dean, and vice dean (according to university regulations) must be a full professor.

When a new professorial chair is created or when a professor retires, the empty chair is announced and all those who apply for it are scrutinized by three experts, who submit to the faculty lists ranking the candidates they consider competent. The faculty then prepares a nomination list and sends it to the chancellor of the universities. The final decision is made in the Ministry of Education. This long, careful, and stressing procedure is admirably adapted to undermine the self-confidence of the candidates and to destroy their contacts with competitors, experts, faculty members, and administrators. Not even the winner escapes serious blows, but once appointed he can lick his wounds, enter his new department in triumph, take his seat in the faculty, and suddenly possess competence for his many administrative duties. The ability to console themselves with the knowledge that they have got through the really important passage-rite, may be the second factor uniting Swedish professors in a closed group with high solidarity. Everyone of them is not only competent but is the best man available. Those not appointed deeply feel their insufficiency (but of course furiously deny it).

All competent professors do not produce competent research. Teaching load, guidance of young candidates and their administrive duties may be obstacles. A comparatively large part of Swedish research is carried out by candidates for the Ph.D. degree and by those Ph.D.'s who wish to qualify themselves for a professor's chair and hope for a glorious treatment by experts, faculty, etc.

Swedish science shares problems and scope with science at large. There are, of course, areas where some Swedish departments are excellent and some where they are rather bad. Swedish researchers contribute to international journals and to some Swedish or Scandinavian journals of high standard. Library facilities are not bad and thus the scientific communication between Sweden and other countries is adequate–at least in the direction *to* Sweden.

19

University departments, until very recently, had their budgets in every detail fixed by the parliament. Most departments could see their own efforts to expand their budget come to a sad end, but also with envy register the few successful cases where strong arguments, new techniques, or efficient lobbying had resulted in new chairs or a considerable increase in resources. This system may have been responsible in part for the relentless competition between Swedish university departments and the resulting distrust, bad feeling, and lack of contacts. As a result, each department has to make a virtue out of every point where it differs from other departments and so, of course, becomes the best of all. This superiority can be maintained and taken quite seriously as long as there is little communication between departments and enough distrust to make a pretense of good friendship natural. Professors are, however, secure in their status and so can afford to be more realistic and have better contacts—at least with their fellow-professors.

The Swedish departments compete either with other departments of their own university or with their own kind of department at other universities. If they are at a serious disadvantage, they try to get help from other departments of their own university against the rivals at other universitites, or from their own kind of department at other universities against dangerous competitors at their own.

Each department and most of its staff has considerable freedom to choose research areas, problems, and methods according to their own ideas on what is important and/or rewarding to their career. But at least the chairmen of the departments are very conscious that there are better chances to persuade the Parliament to expand their budget if they can present research results or plans on problems appealing to this set of political thinkers.

The competition between departments in front of judges who are anxious to prove their political ability and common sense tends to entangle the official freedom of research or at least to make research more prudent, guarded, heavy; and researchers are anxious to avoid a playful approach or controversial problems. Recently a reaction in the opposite direction is felt, but it cannot for a long time influence the composition of the scientific staff under investigation. The majority of Swedish researchers at the professorial level are expected to have worked hard and conscientiously, forcing themselves to overcome obstacles or adapt stubborn theories to rigid data.

Scientists who tend to take research so seriously need a lot of sympathy and appreciation from their families and their friends to stand

the strain. They can ask for this support and get it because research is so highly respected by everybody. It is suspected that researchers use their families and acquaintances for comfort and solace, but their research remains their major sphere of interest. Swedish researchers are expected to marry later, have less children, take less interest in their families than other groups with a similar branch of education.

The author realizes that his conception of the background may be wrong and cover only some sectors or some types of scientists in Sweden. The picture probably has little value outside Sweden. This study concerns just one case, the case of Sweden, hoping similar research in other countries will provide material for comparisons.

Problem and samples

Scientists will be compared to academically trained citizens at a high level in order to see how they differ in family behavior and social orientation. Scientists are expected to let their research interests dominate their family behaviors and social adaptation. Boalt has previously discussed the problem (Boalt: *The Sociology of Research,* 1969, chapter V; Boalt and Lantz: *Universities and Research,* 1970, chapter 10) and suggested *Who is Who* as a convenient source for information.

The Swedish *Who is Who (Vem är det)* certainly is easily available and so are the data about 10 000 prominent Swedes, but there are, of course, a number of disadvantages.

1. All full professors are included in the Swedish *Who is Who,* but only a part of the associate professors and just a few of the assistant professors. The sample of scientists used thus is selected rather from the status aspect, less from the research aspect. This also means that young researchers are scantily represented in our sample.

2. Scientists should be compared with other groups with a similar education and high enough status to be included in *Who is Who.* Choosing these groups is important and difficult. Social scientists, for instance, can be compared with civil servants, trained academically in social sciences. This means that former social scientists who have given up science and chosen a career as school teachers (headmasters, etc.), journalists, librarians, etc., are excluded. It is not possible to collect an acceptable sample from such groups because they are too small. But the comparison group of higher civil servants in the central government administration (which is large enough), may be unique in some respects.

3. *Who is Who* uses only data given by the persons included in it. If they prefer to ignore their marriage, their divorce, or their former job, *Who is Who* ignores it, too. The selection of facts is in their own hands and up to a point the formulation of facts, also. They are in this way able to build up their public façade. It is hoped, however, that they are not sophisticated enough to realize the interesting implications of the innocent looking data they give. There may be cracks in their façade, visible but not obvious.

4. Technically the data in *Who is Who* must be trusted, although it is known from bitter experience that reliability as well as validity is not very high. All that can be done is to use additional information, where it is available. There is a larger book *Vem är vem* in five volumes, taking up most of those mentioned in *Vem är det* and giving considerably more information about them. It has, however, only had two editions and the last one is now a bit outmoded.

Samples have been taken from all the important research faculties: social sciences, humanities, law, theology, commerce, engineering, medicine, agriculture, natural science. The female researchers are few in all these fields, numbering only 50. As they are expected to behave differently from men, at least in family matters, they are placed in a special group. The result is ten samples of researchers, nine of them including only men, and one including only women. These samples of researchers are compared in most cases with counterparts from the same academic field but now well advanced in other sectors of the Swedish society. Social scientists are compared with higher civil servants trained in social subjects and holding posts at the same level as full professors or above. The humanity researchers in the same way have as counterparts teachers, headmasters, and superintendents in the school system, high enough in the hierarchy to be included in *Who is Who*. The law researchers are compared with judges, the theologians with bishops and deans (bishops above their level but deans at the same level as professors), and for researchers in commerce and business administration, directors trained at a faculty of commerce were used as counterparts. The directors trained at a faculty of engineering could, of course, be used as counterparts to the researchers in the engineering field. The medical researchers could be compared to head physicians, the researchers in agriculture, etc., with high forestry officers, but no adequate counterpart to natural scientists was found. Interest in a group of Army officers evolved. They lack academic training but possess considerable status in the Swedish society, at least if they have reached the level needed for *Who is Who*: colonel

Table 1. *Size of sampled groups of researchers and their counterparts*

Group of Researchers	Size	Counterparts	Size
Social Scientists	80	Civil Servants	41
Researchers in Humanities	100	Teachers, Headmasters, etc.	100
Researchers in Law	53	Judges	100
Researchers in Theology	32	Bishops, Deans	40
Researchers in Commerce,		Directors from Commerce	100
Business Administration	28		
Scientists in Engineering	100	Directors from Engineering	100
Medical Researchers	100	Head Physicians, etc.	100
Researchers in Agriculture, Forestry	71	Higher Forestry Officers	51
Researchers in Natural Science	100	Officers in Army, Navy, Air Force	100
Female Researchers	50		

commanding a regiment or the rank of general (brigadier, general-major, etc.) or the corresponding positions in the Navy or the Air Force.

Some of these groups were small, the professors in commerce, business administration, etc., numbering only 28; the professors in theology, numbering 32. If *Who is Who* contained less than 100 members of a group, all of them have been included in the sample. If the group was larger, a random sample of 100 was taken. The samples and their size are presented in Table 1.

Variables

Thirty-two variables were taken from the Swedish *Who is Who (Vem är det* 1969); income data, two variables, from *Sveriges Taxeringskalender 1968*; two variables on hobbies and club memberships from *Vem är vem*; and two variables from the usual Swedish reference books, type *Encyclopedia Britannica,* down to the compressed one volume editions. These variables were divided in three groups, belonging to (A) the role of researcher, (B) the family role, and (C) the social role. The variables are:

A. Variables belonging to the researcher's role (or to the career pattern)

1. *Family name* of researcher classified after number of pages given the name in the Stockholm population register in 1967. Step 1: More than 40 columns; Step 2: 39–6; Step 3: Less than 6, not nobility; Step 4: Nobility. A common name may in some instances mean a slight handicap, and nobility sometimes an advantage.

23

2. *Age*. The researcher must have time to work, publish, get along in the hierarchy, reap his reward in faculty, academy or research council.

3. *Academic Performance* from *one* (no school-leaving examination) to *ten* (declared competent for a full professor's chair).

4. *University Loyalty I*. A change of university between bachelor's degree and master's degree may in Sweden indicate a maladjustment at the first university and thus a drawback.

5. *University Loyalty II*. Going to another university after master's degree is unusual in Sweden and probably indicates some interest conflict at the department with the staff there.

6. *Father's social class* according to the three classes in Swedish election statistics, based on occupation titles. These classes may be termed upper, middle, and lower class.

7. *Place of residence,* starting with (1) rural area, (2) towns below 100 000 inhabitants and without university, (3) Uppsala, Lund, Umeå, (4) Stockholm, Gothenburg, and Malmö, (5) Scandinavia outside Sweden, (6) Outside Scandinavia.

8. *Status according to encyclopedias,* starting with reference works giving many names and ending with those with few Swedes. (1) *Vem är vem,* (2) *Vem är det 1969,* (3) *Bonniers lexikon,* (4) *Lilla uppslagsboken,* (5) *Norstedts uppslagsbok,* (6) *Lilla Focus,* (7) *Prismas uppslagsbok,* (8) *Who is who in Europe 1966–67,* (9) *The World's Who is Who in Science,* (10) *The International Who is Who.* Our subjects are given the rank of the highest ranking source incorporating their name.

9. *Number of lines* given the subject in *Vem är det 1969.*

10. *Number of reference books* listed for variable 8 giving the name of the subject.

11. *Number of academies* or learned societies, which have made him a member, corresponding member, etc.

12. *Number of Swedish honorary doctor's degrees* given him.

13. *Number of government committees,* which the subject, according to his own information to *Vem är det,* has been a member of.

14. *Number of memberships in research councils* enumerated by the subject.

15. Number of enumerated international commissions.

16. Number of enumerated foreign guest professorships.

17. *Number of academic positions* as president, vice president, dean, vice-dean, or chairman of a department.

18. *Number of published works* enumerated in *Vem är det.*

19. *Name of doctor's thesis* given in *Vem är det.* It is seldom given by

very productive researchers, but in some faculties it may indicate high quality.

20. *Number of distinctions* conferred upon the subject, according to *Vem är det*.

21. *Number of foreign honorary doctor's degrees* enumerated by the subject.

22. *Researcher's status* measured as a sum of the variables 11, 12, 14, 15, 16, 18, 19, and 21.

23. *General status* measured as a sum of the variables 8, 9, 10, 13, and number of inventions, patents, etc., enumerated.

24. *Academic power* measured as a sum of the variables 11, 13, 14, 15, and 17.

(Observe that the three last variables, 22, 23, and 24, are constructed as sums and so tend to give positive correlations with the variables included in them. There should also be a positive correlation between 22 and 24, as they have variables 11, 14, and 15 in common.)

B. Variables belonging to the family role

25. *Number of marriages* enumerated in *Vem är det*. In Swedish society divorce and remarriage are considered a threat to the marriage ideology and therefore a low number of marriages is given a higher value.

26. *Number of children* enumerated in *Vem är vem*.

27. *Educational level of the subject's spouse* measured by the same scale as variable 3.

28. Number of years between first examination (B.A., etc.) and appointment to full professor.

29. *Age at doctor's dissertation.* An early dissertation is considered a sign of scientific talent and could therefore be included in the research role, but we consider its effect on family behavior more important (the »union card» syndrome).

30. Age of (first) appointment to full professor.

31. *Income.* Data taken from *Sveriges taxeringskalender 1968*. Income decides standard of living.

32. *Income of the subject's spouse* taken from the same source as variable 31. This income is important in deciding the standard of living.

33. *Nearness between first marriage and first child.* The later the child arrives after marriage, the less anxious we suspect the subject to

be for children. There may, however, also be an economic factor responsible: children are expensive.

34. *Nearness between first and second child.* The second child should replicate the tendency from the first child.

C. Variables belonging to the social role

35. *Number of clubs* enumerated by the subject in *Vem är vem.*
36. *Number of hobbies* enumerated by the subject in *Vem är vem.*

The reader may be a bit surprised that variables like age at dissertation (29), age at appointment to full professor (30) and income (31) are included in the family role, not in the research role. But it must be remembered that we are looking for disadvantages which research engagement may bring to family interests and family life. Of course, an early marriage, many children and a crowded apartment in the same way is a serious handicap to the researcher, often delaying his dissertation and his scientific career.

The two variables 35 and 36, number of clubs and hobbies, are of course not very tempting from our view. It was decided, however, to include them, taking the small chance that they may give some kind of information, possibly indicating a tendency to use such behaviors as compensation for research or family.

CHAPTER 3

The summation theory and its adaptation to the problem

The author has previously discussed the career problems of the researchers in *The Sociology of Research* (1969, chapter II) and *Universities and Research* (1970, chapter 10), using his "summation" theory. These ideas are adapted to the present problem.

Sociologists believe that people tend to act along the same lines in similar situations. They also believe that some kind of behaviors tend to accompany, support, one another, or are stimulated by the same circumstances and just represent two different aspects of one larger behavior-complex. For instance, researchers who have published some excellent treatises are expected to be appointed to professors, mentioned in encyclopedias, elected to academies, research councils, and high academic positions. On the other hand such behaviors are not expected to be too closely related. Good researchers probably are anxious to get a chair, even in an academy, but they may have sense enough to avoid little rewarded positions in academic administration or membership in hard working government committees.

Researchers with a fine publication list are also expected to be little interested in modern sculpture, drugs, tin soldiers, or gluttony, simply because these take a lot of time and there probably exists an unwillingness to spend time and/or money this way. There are, however, no such data about private interests or behaviors of this type available, although *Vem är vem* certainly gives some data about stamp-collecting, gardening and interest in railway time tables.

Marriage and most behaviors at home or towards the children in the same way should tend to accompany one another. He who marries early should also have children early, more children and probably be older when appointed to professor, as he has had to devote more time to earn the livelihood of his family and more interest to extra-academic behaviors with wife and children. Income is a difficult variable as researchers who marry young on the one hand need more money and try to get it, on the other hand income partly depends on university degree

and academic merits. If marriage delays their career, they risk a lower income although they need a higher one. Probably the situation on the labor-market will decide the outcome, but theoretically we prefer to expect marriage and children to press the researcher to a higher income. Probably a researcher marries a girl from his own academic circle, and then she can use her merits in the labor market. She is expected to be anxious to keep her job and earn as much as possible in order to "relieve the husband's burden", and in order to facilitate his academic career. On the other hand her researcher husband then will have to lend a hand with housework, shopping or even bring the children to or from the nursery school, which may delay him all the same.

The social variables, clubs and hobbies, do not seem to have much in common. The more time devoted to hobbies, the less time to clubs, etc. This, however, may be wrong for two reasons. First, they may both depend on another factor: very active people engage in a number of rather divergent behaviors. Second, enthusiastic researchers may be less enthusiastic for anything else and so clubs and hobbies may accompany each other simply because both are shunned by so many researchers. Something similar may be true for the enthusiastic family men.

The different variables labeled "research variables" are expected to tend to accompany one another, i.e., to form a cluster. The family variables should form a second cluster and the two social factors, a third. The research variables are expected not only to be positively correlated with one another, but also to show a tendency to *negative* correlations with the variables belonging to the family cluster and the social cluster. Research is so highly valued in Swedish society that all the variables connected with it get permeated by some common set of scientific values and so tend to form a cluster, pushing aside behaviors based on other values. But less successful researchers, unable to attain these scientific values, should have more need of appreciation in interaction with persons they appreciate and like. The family should be the best available group or remedy, based on important values, binding together the family variables to a cluster.

If one sample after another is taken and separate calculations are made for all the correlations between the 36 variables, it is expected that the samples of researchers should show a tendency to *positive* correlations within the research cluster and the same tendency within the family cluster, but show *negative* correlations between variables belonging to different clusters.

What about the samples of civil servants and other comparison

groups? Several of the research variables will be useless in their samples. They seldom have been appointed professors, possessed academic power, etc. The research cluster in their case is reduced and transformed to a career cluster. Still, in the Swedish society, career is an important thing—at least among those who have made a successful one. There is a good chance that a weak tendency to form a career cluster may appear in the matrix, although when it is compared with the matrix of the corresponding researchers' sample, the last matrix is expected to have far more higher positive correlations within the researcher's cluster and far more negative correlations between the variables from different clusters.

If a matrix shows a division of variables between different clusters, with a high percent of positive correlations between the variables belonging to the same cluster and a high percent of negative correlations between variables belonging to different clusters, such a pattern is interpreted as an indication that the different clusters compete with one another and are able to compensate one another. This is called the *compensation pattern*. Samples of researchers should show a more clear-cut compensation pattern than the corresponding samples of non-researchers.

But the sample in itself has a profound effect on the pattern of the matrix. Suppose a sample of researchers was taken covering a very broad register, from the youngsters just starting on graduate work up to famous Nobel prize winners. Then the top researchers would tend to be older, married, to have children, income, maybe even clubs or hobbies. The result then might be positive correlations between all variables, uniting them to one single cluster in the matrix, exposing a pattern called *the unified value pattern* (as it gives the impression that some tend to get everything in research as well as in family life or company, while others get very little). A statistician would say that the variance *between* the classes totally dominates the variance *within* the classes, thus turning the author's expectations upside down. But if just one class was taken, one competence level of researchers, then there would be no variance between classes and there would be a chance to get a rather strong compensation pattern.

A very wide distribution of researchers thus can be expected to give a unified value pattern in the correlation matrix, a very narrow distribution should give a compensation pattern. The sample in the middle between these extremes should show the two tendencies in balance with each other. The variance between classes ought to be as strong as the variance within classes, that is the majority of the correlations between

Table 2. *Sample of social scientists*

Variables	A. Research cluster													
	1	2	3	4	5	6	7	8	9	10	11	12	13	14
A. Research cluster														
1. Family name	■	+.15	+.11	+.05	+.15	+.16	+.16	−.01	+.21	+.03	+.05	−.05	+.03	−.03
2. Age		■	+.11	−.10	+.04	+.15	−.07	+.40	+.56	+.52	+.49	+.25	+.09	+.03
3. Academic performance			■	+.06	+.01	+.09	+.03	+.19	+.16	+.29	+.27	+.15	+.02	+.12
4. University loyalty I				■	+.48	−.11	−.14	−.07	−.02	−.03	+.10	−.08	−.00	+.08
5. University loyalty II					■	−.01	+.02	−.05	+.11	+.10	+.15	−.09	−.02	+.07
6. Father's social class						■	+.05	+.16	+.23	+.29	+.10	+.06	+.09	+.02
7. Place of residence							■	+.18	+.19	+.12	−.30	−.07	+.11	+.04
8. Status according to encyclopedias								■	+.48	+.83	+.31	+.30	+.08	+.35
9. Number of lines									■	+.65	+.50	+.29	+.40	+.28
10. Number of reference books										■	+.49	+.41	+.16	+.41
11. Academies etc.											■	+.55	+.07	+.08
12. Swedish honorary doctor's degrees												■	+.28	+.05
13. Government committees													■	+.17
14. Memberships in research councils														■
15. Enumerated international commissions														
16. Foreign guest professorships														
17. Academic positions														
18. Published works														
19. Name of doctor's thesis given in 'Vem är det'														
20. Distinctions														
21. Foreign honorary doctor's degrees														
22. Researcher's status														
23. General status														
24. Academic power														
B. Family cluster														
25. Number of marriages														
26. Number of children														
27. Educational level of the subject's wife														
28. Number of years between first examination and appointment to full professor														
29. Age at doctor's dissertation														
30. Age at appointment to full professor														
31. Income														
32. Income of the subject's wife														
33. Imminence between first marriage and first child														
34. Imminence between first and second child														
C. Social cluster														
35. Number of clubs														
36. Number of hobbies														

variables from different clusters would be very low, about zero, and about half of them positive. This pattern is called the *compromise pattern*.

Which patterns are expected from the matrices of our own samples, compensation, compromise or unified value patterns? It is hoped to find clearcut compensation patterns in the matrices of the researchers' samples, but some of them may be a rather mixed set, not quite permeated by the common set of research values and then a compromise

										B. Family cluster										C. Social cluster	
15	16	17	18	19	20	21	22	23	24	25	26	27	28	29	30	31	32	33	34	35	36
+.02	−.14	.00	+.16	+.02	+.19	+.04	+.13	+.15	+.05	−.20	+.11	−.04	+.03	−.12	−.03	−.05	+.16	−.04	−.04	−.32	−.08
+.19	−.12	−.09	+.56	−.27	+.56	+.34	+.59	+.55	+.32	−.15	+.04	−.29	+.49	+.04	+.47	−.12	−.02	−.15	−.13	−.09	−.15
+.13	+.13	−.04	+.28	−.19	+.17	+.14	+.32	+.19	+.18	−.20	+.13	+.06	+.12	−.22	+.44	−.02	+.11	+.14	−.04	−.22	−.11
−.37	+.06	−.04	+.07	+.16	+.04	+.01	+.02	−.05	−.13	+.01	+.20	+.04	+.20	−.07	−.09	+.09	+.12	+.04	+.16	+.04	+.11
−.17	+.05	+.09	+.15	+.22	+.07	.00	+.12	+.08	.00	−.08	+.11	−.15	+.02	−.02	−.03	−.04	−.10	.00	−.11	+.04	+.16
+.16	+.02	+.05	+.17	−.06	+.06	+.11	+.19	+.25	+.15	−.10	−.01	+.07	+.23	−.29	−.16	+.01	+.26	−.07	−.16	−.12	+.09
+.21	−.05	−.06	+.18	+.13	−.08	−.03	+.11	+.20	+.02	−.20	−.16	+.13	−.06	−.17	−.02	+.16	+.04	+.34	+.16	−.09	−.12
+.32	−.14	+.10	+.51	−.09	+.28	+.31	+.56	+.65	+.34	−.11	+.09	−.11	+.04	−.29	−.09	+.35	+.15	+.14	+.02	−.11	−.26
+.43	+.07	+.06	+.83	−.06	+.52	+.49	+.88	+.96	+.65	−.26	+.10	−.12	+.22	−.19	+.07	+.37	+.22	+.06	−.10	−.07	−.12
+.39	−.08	+.15	+.69	−.11	+.40	+.39	+.75	+.78	+.51	−.21	+.19	−.20	+.12	−.37	−.13	+.32	+.19	+.07	−.01	−.10	−.22
+.19	+.10	+.22	+.46	−.17	+.59	+.53	+.64	+.49	+.55	−.05	+.06	−.23	−.01	−.18	−.16	+.15	+.11	−.19	−.16	+.04	−.12
+.45	−.02	+.25	+.19	−.31	+.51	+.65	+.39	+.37	+.59	+.06	+.13	−.23	−.15	−.26	−.20	+.21	−.45	+.05	+.02	−.03	−.09
+.38	−.01	+.08	+.16	−.08	+.23	+.27	+.24	+.52	+.80	+.02	+.11	−.01	−.08	−.13	−.04	+.22	+.05	−.06	−.14	.00	−.09
−.04	−.04	+.10	+.28	+.07	+.04	+.05	+.29	+.34	+.24	−.17	+.29	−.08	+.01	−.02	−.05	+.36	+.04	+.11	+.07	−.02	−.07
■	+.14	−.12	+.16	−.15	+.23	+.39	+.38	+.49	+.67	+.07	−.18	−.10	−.14	−.19	−.09	+.17	−.24	+.11	−.04	−.05	−.15
	■	−.05	−.01	+.09	−.04	+.10	+.11	+.02	+.08	+.05	−.02	+.23	−.01	−.11	−.13	−.04	+.28	+.12	−.02	−.05	+.03
		■	+.04	+.07	+.13	+.09	+.06	+.09	+.19	+.06	+.07	−.02	−.19	−.06	−.16	+.30	+.15	+.06	−.08	−.03	−.09
			■	−.22	+.43	+.39	+.95	+.81	+.38	−.34	+.12	−.09	+.36	−.27	+.11	+.29	+.33	+.15	−.04	−.07	−.09
				■	−.22	−.19	−.24	−.09	−.16	+.12	−.03	+.27	−.16	+.18	−.14	+.09	+.53	−.10	+.38	+.09	−.10
					■	+.76	+.55	+.52	+.49	−.03	+.15	−.18	+.16	−.12	+.08	−.05	−.09	+.05	−.11	−.06	−.12
						■	+.56	+.50	+.54	+.06	+.23	−.15	+.02	−.24	−.10	+.04	−.11	+.05	+.05	−.03	−.04
							■	+.87	+.59	−.27	+.11	−.14	+.26	−.31	+.02	+.30	+.19	+.10	−.06	−.06	−.12
								■	+.74	−.23	+.13	−.13	+.16	−.26	+.01	+.41	+.21	+.09	−.10	−.08	−.18
									■	+.04	+.06	−.15	−.11	−.23	−.14	+.32	.00	+.01	−.16	−.01	−.17
										■	−.21	+.03	−.19	+.10	−.08	+.06	+.09	+.13	+.20	+.03	−.05
											■	−.17	+.11	−.06	+.08	+.10	+.16	+.07	+.17	−.01	+.10
												■	+.25	−.18	+.02	−.02	+.47	+.20	+.01	+.01	+.01
													■	+.15	+.90	−.21	+.15	−.11	+.05	.00	−.01
														■	+.57	−.12	+.15	−.25	+.06	+.20	+.19
															■	−.25	+.05	−.04	+.02	.00	−.12
																■	+.12	+.21	−.01	−.04	−.11
																	■	+.31	+.17	−.08	+.17
																		■	+.07	−.09	−.04
																			■	−.04	−.05
																				■	−.04
																					■

pattern may appear. It is not expected to find unified value patterns among the researchers. That would mean that their research was not based on a strong set or scientific values – and why then call such a sample researchers? In some cases the career efforts of the comparison samples may be so efficiently integrated that they may show a weak compensation pattern, but in general compromise patterns or even unified value patterns are expected. This is because they ought to be more mixed, have a broader distribution on the career values.

31

Table 3. *Sample of civil servants*

Variables	\multicolumn{14}{c}{A. Research cluster}													
	1	2	3	4	5	6	7	8	9	10	11	12	13	14
A. Research cluster														
1. Family name	■	+.31	+.11	.00	−.05	+.40	+.14	−.01	+.09	+.01	+.02	+.08	−.18	−.26
2. Age		■	+.46	.00	+.11	+.38	−.21	−.02	+.28	+.04	+.47	+.20	−.12	−.04
3. Academic performance			■	.00	−.50	+.18	−.17	+.30	+.56	+.22	+.29	.00	−.03	+.40
4. University loyalty I				■	.00	.00	.00	.00	.00	.00	.00	.00	.00	.00
5. University loyalty II					■	+.66	−.13	+.36	−.59	+.34	+.28	.00	+.32	+.18
6. Father's social class						■	+.09	+.06	−.04	+.02	+.35	+.13	−.15	+.18
7. Place of residence							■	−.04	−.19	−.13	−.17	+.02	−.22	+.02
8. Status according to encyclopedias								■	+.29	+.81	−.10	−.08	+.24	+.50
9. Number of lines									■	+.28	+.14	−.15	+.43	+.30
10. Number of reference books										■	−.10	−.06	+.22	+.35
11. Academies etc.											■	+.35	−.13	+.16
12. Swedish honorary doctor's degrees												■	−.17	−.03
13. Government committees													■	+.14
14. Memberships in research councils														■

15. Enumerated international commissions
16. Foreign guest professorships
17. Academic positions
18. Published works
19. Name of doctor's thesis given in 'Vem är det'
20. Distinctions
21. Foreign honorary doctor's degrees
22. Researcher's status
23. General status
24. Academic power

B. Family cluster
25. Number of marriages
26. Number of children
27. Educational level of the subject's wife
28. Number of years between first examination and appointment to full professor
29. Age at doctor's dissertation
30. Age at appointment to full professor
31. Income
32. Income of the subject's wife
33. Imminence between first marriage and first child
34. Imminence between first and second child

C. Social cluster
35. Number of clubs
36. Number of hobbies

These expectations will be tested on some samples, starting with the two best known: the sample of social scientists and its counterpart, the civil servants trained in social science; then the law researchers and, as their counterpart, the judges.

										B. Family cluster										C. Social cluster	
15	16	17	18	19	20	21	22	23	24	25	26	27	28	29	30	31	32	33	34	35	36
+.07	.00	.00	+.15	+.09	+.19	.00	+.12	−.02	−.15	−.21	+.15	−.17	.00	+.18	.00	+.07	+.33	+.01	−.09	+.14	+.05
+.11	.00	.00	+.24	+.18	+.55	.00	+.36	+.12	+.07	−.14	+.10	−.26	.00	−.28	.00	−.26	+.36	−.14	−.04	+.23	+.11
+.21	.00	.00	+.55	+.59	+.08	.00	+.60	+.41	+.17	−.25	+.29	+.15	.00	+.43	.00	−.07	+.51	−.28	+.11	+.32	+.30
.00	.00	.00	.00	.00	.00	.00	.00	.00	.00	.00	.00	.00	.00	.00	.00	.00	.00	.00	.00	.00	.00
+.35	.00	.00	−.29	+.40	+.31	.00	+.04	−.10	+.56	−.13	−.13	−.65	.00	−.73	.00	+.34	−.10	−.11	−.54	+.25	+.19
+.23	.00	.00	−.18	+.18	+.35	.00	+.11	−.07	+.08	−.11	+.08	+.07	.00	−.20	.00	+.05	+.22	−.20	−.04	+.07	+.22
+.28	.00	.00	−.04	+.04	.00	.00	+.04	−.22	−.13	−.11	+.11	+.03	.00	+.17	.00	+.27	.00	.00	.00	−.16	+.03
+.27	.00	.00	−.01	+.30	−.17	.00	+.12	+.60	+.33	−.03	+.19	−.16	.00	−.13	.00	+.48	−.37	−.38	−.09	+.39	+.11
+.35	.00	.00	+.56	+.45	+.27	.00	+.60	+.26	+.57	−.45	+.36	−.11	.00	+.75	.00	+.22	+.13	−.04	+.04	+.21	+.15
+.39	.00	.00	+.03	+.17	−.15	.00	+.19	+.56	+.35	−.10	+.22	−.24	.00	+.03	.00	+.55	−.18	−.35	+.02	+.05	+.12
+.06	.00	.00	+.12	+.30	+.30	.00	+.44	−.01	+.20	.00	+.05	−.22	.00	−.42	.00	−.04	.00	+.04	+.16	+.29	.00
+.11	.00	.00	−.05	−.06	+.08	.00	+.15	−.18	−.02	.00	+.14	−.08	.00	.00	.00	.00	.00	+.10	+.21	−.04	−.04
+.02	.00	.00	−.10	+.01	+.15	.00	−.10	+.73	+.86	−.05	+.21	−.31	.00	−.21	.00	+.18	−.36	+.12	−.14	−.04	−.08
+.24	.00	.00	+.01	+.36	−.13	.00	+.24	+.39	+.34	.00	+.10	−.11	.00	−.08	.00	+.24	.00	−.36	−.12	−.06	+.33
■	.00	.00	+.20	+.30	+.31	.00	+.60	+.32	+.43	−.59	+.17	−.09	.00	−.26	.00	+.37	.00	−.18	+.08	+.01	+.22
	■	.00	.00	.00	.00	.00	.00	.00	.00	.00	.00	.00	.00	.00	.00	.00	.00	.00	.00	.00	.00
		■	.00	.00	.00	.00	.00	.00	.00	.00	.00	.00	.00	.00	.00	.00	.00	.00	.00	.00	.00
			■	+.35	−.02	.00	+.83	+.29	+.02	−.52	+.43	+.18	.00	+.50	.00	+.04	+.16	+.08	−.01	+.15	+.16
				■	+.03	.00	+.49	+.36	+.23	−.34	+.33	+.02	.00	−.12	.00	+.23	−.37	+.08	+.10	+.18	+.31
					■	.00	+.20	+.16	+.32	−.31	−.08	−.27	.00	−.45	.00	−.02	−.24	+.15	−.06	+.15	−.09
						■	.00	.00	.00	.00	.00	.00	.00	.00	.00	.00	.00	.00	.00	.00	.00
							■	+.36	+.29	−.61	+.41	+.01	.00	+.11	.00	+.19	+.16	−.04	+.06	+.19	+.23
								■	+.20	−.30	+.36	−.25	.00	+.38	.00	+.39	−.05	−.13	−.06	+.20	+.10
									■	−.27	+.27	−.38	.00	−.49	.00	+.29	−.36	+.01	−.06	+.04	+.04
										■	−.44	−.22	.00	−.08	.00	−.01	.00	−.10	−.10	.00	−.30
											■	−.11	.00	+.31	.00	+.13	+.17	+.36	+.33	.00	+.37
												■	.00	+.69	.00	−.15	+.55	+.11	+.35	−.09	+.02
													■	.00	.00	.00	.00	.00	.00	.00	.00
														■	.00	−.04	+1.0	+.13	+.86	−.26	−.07
															■	.00	.00	1.00	.00	.00	.00
																■	−.30	+.11	−.04	−.08	+.23
																	■	−1.0	+1.0	−.37	.00
																		■	−.01	−.16	+.13
																			■	−.09	+.17
																				■	−.07
																					■

The matrices of social scientists and of their counterparts among civil servants

The 24 variables included in the research cluster (see Table 2) actually tend to be positively intercorrelated in the matrix of intercorrelations from the social scientists' sample, as 216 out of 276 are positive (78 %). The family variables are positive in 30 cases out of 45 (67 %). But the 240 correlations between 24 research variables on the one hand and the

Table 4. *Sample of researchers in jurisprudence*

Variables	A. Research cluster													
	1	2	3	4	5	6	7	8	9	10	11	12	13	14
A. Research cluster														
1. Family name	■	+.10	+.05	+.44	+.00	+.01	+.14	+.20	+.19	+.20	+.13	+.22	+.03	−.10
2. Age		■	+.18	+.05	+.19	+.03	+.08	+.42	+.68	+.62	+.49	+.23	+.35	+.05
3. Academic performance			■	+.38	+.23	+.24	−.22	+.24	+.09	+.22	+.22	+.07	+.01	+.05
4. University loyalty I				■	+.30	+.12	+.20	+.07	+.22	+.07	+.08	−.20	+.08	+.07
5. University loyalty II					■	+.06	−.04	+.18	+.10	+.18	+.16	−.31	+.12	+.05
6. Father's social class						■	+.30	−.04	+.12	+.11	+.12	+.10	+.01	+.07
7. Place of residence							■	+.28	+.29	+.28	+.01	+.04	+.16	+.19
8. Status according to encyclopedias								■	+.55	+.87	+.50	+.36	+.33	+.15
9. Number of lines									■	+.76	+.51	+.31	+.48	−.02
10. Number of reference books										■	+.63	+.38	+.38	+.20
11. Academies etc.											■	+.29	+.14	+.01
12. Swedish honorary doctor's degrees												■	−.24	−.06
13. Government committees													■	+.05
14. Memberships in research councils														■
15. Enumerated international commissions														
16. Foreign guest professorships														
17. Academic positions														
18. Published works														
19. Name of doctor's thesis given in 'Vem är det'														
20. Distinctions														
21. Foreign honorary doctor's degrees														
22. Researcher's status														
23. General status														
24. Academic power														
B. Family cluster														
25. Number of marriages														
26. Number of children														
27. Educational level of the subject's wife														
28. Number of years between first examination and appointment to full professor														
29. Age at doctor's dissertation														
30. Age at appointment to full professor														
31. Income														
32. Income of the subject's wife														
33. Imminence between first marriage and first child														
34. Imminence between first and second child														
C. Social cluster														
35. Number of clubs														
36. Number of hobbies														

10 family variables on the other are expected to be negative and they are so only in 120 cases (50 %). The two social variables are correlated − .04, but 39 out of 48 correlations with the research cluster are negative (81 %), and 9 out of their 20 correlations with the family cluster (45 %). This is a compromise pattern or possibly a weak compensation pattern. However, 78 % of positive correlations in the research cluster to some extent is the result of variables 22, 23, and 24 calculated as sums of other variables in the research cluster. If these are excluded, the result

	B. Family cluster																				C. Social cluster	
15	16	17	18	19	20	21	22	23	24	25	26	27	28	29	30	31	32	33	34	35	36
+.14	.00	+.02	+.25	+.06	+.10	+.09	+.25	+.19	+.12	−.05	−.04	−.33	−.20	−.26	−.15	.00	−.14	+.12	+.06	.00	−.02
+.17	.00	+.46	+.63	−.22	+.66	+.22	+.64	+.67	+.54	−.03	.00	−.26	+.14	−.29	+.11	−.10	+.13	−.01	−.12	.00	−.16
−.03	.00	+.09	+.16	+.21	+.16	+.05	+.17	+.13	+.10	+.02	.00	−.14	.00	−.35	.00	−.18	−.18	.00	−.14	.00	+.10
+.22	.00	+.17	+.28	+.10	+.08	+.09	+.27	+.18	+.17	+.05	−.07	−.10	−.36	−.49	−.35	.02	−.25	+.08	−.10	.00	+.18
−.14	.00	+.12	+.11	−.05	−.10	+.06	+.10	+.14	+.12	+.03	−.07	−.16	−.08	−.09	−.11	.10	+.10	−.03	−.14	.00	+.13
+.02	.00	−.01	+.10	−.13	+.19	+.06	+.12	+.09	+.07	+.03	+.11	−.10	−.18	−.34	−.16	+.11	−.34	+.07	−.11	.00	−.05
+.08	.00	+.13	+.15	−.05	+.13	+.15	+.15	+.31	+.15	+.01	−.36	−.19	−.15	−.50	−.17	+.11	−.23	−.06	−.36	.00	+.16
+.29	.00	+.35	+.43	−.10	+.19	+.38	+.55	+.70	+.56	−.05	+.10	−.18	−.17	−.38	−.18	−.08	+.36	−.09	−.05	.00	+.15
+.40	.00	+.32	+.81	−.19	+.47	+.47	+.84	+.95	+.68	−.22	+.01	−.21	−.19	−.52	−.23	−.07	+.44	−.06	−.19	.00	+.02
+.36	.00	+.50	+.58	−.16	+.28	+.55	+.73	+.85	+.69	−.12	+.11	−.18	−.22	−.43	−.22	−.13	+.40	−.11	−.14	.00	.00
+.25	.00	+.25	+.46	−.16	+.12	+.22	+.66	+.53	+.63	+.05	+.14	−.04	−.09	−.34	−.06	−.17	+.30	−.23	−.07	.00	−.03
+.13	.00	−.10	+.31	+.02	+.22	+.47	+.41	+.25	.00	−.03	+.36	−.09	+.09	+.02	+.23	−.22	+.79	+.09	−.04	.00	−.12
+.21	.00	+.25	+.09	−.19	+.42	−.08	+.11	+.65	+.78	−.23	−.15	−.01	−.05	−.39	−.15	+.40	−.25	−.19	+.33	.00	+.10
+.09	.00	+.43	−.15	−.10	−.07	+.04	−.06	+.05	+.16	−.02	.00	+.01	−.08	−.14	−.10	+.07	−.16	+.03	+.14	.00	+.17
■	.00	+.24	+.25	−.31	+.20	+.22	+.45	+.40	+.57	+.12	−.12	−.18	+.08	−.28	−.01	+.06	−.01	+.08	−.02	.00	−.15
	■	.00	.00	.00	.00	.00	.00	.00	.00	.00	.00	.00	.00	.00	.00	.00	.00	.00	.00	.00	.00
		■	+.15	−.27	+.15	+.04	+.23	+.39	+.49	−.03	−.11	−.32	−.21	−.21	−.22	−.07	−.21	+.04	−.23	.00	−.02
			■	−.08	+.36	+.46	+.94	+.69	+.34	−.05	+.04	−.18	−.14	−.45	−.17	−.23	+.50	+.03	−.35	.00	−.04
				■	−.07	+.05	−.14	−.21	−.31	+.28	−.03	+.19	−.16	+.08	−.07	−.15	+.47	−.03	−.01	.00	+.15
					■	−.07	+.31	+.47	+.39	−.01	+.01	−.23	+.25	−.31	+.23	+.25	−.20	+.09	+.18	.00	−.05
						■	+.58	+.42	+.12	−.02	+.07	+.11	−.27	−.13	−.22	−.37	+.75	−.02	−.27	.00	−.08
							■	+.76	+.52	.00	+.06	−.15	−.15	−.47	−.16	−.25	+.55	−.02	−.30	.00	−.07
								■	+.81	−.22	.00	−.20	−.19	−.55	−.24	+.02	+.35	−.11	−.08	.00	+.06
									■	−.10	−.08	−.12	−.08	−.51	−.15	+.19	−.09	−.19	+.14	.00	+.01
										■	−.27	−.18	+.15	+.08	+.19	+.12	+.02	+.20	−.08	.00	−.04
											■	+.02	−.05	+.17	+.03	.00	+.38	+.38	+.51	.00	+.10
												■	−.13	+.11	−.10	−.18	+.36	−.31	−.02	.00	.00
													■	+.33	+.95	+.08	−.48	−.25	+.17	.00	−.03
														■	+.42	−.10	+.20	−.05	+.25	.00	−.15
															■	+.02	−.41	−.29	+.18	.00	−.01
																■	−.57	+.03	+.37	.00	+.13
																	■	+.08	−.16	.00	−.01
																		■	−.19	.00	−.31
																			■	.00	+.20
																				■	.00
																					■

is 156 positive correlations out of 210, 74 % instead of 78 %, not a serious reduction, however.

Our attention is now turned to Table 3, the correlations of the civil servants' sample. Four of the 24 variables in the research cluster are irrelevant for this sample: variables 4, change of university; variable 16, number of guest professorships; variable 17, academic top positions; and variable 21, number of foreign doctor's degrees. The research cluster is thus reduced to a corresponding career cluster containing 20 varia-

35

Table 5. *Sample of judges*

Variables	A. Research cluster													
	1	2	3	4	5	6	7	8	9	10	11	12	13	14
A. Research cluster														
1. Family name	■	+.02	+.03	.00	.00	+.11	−.04	−.02	+.04	+.03	+.03	.00	−.02	+.04
2. Age		■	+.02	.00	.00	−.21	+.04	−.12	+.06	.00	+.13	+.16	−.15	+.01
3. Academic performance			■	.00	.00	−.16	+.11	−.04	+.03	−.01	−.04	−.04	+.05	−.02
4. University loyalty I				■	.00	.00	.00	.00	.00	.00	.00	.00	.00	.00
5. University loyalty II					■	.00	.00	.00	.00	.00	.00	.00	.00	.00
6. Father's social class						■	+.07	+.04	+.03	+.12	+.05	+.09	+.16	+.09
7. Place of residence							■	+.20	+.21	+.26	+.23	+.23	+.10	+.15
8. Status according to encyclopedias								■	+.54	+.76	+.35	+.42	+.37	+.14
9. Number of lines									■	+.58	+.66	+.70	+.59	+.19
10. Number of reference books										■	+.40	+.59	+.30	+.26
11. Academies etc.											■	+.81	+.19	+.28
12. Swedish honorary doctor's degrees												■	+.15	+.41
13. Government committees													■	−.05
14. Memberships in research councils														■
15. Enumerated international commissions														
16. Foreign guest professorships														
17. Academic positions														
18. Published works														
19. Name of doctor's thesis given in 'Vem är det'														
20. Distinctions														
21. Foreign honorary doctor's degrees														
22. Researcher's status														
23. General status														
24. Academic power														
B. Family cluster														
25. Number of marriages														
26. Number of children														
27. Educational level of the subject's wife														
28. Number of years between first examination and appointment to full professor														
29. Age at doctor's dissertation														
30. Age at appointment to full professor														
31. Income														
32. Income of the subject's wife														
33. Imminence between first marriage and first child														
34. Imminence between first and second child														
C. Social cluster														
35. Number of clubs														
36. Number of hobbies														

bles. In the same way the family cluster is reduced to 8 because 28, number of years between first examination and appointment to professor, and variable 30, age at appointment to professor, cannot be used. The social cluster still holds 2 variables. The career cluster contains 138 positive correlations out of 190 (73 %), the family cluster contains 14 positive out of 28 (50 %), and the two social variables remain uncorrelated (− .07). The 168 correlations between 21 career variables and 8 family variables should show a tendency toward negative correla-

36

										B. Family cluster										C. Social cluster	
15	16	17	18	19	20	21	22	23	24	25	26	27	28	29	30	31	32	33	34	35	36
−.02	.00	.00	−.02	+.02	+.09	+.02	−.01	+.02	−.02	−.27	+.25	+.13	.00	.00	.00	−.04	+.14	+.05	+.16	+.07	+.08
+.12	.00	.00	+.04	+.04	+.39	+.29	+.13	.00	−.03	+.02	−.05	−.16	.00	.00	.00	−.37	−.08	−.17	−.03	+.02	+.02
−.04	.00	.00	+.07	+.89	−.09	−.01	.00	+.03	+.01	−.01	+.14	−.06	.00	.00	.00	+.06	.00	+.03	−.10	−.04	−.04
.00	.00	.00	.00	.00	.00	.00	.00	.00	.00	.00	.00	.00	.00	.00	.00	.00	.00	.00	.00	.00	.00
.00	.00	.00	.00	.00	.00	.00	.00	.00	.00	.00	.00	.00	.00	.00	.00	.00	.00	.00	.00	.00	.00
−.10	.00	.00	+.02	−.20	−.02	−.08	−.04	+.08	+.08	−.13	+.05	+.14	.00	.00	.00	+.16	+.31	+.07	+.05	−.12	+.07
+.21	.00	.00	+.15	+.08	+.05	+.08	+.26	+.22	+.22	−.03	−.04	+.13	.00	.00	.00	+.23	+.22	+.14	−.14	−.19	−.27
+.25	.00	.00	+.43	−.05	+.23	+.01	+.43	+.66	+.46	−.10	−.02	+.15	.00	.00	.00	+.22	+.18	−.07	+.09	−.13	−.15
+.65	.00	.00	+.64	−.03	+.57	+.49	+.85	+.96	+.87	−.26	+.13	−.05	.00	.00	.00	+.19	+.36	+.05	+.07	−.14	−.14
+.30	.00	.00	+.47	−.04	+.30	+.07	+.51	+.65	+.44	−.13	+.03	+.09	.00	.00	.00	+.04	+.26	−.07	+.02	−.12	−.14
+.55	.00	.00	+.46	−.03	+.51	+.54	+.79	+.59	+.57	−.21	−.04	+.06	.00	.00	.00	+.19	+.20	+.05	−.28	−.09	−.10
+.53	.00	.00	+.67	−.03	+.60	+.37	+.84	+.61	+.51	−.13	+.03	+.06	.00	.00	.00	+.02	+.28	−.02	−.02	−.08	−.09
+.08	.00	.00	+.34	−.09	+.20	+.09	+.23	+.75	+.80	−.18	+.12	−.13	.00	.00	.00	+.39	+.07	+.13	+.04	−.12	−.21
−.05	.00	.00	+.38	−.02	+.10	−.02	+.25	+.14	+.02	−.02	−.12	−.07	.00	.00	.00	+.03	−.18	−.21	+.06	−.05	−.06
■	.00	.00	+.16	−.03	+.48	+.70	+.82	+.54	+.64	−.05	−.03	+.13	.00	.00	.00	−.11	+.47	+.09	+.03	−.04	−.06
	■	.00	.00	.00	.00	.00	.00	.00	.00	−.08	+.03	−.05	.00	.00	.00	+.19	+.11	−.08	+.01	−.10	−.03
		■	.00	.00	.00	.00	.00	.00	.00	−.01	+.13	−.04	.00	.00	.00	−.01	.00	+.01	−.15	−.03	−.03
			■	+.01	+.38	+.08	+.67	+.60	+.41	.11	+.09	.00	.00	.00	.00	+.66	+.48	+.01	+.11	+.12	−.04
				■	−.04	−.01	−.02	−.05	−.09	−.01	−.02	−.04	.00	.00	.00	−.07	.00	+.11	+.01	−.03	−.03
					■	+.34	+.59	+.49	+.47	−.11	−.01	+.07	.00	.00	.00	+.06	+.37	+.02	−.02	−.09	−.08
						■	+.60	+.42	+.50	−.24	+.11	−.04	.00	.00	.00	+.27	+.31	+.07	+.07	−.15	−.19
							■	+.74	+.71	−.19	+.06	−.02	.00	.00	.00	+.27	+.37	+.14	+.01	−.13	−.20
								■	+.92												
									■												
										■	−.53	−.04	.00	.00	.00	+.02	−.43	−.15	+.37	+.09	+.01
											■	+.07	.00	.00	.00	−.06	+.51	+.34	+.13	+.05	+.11
												■	.00	.00	.00	−.17	+.42	+.16	−.27	−.04	+.11
													■	.00	.00	.00	.00	.00	.00	.00	.00
														■	.00	.00	.00	.00	.00	.00	.00
															■	.00	.00	.00	.00	.00	.00
																■	−.15	+.09	−.03	−.10	−.18
																	■	+.26	−.28	.00	−.07
																		■	+.14	−.04	−.03
																			■	+.05	+.10
																				■	+.21
																					■

tions, but only 95 cases are like that (55 %). The 42 correlations between career variables and social variables are negative only in 7 cases (17 %), and then the 16 correlations between the family variables and the social variables are negative in 9 cases (55 %). Actually all three clusters are hardly correlated at all with one another, thus they show a tendency toward a compromise pattern.

In regard to the comparison between the samples, the matrix of the researchers' sample was expected to show more of a compensation pat-

tern and the matrix of their counterparts more of a unified value pattern. Then the researchers should have a higher percent positive correlations within the research cluster (as research values tend to integrate the variables) than their counterparts, the civil servants. The outcome was 78 % against 73 %. The researchers were expected a higher percent negative correlations between research cluster and family cluster (as marriage and children may delay research or successful research delay marriage) than the teachers. But this does not hold true. The percent is lower among the researchers: 50 % against 55 %.

There are at least three reasons for the failure of the theory:

1. The social scientists may be too mixed, have too broad a distribution of scientific ability. This is the most acceptable explanation from our point of view.

2. The variables may have too low reliability and/or validity to allow a more clearcut pattern.

3. The theory may be completely or partly wrong.

The first points are both reasonable but not possible to test. The third point, however, can be tested on the remaining samples. If the predictions break down completely, the theory must be wrong.

The matrices of jurisprudence researchers and of their counterparts, judges

The research cluster has 23 variables among the jurisprudence researchers, as variable 16, number of guest professorhips proved to be irrelevant in Table 4. We expect the 253 intercorrelations between them to be positive and so they are in 215 cases (85 %). The family cluster has 10 variables and 45 intercorrelations, 23 of them positive (51 %). The clubs proved useless in this sample and so there remains a single variable in the social cluster, the hobbies.

The 23 research variables are expected to have negative correlations with the ten family variables. They are negative in 155 cases out of 230 (67 %). The 23 correlations between research variables and hobbies are negative, as they should be, in only 11 cases (48 %) and then eventually family variables and hobbies are negative in 4 cases of 10 (40 %).

This can be considered a reasonable compensation pattern as the research cluster is well integrated and negatively correlated with the family cluster. This family cluster, on the other hand, is not integrated and the only remaining social variables, hobbies, does not behave at all.

What about the judges (Table 5)? The career cluster contains 20 variables, as variables 4, 5, 16, and 17 are irrelevant, that is, give only zero correlations. The remaining 20 variables have 190 intercorrelations, 145 positive (76 %). The family cluster in the same way has lost variables 28, 29, and 30; thus it is reduced to 7 variables with 21 intercorrelations, 11 of them positive (52 %). The two social variables are correlated + .21.

The 20 career variables have 140 intercorrelations with the 7 family variables, expected to be negative. They are negative in 45 cases (32 %). The 40 intercorrelations between the research cluster and the social cluster are negative in 35 cases (88 %). The 14 intercorrelations between the family cluster and the social are negative in 9 cases (64 %).

The strong tendency to positive correlations between the career cluster and the family cluster makes it impossible to call this a compensation pattern, rather a unified value pattern, if we−as usual− disregard the social variables.

Our second pair of samples from the jurisprudence area thus supports our prediction that samples of researchers would show a tendency towards the compensation pattern, indication that successful research may counteract family commitment or family life may be a compensation for research, which is not too rewarding. The sample of judges has a lower percent positive correlations in the career cluster, 76 % against 85 % among the researchers and a strong tendency towards the unified value pattern, as only 32 % of the correlations between the career cluster and the family cluster are negative, to be compared to 76 % among the researchers.

In this case our comparison has come out as we expected. We have one case against our expectations and one for. What about the remaining cases?

CHAPTER 4

A comparison between researchers and non-researchers with similar academic training

A comparison of matrices, using 36 variables

It was originally expected that the scientific work would press the researchers hard, forcing them—at least the successful ones—to withdraw from family life and early marriage, many children may in the same way delay or diminish research. If we compare researchers to non-researchers academically trained in the same field and now up to the same status level as our samples of researchers, we can test four hypotheses:

1. Researchers' research behavior should be better integrated than the corresponding career behaviors of their counterparts; that is, the matrix of a researchers' sample should have a higher percent positive intercorrelations in the research cluster than the corresponding career cluster of the relevant non-researchers' sample.

2. Researchers' family cluster should tend to have a higher percent negative correlations than that of the non-researchers.

3. The research or career cluster should dominate over the family cluster and thus in all samples have a higher percent positive correlations within the cluster than the family cluster.

4. As the behavior in the family cluster tends to counteract or compensate the dominating research or career variables, this compensation tendency should lessen the integration of the family cluster, that is, the sample with a higher percent negative correlations between research and family clusters should *not* have a higher percent positive intercorrelations within the family cluster.

We now turn to the empirical material and for each of the 16 samples, forming 8 pairs of one researchers' sample and one sample of counterparts (trained at the same faculty but no longer researchers), we use the matrices (the last 14 of these are given as appendix 3) to compute:

Table 6. *Intercorrelations from the matrices of 16 samples*

Sample of researchers	Researchers' sample, percent		
	Positive within research cluster	Negative between research and family cluster	Positive within family cluster
Social scientists	78	50	67
Researchers in			
humanities	61	51	40
law	85	67	51
theology	70	55	36
commerce	68	47	40
Scientists in engineering	77	44	44
Medical researchers	72	55	67
Researchers in forestry, etc.	71	58	58

Sample of counterparts	Non-researchers' sample, percent		
Civil servants	73	55	50
Teachers	52	42	49
Judges	76	32	52
Bishops, deans	69	52	42
Directors (commerce)	74	46	40
Directors (engineers)	68	45	42
Head Physicians	65	50	69
Forestry Officers	69	50	38

1. Percent of positive intercorrelations in the research or career cluster.
2. Percent of negative intercorrelations between the research and the family cluster.
3. Percent of positive intercorrelations within the family cluster.
   Table 6 presents the data.

We use these data to test our four hypotheses:

1. The researchers' research cluster should have a higher percent positive intercorrelations than the career cluster of the counterparts. The research cluster is higher in 7 out of 8 cases.

2. The percent of negative correlations between research and family cluster should be higher in the researchers' sample than in their counterparts'. They are so in 6 out of 8 cases.

3. The research or career cluster should have a higher percent of positive correlations than the corresponding family cluster. They are higher in 15 out of 16 cases.

4. In each pair of samples, the sample with a higher percent of negative correlations between research and family cluster should *not* have a higher percent of positive intercorrelations in the family cluster. The hypothesis is supported by 7 out of 8 cases.

Seven cases out of eight can be considered statistically significant; three of the hypotheses passed the test and the fourth was rather near. Our idea that researchers tend to be delayed, handicapped by early marriage, and that less successful researchers may compensate their scientific failure with a successful marriage and home is supported by our data. It is easy to point out a technical weakness in our data, to some degree responsible for the support they give our hypotheses: The researchers' samples nearly always contain 24 variables in the research cluster and 10 in the family cluster, the samples of the non-researchers (except the sample of bishops and deans) contain only 20 variables in the career cluster and 7 in the family cluster. The 7 variables lacking in the matrices of the non-researchers may be responsible for the higher percent of positive correlations in the research clusters of the researchers and for their higher percent of negative correlations between the research (career) cluster and the family cluster.

A comparison between the matrices of researchers and non-researchers using 20 research (or career) variables and 7 family variables

Only 20 variables in the research cluster are used, getting rid of those lacking in the corresponding sample of non-researchers, and always cutting them down to 20 in order to possibly make better comparisons between pairs for samples. In the same way only 7 variables in the family cluster are used, getting rid of variables 28, 29, and 30. We should then get the same number of intercorrelations within the research or career cluster (190), within the family cluster (21) and between the research and the family cluster (140). In this way, just the number of positive/negative correlations instead of percents can be given.

The sample of higher forestry officers, however, has only 19 variables in the career cluster, as variable 23, change of university, in their case is useless. There is only one faculty of forestry in all of Sweden. In order to make the data comparable, we have to add 1/19 of the negative correlations between the career and the family cluster.

Table 7. *Number of positive correlations within the research, the career and the family clusters and number of negative correlations between the research and the family clusters*

Sample of researchers	Researchers' sample, correlations		
	Positive within research cluster	Negative between research and family cluster	Positive within family cluster
Sum of all correlations	190	140	21
Social scientists	161	65	16
Researchers,			
humanities	136	68	10
law	162	83	11
theology	128	80	8
commerce	136	52	9
Scientists in engineering	152	56	11
Medical researchers	143	68	13
Researchers in forestry, etc.	145	77	15
Naturalists	136	68	11

Sample of nonresearchers	Non-researchers sample, correlations		
Sum of all correlations	190	140	21
Civil servants	138	67	9
Teachers	97	65	8
Judges	145	56	11
Bishops, deans	134	70	10
Directors (commerce)	140	45	13
Directors (engineering)	127	48	11
Head physicians	129	43	16
Forestry officers	131[a]	70[a]	10
Officers	128	55	16

[a] Data corrected.

When a comparison is made between the number of positive correlations within the research or career cluster (190 correlations all together) and the number of positive correlations within the family cluster (21 correlations), it must be done by multiplying the latter number by 9 (Table 7).

The data from the eight pairs of samples is used to test the four hypotheses once more:

1. The researchers' matrices should have more positive intercorrelations within the research cluster than the corresponding non-researchers. They are higher in six out of eight cases.

43

2. The researchers matrices should have more negative intercorrelations between the research and the family cluster than the corresponding samples of non-researchers. The number of negative correlations is higher among the researchers in seven out of eight cases.

3. The number of positive correlations within the research or career cluster should be higher than within the corresponding family clusters when multiplied by 9. They are higher in 15 out of 16 cases.

4. Within each pair of samples, the sample with a higher number of negative correlations between the research and the family clusters should *not* have a higher number of positive correlations within the family cluster. They are not higher in seven out of eight cases.

These new and more rigid tests, where the number of variables are kept constant, give a much more favorable result. The system of hypotheses remains, even if the expected clearcut compensation patterns are not found. It is now believed that the samples of researchers have too broad a distribution of scientific ability to allow the compensation pattern to show. Nonetheless, the last table seems to indicate that researchers give their research behavior a priority over their family behavior—unless they get little reward from their research or the family commands too much of their interest or they seek consolation from the family when their scientific results do not fulfill their expectations.

But how are the exceptions to be explained? Why do the pairs of samples in the social area, the theological area, and the commerce area not follow the general trend? Reasons can easily be found afterwards: The careers ranging from teacher to high-level administrator may be more frustrating to their families than scientific work. The bishops and deans have often been selected among the most famous theology professors. The directors with a commercial-academic training may have a career more demanding than that of their scientific counterparts.

It should be possible to test these ideas in a more methodological way. Let us start by admitting that our hypothesis about research work as more demanding than anything else may be wrong in some cases. There are, after all, more difficult and more stressing jobs than the scientists', but they probably are high up in the hierarchy, thus too few to be useful as counterparts to the more numerous researchers. Then we come down to a simple truth: The results obtained from comparing samples of researchers with samples of non-researchers totally depend on the samples selected.

A reasonable choice of samples has been made. The results still are

relevant and interesting, at least to researchers. A control can be made. Suppose that this is no more than a special case of a general tendency, the more priority a career is given, the more family life is used to compensate frustrations in the career. The results then would have little relevance for the specific *academic* careers and *academic* society.

This control must be tried one way or another; it is the subject of the next chapter.

CHAPTER 5

The interaction between career cluster and family cluster studied in 19 samples

It was expected from the start to find clearcut compensation patterns in the samples of researchers, indicating that their scientific work was very important to them and counteracted their family responsibilities, unless the research work gave so little reward that they tended to compensate their frustration within their family. However, very clearcut compensation patterns were not found, but only a stronger tendency towards this ideal among the researchers than among their counterparts of non-researchers. The results have been explained in two ways. First, a very homogenous sample of good researchers is needed to get clearcut compensation patterns. It is doubtful that the researchers occupying top positions always are top researchers. It is possible they may be deluged by administrative work once they have been appointed to full professors. If so, something between the compensation pattern and the compromise pattern can only be expected. Second, researchers need not always have a worse career burden than all other comparable groups. There might be samples still worse off than the corresponding researchers, or even those which have such groups represented in our samples of counterparts. In this case, an attempt at generalization should be made: the heavier the career burden, the less family life can support the career and the more importance family and home have as a refuge from the career. This should hold for samples of researchers as well as for samples of non-researchers.

Evidently there is a need for measures of career burden, of the assistance family can give career and of family importance. For this purpose we use three variables out of the matrices:

1. Career burden is measured by the number of positive intercorrelations within the career cluster of 20 variables, giving a total of 190 correlations.

Table 8. *Career burdens, family assistance and family importance in 10 samples of researchers*

Sample	Career burden	Family assistance	Family importance
Researchers in law	162	57	11
Social scientists	161	75	16
Scientists in engineering	152	84	17
Scientists in forestry, etc.	145[a]	63[a]	15
Medical researchers	143	72	16
Researchers in humanities	136	72	11
Researchers in commerce	136	88	11
Naturalists	136	72	11
Researchers in theology	128	60	11

[a] Data corrected.

2. Family assistance (to career) we try to measure as the number of positive correlations between 20 career variables and seven family variables (140 correlations).

3. Family importance we intend to measure as the number of positive intercorrelations out of the 21 possible between the seven family variables.

What is expected? If a study is made of the interaction between these three variables, characterizing the correlation matrix of each sample, the effect of the career burden is expected to create a clearcut compensation pattern, here given the form of three hypotheses:

1. A negative rank order correlation between career burden and family assistance to the career. (This means that the family tends to be a distraction in the most pressing careers.)

2. A positive rank order correlation between career burden and family importance as a refuge.

3. A negative rank order correlation between family assistance and family importance as a refuge from the career.

If a ranking list was made of all our *19* samples, we probably would find some tendencies in these directions as the samples of researchers generally have a higher career burden, less help in their career from the family and more need of a refuge in the family than the corresponding samples of non-researchers. In order to get rid of this effect, it is necessary to keep the samples of researchers apart from the samples of their counterparts and to make two different ranking lists. Let us start with our 9 samples of researchers (Table 8).

Table 9. *Career burdens, family assistance and family importance in nine samples of non-researchers*

Sample	Career burden	Family assistance	Family importance
Judges	145	84	14
Directors (commercial training)	140	95	13
Civil servants	138	73	14
Bishops, deans	134	70	10
Higher forestry officers	131[a]	70[a]	10
Head physicians	129	97	16
Officers in army, navy, and Air Force	128	85	16
Directors (engineers)	127	92	11
Teachers, headmasters, etc.	97	75	10

[a] Data corrected.

A negative rank correlation was expected between career burden and family assistance. It is only – .14. The expected positive correlation between career burden and family importance is +.60 and the expected negative correlation between family assistance (to career) and family importance (as a refuge from career) – .13. In two cases out of three, the expectations are *not* fulfilled.

The nine samples of non-researchers are now examined (Table 9).

A negative rank correlation between career burden and family assistance to career is expected. It is only – .11. The expected positive correlation between career burden and family importance as a refuge from career is only +.17 and the expected negative correlation between family assistance to career and family importance as a refuge is +.59. All three correlations thus contradict the expectations.

The theory just tested has to be discarded as five tests out of six failed. Career burden cannot be made responsible for the variances in family assistance or family importance between our samples. This means, however, that the differences (in career burden) found in the previous chapter between researchers and non-researchers with the same type of academic training cannot be dismissed. On the contrary, there are now better reasons to believe that the researchers in each area tend to behave differently in the family life sphere than their counterparts of non-researchers. We may have found something unique in the family life of researchers – at least in Sweden.

Still, there are two high rank correlations in these two tables giving interesting information. Why do the samples of researchers have such a strong correlation between career burden and family importance when

Table 10. *Connections (number of positive correlations out of 7) between career burden and importance of seven family variables among researchers and non-researchers*

Sample	Career burden	25	26	27	31	32	33	34
Researchers								
17. Law	162	3	4	2	3	4	4	2
15. Social science	161	4	4	4	4	6	5	5
12. Engineering	152	3	3	3	3	3	6	3
14. Forestry	145	3	4	3	4	6	4	6
11. Medicine	143	5	5	6	5	3	3	5
10. Humanities	136	2	4	2	3	2	5	4
7. Commerce	136	5	3	2	3	2	2	4
6. Theology	128	3	5	5	3	1	2	3
Non-researchers								
17. Law	162	5	5	4	2	3	6	3
15. Social science	161	5	5	4	3	3	4	4
12. Engineering	152	3	3	3	2	2	5	4
14. Forestry	145	3	4	2	3	2	1	5
11. Medicine	143	3	5	6	6	3	4	5
10. Humanities	136	2	3	2	1	3	4	5
7. Commerce	136	2	3	5	6	3	3	4
6. Theology	128	3	2	4	2	2	4	3

the non-researchers have such a weak one and why do the non-researchers show such a high correlation between family assistance to career and family importance as a refuge, when researchers do not?

Differences in family patterns between researchers and non-researchers

It was discovered that family importance (number of positive correlations within the family cluster) tended to correlate with career burden (number of positive correlations within the career cluster) only among the researchers' samples but with family assistance (number of negative correlations between the career cluster and the family cluster) only among the samples of non-researchers. It is now the intent of the author to find out which of the family variables can be made responsible for these differences.

If a comparison is made between researchers and non-researchers, an exclusion must be made of natural scientists and officers, as they have no counterparts. Connections must be sought between career burden (positive correlations within career cluster) on the one hand and the family variables on the other. This is done among the samples of re-

Table 11. *Connections between family assistance and importance of 7 family variables among researchers and non-researchers*

Sample	Family assistance	Family variables						
		25	26	27	31	32	33	34
Researchers								
Medicine	97	5	5	6	5	3	3	5
Commerce	95	5	3	2	3	2	2	4
Engineering	92	3	3	3	3	3	6	3
Law	84	3	4	2	3	4	4	2
Humanities	75	2	4	2	3	2	5	4
Social science	73	4	4	4	4	6	5	5
Theology	70	3	5	5	3	1	2	3
Forestry	70	3	4	3	4	6	4	6
Non-researchers								
Medicine		3	5	6	6	3	4	5
Commerce		2	3	5	6	3	3	4
Engineering		3	3	3	2	2	5	4
Law		2	4	3	2	3	5	3
Humanities		2	3	2	1	3	4	5
Social science		0	4	3	2	3	3	3
Theology		3	2	4	2	2	4	3
Forestry		3	4	2	3	2	2	5

searchers and we do give the corresponding data for non-researchers although they are irrelevant here. Tables similar to the previous ones are constructed, starting with connections, that is number of positive correlations out of the 7 given, between career burden and the seven different family variables (Table 10).

Evidently variables 31, 32, and 33 seem to give the rank orders best correlated with the *career burden* among researchers. The connections between *family assistance* (number of positive correlations between career cluster and family cluster) and *family importance* (number of positive correlations within the family cluster) among the samples of non-researchers is given in Table 11 where we start with the data for researchers although they are irrelevant in this case:

Among the non-researchers variables 27, 31, 32, and 33 follow the descending rank of family assistance better than the remaining variables. If variables 31, 32, and 33 thus are made responsible for both of our two unexpected correlations, how should the result be interpreted?

Variable 31 is income; 32, income of wife; and 33, nearness between marriage and first child. Together these three variables indicate a stable economic ground for marriage and an early child as a result of this or as a reason for it. This little child-economy cluster on the one hand is related to more unified career clusters among researchers, that is nega-

tively correlated to them, and on the other hand, it is positively correlated with the career cluster among non-researchers.

This sounds a bit confusing. It could be seen in this light: good economy and child can help the researchers to integrate his research behavior to a closed cluster, closed even to his helpful family, but the non-researchers instead use economy and child for their career and include them in their career cluster. The female role does not look too attractive in either case. Is she better off feeding and fondling a researcher absorbed in things, he can't even mention to her or does she prefer to use all of her resources, even her children for the career of her husband? The data thus suggest something interesting but only about differences *between* samples. *Groups* of non-researchers making more money and an early first child tend to include these successful production data in their career cluster. But this does not say anything about tendencies *within* these groups, and so we turn our attention in that direction.

CHAPTER 6

The interaction between economy and research within samples

Presented in the previous chapter were samples of researchers and the fact that samples with better economy and family planning showed a more integrated research pattern. The samples of non-researchers making more money and having their first child sooner included these data in their career cluster. This is interesting, but it would be far more interesting to test this idea within the nine samples of researchers instead of just comparing them.

The differences found between samples have no statistical effect on the differences within the samples. It is now assumed that the explanations given to those differences *between* samples should hold also *within* samples: individual researchers with high income, wife with high income, and a first child soon after the marriage should tend to be better researchers!

What is meant by better researchers? A list of 24 research variables was presented, but they were meant more to probe the field than to define research. If the three variables 31 (Income), 32 (Income of wife), and 33 (Nearness between marriage and first child) are to be used as instruments to test the research variables, they require study to be reclassified from an economic point of view.

A sociologist may consider own income, wife's income, and the first child as very important instrumental family behavior. This view is adopted in an attempt which made use of the concepts instrumental and expressive to classify research variables. The following three classes resulted:

1. Instrumental research variables, relevant for systematically planned scientific work. No less than 17 of the 24 research variables are included in this dominant class, which is no surprise. It can hardly be necessary to

explain these 17 cases, but it should be explained why the remaining 7 variables have been excluded.

2. Expressive research variables, relevant to new approaches, thinking little bound by tradition or respect, willingness to take large risks. Only three variables are suggested, all of them concerned with going abroad, since the Swedish research system pays little attention to approaches or traditions not yet accepted here and is unwilling to accept merits acquired from foreign universities. The following related variables are listed:

15. Number of enumerated international commissions.
16. Number of enumerated foreign guest professorships.
21. Number of foreign doctors' degrees enumerated by the subject.

3. Career variables of background type, useful for a career, but in theory less important for research.

1. Family name of researcher, classified according to its status.
6. Father's social class.
9. Number of lines given the subject in *Vem är det 1969*. Researchers often hesitate to give too much material, but career-minded people should have less qualms.
12. Number of Swedish honorary doctor's degrees. Few people have more than one, but these degrees, until recently generally were used to reward very successful persons, using their money or their ability to the advantage of the university.

Hypotheses

It has previously been pointed out that clearcut negative correlations cannot be expected between research variables on the one hand and family variables on the other; unless, of course, the sample is very homogeneous and consists of researchers on the same high level. As clearcut correlations have not been found, it is suspected that the samples are rather heterogeneous, listing researchers of varying ability. If so, expectations should be very modest, as correlations would tend to be low, almost near zero. All is asked for are *tendencies* to the signs of the correlations, positive or negative. These tendencies will indicate where more pronounced interaction between clusters could be expected if more homogeneous samples of researchers were secured.

53

The 19 samples available are divided into three groups:

I. Nine samples of male researchers from (1) Social Science, (2) Jurisprudence, (3) Humanities, (4) Theology, (5) Commerce, (6) Engineering, (7) Medical Research, (8) Forestry and Agriculture, and (9) Naturalists.

II. The sample of female researchers from all fields.

III. Nine samples of non-researchers.

The interaction between the family planning variables 31, 32, and 33 on the one hand, and different classes or research variables on the other are expected to follow different patterns in the three groups of samples. The following seven hypotheses have evolved:

Hypothesis 1. The instrumental family variables 31, 32, and 33 are expected to be positively related to instrumental research variables, as both kinds of variables can be taken as expressions of an instrumentally-oriented personality. The formula from the previous chapter may be preferred: a stable economy and children seem to stimulate research (and/or the other way round).

Hypothesis 2. The expressive research variables 15, 16, 21 (seeking glory abroad) should be negatively correlated with the instrumental family variables 31, 32, and 33. Or it may be said that good economy and a child would tend to prevent foreign assignments.

Hypothesis 3. The career variables of good background 1, 6, 9, and 12 are, of course, instrumental to career but not to research. Among researchers variables 1, 6, 9, and 12 are expected to be negatively correlated to 31, 32, and 33. This could be expressed in another way: Good economy and stable family should be able to compensate a lack of earlier background.

Hypothesis 4. If female researchers are to succeed in research they had better let marriage and especially children wait. They probably would have to be content with less pay, too. Negative correlations are expected between 31, 32, and 33 on the one hand and all the instrumental research variables on the other.

Hypothesis 5. Female researchers would be seriously hampered by marriage, children, and a good job, if they considered working abroad. The husband might be unwilling, the children a nuisance in a new setting and possibly even their good jobs back in Sweden might disappear while they were gone. Variables 31, 32, and 33 then should be negatively correlated to variables 15, 16, and 21 (glory abroad).

Hypothesis 6. Female researchers need a good background just as well as men and a lack of it could be compensated by good economy and a child, just as with men. It is expected that variables 31, 32, and 33 will be negatively correlated to variables 1, 6, 9, and 12 (background).

Hypothesis 7. When an attempt is made to focus on research behavior of non-researchers, admittedly the three classes of variables do not make much sense. It is hoped that no differences will be found at all between their share of negative correlations with variables 31, 32, and 33.

The correlations

From the presented 19 matrices, the number of negative correlations is taken between the variables 31, 32, and 33 on the one hand and the classes of research variables on the other. Nine samples of male researchers and one sample of female researchers are used. Their shares of negative correlations are presented in Table 12.

This table can be used to test the first six hypotheses:

Hypothesis 1. The instrumental research variables should have a low share of negative correlations with 31, 32, 33. It is low: 166/439.

Hypothesis 2. The expressive research variables should have a high share of negative correlations with 31, 32, 33. It is high for at least more than half: 39/74.

Hypothesis 3. The career variables should have a high share of negative correlations with 31, 32, 33. It is high, that is, above 51/102. It is a little more: 55/102.

Hypothesis 4. Female researchers should have a higher share of negative correlations than men between instrumental research variables and 31, 32, 33. Their share is higher: 35/48 compared to 166/439 for men.

Hypothesis 5. Female researchers should have a higher share of negative correlations than men between expressive research variables and 31, 32, 33. Their share is higher: 9/9 against 39/74 for men.

Hypothesis 6. Female researchers should have about the same share of negative correlations as men between career variables and 31, 32, 33. It is, however, lower: 4/9 against 55/102 for men. The hypothesis did not survive the test.

The first five hypotheses came out well. Hypothesis 7 is tested on a similar table of the share of negative correlations between variables 31,

Table 12. *Researchers shares of negative correlations between research variables 1–24 and variables 31, 32, 33*

Class of instrumental variables and expressive variables	Sample of male researchers										Sample of female researchers
	Social science	Law	Humanities	Theology	Commerce	Engineering	Med. res.	For., Agri.	Nat. Science	Sum	
Instrumental research variables											
2.	2/3	2/3	1/3	2/3	1/3	2/3	2/3	2/3	2/3	16/25	3/3
3.	1/3	2/2	1/3	1/2	2/3	2/3	0/3	2/3	1/3	12/25	1/3
4.	0/3	2/3	2/3	1/2	0/3	0/3	3/3	1/3	1/2	10/25	1/3
5.	2/2	1/3	2/3	0/2	0/3	0/3	1/2	1/3	1/2	8/22	1/3
7.	0/3	2/3	0/3	1/2	0/3	0/2	2/3	1/3	1/2	7/24	1/3
8.	0/3	2/3	0/3	0/3	2/3	0/3	0/3	2/3	1/2	7/26	2/3
10.	0/3	2/3	0/3	0/3	1/3	0/3	0/3	2/3	1/3	6/27	3/3
11.	1/3	2/3	2/3	2/3	1/3	0/3	2/3	0/3	1/3	11/27	3/3
13.	0/3	2/3	0/3	2/3	1/3	0/3	0/3	0/3	1/3	6/27	2/3
14.	0/3	1/3	2/3	1/3	2/3	0/3	2/3	1/3	0/3	9/27	2/3
17.	0/3	2/3	1/2	2/2	1/3	2/2	2/3	0/3	2/3	12/24	–
18.	0/3	1/3	3/3	1/3	0/3	1/3	0/3	2/3	2/3	10/27	3/3
19.	1/3	2/3	2/3	0/3	3/3	1/3	2/3	2/3	1/3	14/27	1/3
20.	2/3	1/3	1/3	3/3	0/3	0/3	1/3	1/3	2/3	11/27	3/3
22.	0/3	2/3	2/3	2/3	1/3	1/3	1/3	2/3	1/3	12/27	3/3
23.	0/3	1/3	0/3	2/3	1/3	1/3	0/3	1/3	1/2	7/26	3/3
24.	0/2	2/3	1/3	2/3	1/3	0/3	1/3	0/3	1/3	8.26	3/3
Sum										166/439	35/48
Expressive research variables											
15.	1/3	2/3	1/3	2/3	0/3	1/3	2/3	3/3	2/3	14/27	3/3
16.	1/3	–	0/2	1/3	1/3	3/3	2/3	2/3	3/3	13/23	3/3
21.	1/3	2/3	1/2	3/3	1/3	0/2	1/3	2/2	1/3	12/27	3/3
Sum										39/77	9/9
Career variables											
1.	2/3	1/2	2/3	2/2	1/3	2/3	2/3	2/3	1/3	15/25	1/3
6.	1/3	1/3	2/3	3/3	2/3	2/3	1/3	3/3	1/3	16/27	1/3
9.	0/3	2/3	1/3	2/3	2/3	1/3	1/3	1/3	2/3	12/27	2/3
12.	1/3	1/3	2/3	2/2	1/3	1/2	1/2	2/2	1/3	12/23	–
Sum										55/102	4/9

32, and 33, and the classes of research variables. Table 13 gives the data to be tested.

Hypothesis 7: Non-researchers show no difference between the shares of negative correlations of instrumental research variables, expressive research variables and career variables with variables 31, 32, and 33. There are no differences, as the shares turn out to be 131/344, 13/37,

Table 13. *Non-researchers' shares of negative correlations between research variables 1–24 and variables 31, 32, 33*

Class of instrumental variables and expressive variables	Civil servants	Judges	Teachers	Bishops	Dir. (comm.)	Dir. (engin.)	Head physicians	Forestry officers	Officers	Sum
Instrumental research variables										
2.	1/3	3/3	1/3	1/3	2/3	0/2	0/3	3/3	0/3	8/24
3.	2/3	0/2	0/3	2/3	0/2	0/3	0/3	3/3	0/3	7/25
4.	—	—	1/3	1/2	—	—	1/3	—	—	3/8
5.	2/3	—	1/2	1/3	—	—	2/3	—	—	6/11
7.	0/1	0/3	1/3	1/3	0/3	2/3	2/3	1/3	2/3	9/25
8.	2/3	1/3	2/3	1/3	0/3	1/3	1/3	2/3	0/2	10/26
10.	2/3	1/3	1/3	1/3	0/3	1/3	1/3	2/3	0/2	10/26
11.	1/2	0/3	2/3	1/3	0/3	1/3	2/3	1/3	2/3	8/27
13.	1/3	0/3	1/3	2/3	0/3	1/3	0/3	1/3	2/3	7/19
14.	1/2	1/3	1/2	—	0/2	0/3	1/3	2/2	1/2	—
17.	—	—	—	—	—	—	—	—	—	—
18.	0/3	1/3	0/3	1/3	2/3	0/3	1/3	2/3	2/3	9/27
19.	1/3	0/2	0/3	2/3	—	1/1	1/3	—	1/2	6/17
20.	2/3	0/3	1/3	1/3	0/3	2/3	1/3	1/3	0/3	8/27
22.	1/3	0/3	3/3	1/3	0/3	1/3	1/3	2/3	2/3	11/27
23.	2/3	0/3	2/3	2/3	0/3	0/3	1/3	0/3	3/3	10/27
24.	1/3	0/3	2/3	2/3	0/3	1/3	2/3	1/3	1/2	10/26
Sum										131/344
Expressive research variables										
15.	1/2	1/3	0/3	1/2	2/3	0/2	0/3	3/3	0/3	8/24
16.	—	—	1/2	1/2	—	0/2	1/3	—	—	3/9
21.	—	1/2	—	1/2	—	—	—	—	—	2/4
Sum										13/37
Career variables										
1.	0/3	1/3	2/3	1/2	1/3	2/3	1/3	1/3	2/3	11/26
6.	1/3	0/3	0/2	1/3	1/3	0/3	1/3	0/2	1/3	5/25
9.	1/3	0/3	2/3	2/3	1/3	0/3	1/3	1/3	1/2	9/26
12.	0/1	1/3	—	1/3	0/2	3/3	1/2	2/3	—	8/17
Sum										33/94

and 33/94. Their respective percentages are 38 %, 35 %, and 35 %.

Only one of the seven hypotheses proposed in this chapter has not been able to stand the test this time. The tendencies found *between* samples then may hold also *within* samples. Among male researchers a stable economy and an early first child are related to good research, but neither to work abroad nor to social background. Among female researchers, stable economy and an early first child, on the contrary, are

related to less valuable research, but strongly related negatively to work abroad. The non-researchers do not show similar tendencies.

Theoretically, some of these classes of variables have been described as instrumental or expressive. Using these terms, the results can be rephrased: Among male researchers, instrumental family variables are positively correlated to instrumental research variables, but negatively correlated to expressive research variables and to background variables more useful to a career outside research. Among female researchers, instrumental family variables are negatively correlated to instrumental as well as to expressive research variables. Non-researchers do not show any differences between the three classes of research variables.

The female researchers are a small group, only 50 persons out of the 10 000 included in *Vem är det 1969*. The male researchers number at least 2 000. This, of course, demonstrates efficiently the serious handicaps of women in research work. Still, if only a very select group of women are able to overcome the difficulties and produce high class research, it would be expected of them to have made efficient adaptations. Two of these adaptations may have been found: to accept a low income and to postpone their first child.

Even though our results apply only to Sweden, it must be kept in mind that Sweden has for a long time seriously tried to give women the same rights as men, so it is suspected that female researchers may be still worse off in other countries. As much information as possible should be taken from our Swedish sources about women in research to test this idea.

CHAPTER 7

Difference in role structure and role strain among male and female researchers

In the foregoing, the eventual effects of the specific and uncompromising character of scientific work upon its practioners as compared to parallel groups of non-researchers has been treated. In the light of the findings of that study, a broader analysis of the researcher's situation embracing both male and female scientists was felt to be essential. Thus, the reasoning presented in the preceding chapters is here further developed toward a more comprehensive view of research in terms of instrumentality and expressiveness. The traditional, expressive role of woman as mother and wife is related to the instrumental scientific career, and an attempt is made in a descriptive-exploratory study to shed light upon the relationship between these two roles.

Theoretical background
Sex role ideologies of today

During the last decade, a gradual displacement has taken place in the debate on equality between men and women with reference to, among other things, the terminology employed. From an earlier narrow-minded conception of the problem as 'the feminist question', one is now inclined to use the considerably more adequate designation 'the sex role question'. This view is a new way of looking at the problem, which implies an attempt to reach an overall view of society. To attain this, a capacity for distance-looking that is, freedom from ethnocentric norms and values is necessary. The ethnocentrism in the present case is twofold, as it is simultaneously national and patriarchal. The term 'feminist question' indicates a starting-point and direction and belongs to the same category of concepts as 'the Negro problem', 'the handicap matter' etc. Their frames of reference are the male-governed society, the

white man's world and the healthy man's world, respectively. A change-over to the new appellation 'the sex role question', is not only a sign of enhanced consciousness of the existing complex social relations, it also constitutes and indication, that a broader we-feeling, based on both men and women and with an accompanying weakening of the border-line between in-group and out-group is beginning to manifest itself. Edmund Dahlström surveys lucidly older and newer ideologies concerning the roles of the sexes in *The Changing Roles of Men and Women* (London, 1967). The older ones are:

I) *The traditional* ideological position on sex roles, attached to the bible's religious conceptions, according to which woman is considered a minor, inferior to man;

II) *The early liberal* ideological position on sex roles rooted in the Age of Enlightenment and its ideas of equal worth and equal rights of all human beings. The principal task of women is considered to be located in the home;

III) *The romantic* ideological position on sex roles, which constitutes a selective summary of the two preceding ones. The sexes are considered complementary in their characters, which are perceived as essentially different. The distinctive nature of woman is centered around the functions of home, while man is expected to deal with the external contacts in professional work etc.

IV) The ideological position of *Marxism* on sex roles, with the same basic attitude as the early liberal one concerning the equal rights of the sexes. However, the means considered necessary to attain this equality differ, in so far as the Marxian ideology assumes an independent contribution from the woman in the form of gainful work within a socialistic system to be the only road to equality.

As for the ideologies of the current sex role debate, Dahlström makes a classification along the dimension of conservatism-radicalism with respect to the conception of the traditional structure and function of the family. On the basis of this dimension, the grouping is made in two principal ideologies: 1) *The moderate* ideological position on the sex roles, which stresses that woman occupies two roles. Within the ideology there exists a certain variation, emphasizing either woman's role as housewife or her professional role; 2) *The radical* ideological position, which rejects the idealization of the housewife and strives toward a life-long professional achievement on the part of the woman. Here there is likewise

a variation: on the one hand the liberal-political approach, on the other the Communist outlook, the way it is represented in the Soviet Union.

Another type of classification is made by Caroline Bird (Bird, C., *Born Female,* New York, 1969) on the basis of four distinctive clusters of attitudes to the respective roles of the sexes without any attempt to connect on to specific political ideologies. The attitude clusters can be described along a continuum of degree of sex role traditionalism, where the most pro-traditional extreme is characterized by a patriarchal centering around the man with the woman as a second-hand person, while the anti-traditional extreme considers both sexes as goals in themselves.

The dominant attitude in *Old Masculinism* is, that womans's anatomy determines her social functions and confines her to home and child-rearing, as she is considered mentally and physically incapable of managing a man's job. Advocates of this attitude are, according to Bird, Sigmund Freud, most doctors, business men, lawyers, legislators, self-employed craftsmen, farmers and most women, especially nurses, secretaries, company housekeepers and housewifes.

The overt activity of advocates of this outlook is relatively low in the public Swedish debate, a fact which does not imply that their number is small. In a wider time perspective there are several striking examples from parliamentary debates, mass media etc., which taken together give a fairly good notion of the prevalence of Old Masculinism in Sweden. As a typical example of books representing this approach I choose *The Psychology of Sex* by Oswald Schwarz (England, 1965), who claims that woman unlike man *is* her body and her womb and therefore uncapable of abstract and logical reasoning.

New Masculinism endeavours to modernize the traditional role of woman in engaging her in gainful employment and 'widen her horizon', 'explode the myth' etc. All on condition that this activity does not infringe upon the privileges of man. Woman is considered the bearer of specific sex-determined aptitudes, which give her a special position as idealistic and altruistic worker. As examples of spokesmen for this opinion, Bird mentions David Riesman and Margaret Mead. The location of this attitude on the traditionalism continuum is debatable, as it contains several factors, which need not necessarily be interpreted as expressions of the same basic outlook. It is, for example, hard to imagine a consistent development of the specific traits mentioned above (humanity, sympathy, antidestructiveness etc.) without an accompanying alteration of the role of man and, consequently, of his privileges. New Masculinism thus can be said to comprise two variants, the first one

61

giving woman some kind of cleaning function in the form of more or less casual gainful work preferably in fields neglected by man, and without any notable restructuring of man's role as a consequence. The second and less traditional variant certainly should further build upon this healing and restoring task but now with broader social implications even as far as man is concerned. As a representative of the former variant, I choose the work *Women's two roles* by Alva Myrdal and Viola Klein (London, 1956), while I consider *On the Subjection of Women* by John Stuart Mill (New York, 1869), *Kärleken och äktenskapet, del I och II* ('Love and Marriage') composed by Ellen Kay (Stockholm, 1923) and *The Natural Superiority of Women* by Ashley Montagu (New York, 1968) examples of the latter category within New Masculinism.

A distinctive trait in *Old Feminism* is a firm declaration of woman's equality to man. Bird describes the attitude as competitive, where the competition with man becomes a means of self-assertion and is employed as a proof of the ability of woman. Unlike the former clusters of attitudes, the emphasis in the present one is on identical activities for men and women, the ideal towards which woman strives being that of man. No example of advocates of this attitude is given by Bird, but she considers if frequent above all among unmarried professional women. The outlook is probably not uncommon either among the pioneers of the emancipation of women or among the feminists of today.

Finally, *New Feminism* falls near to the radical sex role ideology in Dahlström's analysis. It implies a rejection of the traditional sex roles and a reorientation toward a wider freedom of choice for both men and women. To obtain this, a radical change of functions as well as structure of the two sex roles is necessary. Representative of this approach are in my opinion i.a.: *The Changing Roles of Men and Women* published in English in 1967 (op.cit.) and *The Feminine Mystique* by Betty Friedan (England, 1965).

The above attempt to chart the present sex role attitudes by means of Bird's four categories is assuredly not exhaustive, and many a nuance is inevitably wiped out in this type of classification. Nevertheless, it provides us with a certain essential lucidity and serves as a background to the subsequent reasoning.

Definition of 'sex role'

Every society described in the social anthropological literature prescribes different attitudes and behavior of men and women. Their way of being designed and distributed between the sexes varies to a great extent from culture to culture, so that what is unthinkable for men in one society is considered solely a 'man's work' in another etc. Each society has its own explanation to the prevailing role assignment, and it is usually connected with the physiological differences between the sexes, the implications of those differences being interpreted in culturally determined ways. A comparative study of various cultures shows that the social consequences of sex affiliation are entirely dependent on the cultural prescriptions. This also to a very great extent applies to the psychological differences between men and women, which on closer examination exhibit such a large variation from one society to another, that their alleged biological anchorage can be of little validity.

The term 'sex role' refers here with Harriet Holter's definition (in Dahlström, E., et al., *Kvinnors liv och arbete,* Stockholm, 1963) to: 'among other things those expectations of activities and personal traits, of rights and duties which the sex of a person raises in the environment'. Thus, the role is ascribed, not achieved, wherefore the individual in being born is captured in the network of expectations being attached to the sex in his/her particular culture.

Instrumentality-Expressiveness

The conceptual couple instrumental–expressive derives originally from Talcott Parsons' (in Merton, Brown and Cottrell, *Sociology Today,* New York, 1959) analysis of social systems. He there indicates four separate functions, which have to be fulfilled in order to make the system or the society work. Two of them are instrumental and attached to the means (the instruments) of an activity, while two functions are expressive and centered around immediate goals. The functions are further characterized along another dimension related to external and internal orientation respectively, and can therefore be depicted in a fourfold table (Figure 1) where each axis represents one dimension.

Of particular interest in this connection is the validity of the functions, which, according to Parsons, is not restricted to societies but is also applicable to other forms of social systems. Parsons here connects on to Bales' (Parsons, Bales & Shils, *Working Papers in the Theory of*

	Instrumental	Consummatory (expressive)
External	A. Adaptive Function (integrating of means toward determined goals)	G. Goal-Attainment Function
Internal	L. Pattern-Maintenance and Tension-Management Function	I. Integrative Function (enhancement and preservation of solidarity)

Figure 1. *Parson's schedule of functional problems*

Action, Glencoe, Ill., 1953) schedule for leadership in small groups: two principal complexes of needs have to be satisfied if the group is to function adequately. One consists of instrumental needs, expressed in the ambition to raise and organize means and resources with the aim of reaching certain more or less distant goals. These functions are administered by a task- or production-oriented leader. To meet the expressive needs, another set of qualities is required, as it is a matter of creating solidarity and an emotionally rewarding climate of social intercourse within the group. The leader of these functions can be called interaction or expressive leader. Instrumental functions are thus goal-oriented but in the long view, so that the means constitute the central factor. The expressive functions, on the other hand, are self-sufficient in so far as they represent goals in themselves. Many a group has a dominating trait of either instrumentality or expressiveness, a case in point being the Calvinistic movement. According to Allardt (*Samhälls-struktur och sociala spänningar,* Tammerfors, 1965) the conduct of the Calvinists can be described as instrumental with dogmatism, long-term goals and a special emphasis on rationalism as chief components.

Bales' schedule likewise is assumed to have a relatively high degree of generalizable applicability, something which is demonstrated in a mapping out of the role relations in the family. The father is alloted to the role of instrumental leader, since he is the one who preferably handles the contacts with the external world, while the mother performs the function of expressive leader and attends to the internal emotional affairs of the family.

That this role assignment has its counterpart in actual relationships is demonstrated in i.a. a study carried through by Zelditch (in Parsons & Bales, *Family Socialization and Interaction Process,* Glencoe, 1955) on 56 randomly selected cultures. In most of these societies, woman seems

to perform an expressive role, characterized by comforting, mediating and conflict reducing functions within the family, whereas the man, as expected, occupies the instrumental role with its principal orientation towards external 'executive' relations with gainful work etc. Moreover, he exercises the task of personifying the ultimate instance of punishment and control within the family.

March (in Bell & Vogel, *The Family,* New York, 1968) shows that when it comes to political issues, husband and wife tend to specialize in separate spheres at which the husband preferably engages in matters of wider range, while the wife is principally interested in local issues. Furthermore, Stroedtbeck and Mann (*Sex Role Differentiation in Jury Deliberations,* Sociometry, 19, 1, 1956) also have come to the conclusion that the behavior of husband and wife can be classified according to Bales' schedule. Thus, the role of father and husband contains to a greater extent instrumental-adaptive questions and answers, while the mother-and-wife role shows a larger amount of positively expressive-adaptive behavior.

In order to further add to the content of the two concepts instrumental and expressive, a list of a number of traits, being calssified according to association to either the masculine instrumental role or the feminine expressive role is reproduced (Table 14). The personality traits are part of a child study carried out by Orville Brim on the basis of an investigation by Helen Koch (in Backman & Secord, *Problems in Social Psychology,* New York, 1966).

Briefly, the masculine instrumental traits can be said to express a strongly goal-oriented and actively extravert behavior with elements of self-assertion and originality, and with a negative evaluation of indecision and uncertainty. The feminine expressive role however, is characterized by a well-behaved lack of independence and adaption to authorities with streaks of negatively valued behavior in the form of pettiness in various matters, fierce appearance and inability to accept failure.

Spacial segregation in sex roles

The spacial differentiation between the central spheres of interest of men and women which is describable in terms of secondary and primary group relations is emphasized by a number of authors. Erik Erikson (in Bell & Vogel, op.cit.) assumes that the anatomical differences serve as a basis for the shaping of the sex roles in so far as the female anatomy is

Table 14. *Personality traits assigned to the masculine* (*instrumental*) *or the feminine* (*expressive*) *role*

Trait name	Pertains primarily to instrumental (I) or expressive (E) role	Trait is congruent (+) or incongruent (−) characteristic of role
1. Tenacity	I	+
2. Aggressiveness	I	+
3. Curiosity	I	+
4. Ambition	I	+
5. Planfulness	I	+
6. Dawdling and procrastinating	I	−
7. Responsibleness	I	+
8. Originality	I	+
9. Competitiveness	I	+
10. Wavering in decision	I	−
11. Self-confidence	I	+
12. Anger	E	−
13. Quarrelsomeness	E	−
14. Revengefulness	E	−
15. Teasing	E	−
16. Extrapunitiveness	E	−
17. Insistence on rights	E	−
18. Exhibitionism	E	−
19. Unco-operativeness with group	E	−
20. Affectionateness	E	+
21. Obedience	E	+
22. Upset by defeat	E	−
23. Responds to sympathy and approval from adults	E	+
24. Jealousy	E	−
25. Speedy recovery from emotional disturbance	E	+
26. Cheerfulness	E	+
27. Kindness	E	+
28. Friendliness to adults	E	+
29. Friendliness to children	E	+
30. Negativism	E	−
31. Tattling	E	−

inner-space centered, while the male anatomy stresses outer-space. Starting out from this physical reality, the sex roles then have been elaborated with consequences reaching far beyond the physiologically given prerequisites. Jessie Bernard (*Academic Women,* 1964) employes the terms 'domestic relations' and 'foreign relations' to indicate the functions of woman and man respectively. This division of spheres is, according to Bernard, applicable even outside the home, so that most gainfully employed women handle the inner contacts and the service, while the men deal with the exterior world in the guise of e.g. customers, competitors or government.

To sum up, the term instrumental can be said to contain the following components: orientation toward long-term results and objects; a ra-

tional organisation of means and resources to reach these; efficiency seeking and cumulative activity. The term expressive has the content as follows: short-term goal-oriented activeness with its interest focused on interpersonal relations and conflicts; immediate need satisfaction and lack of cumulativity; emotional anchorage and dependence.

Apollonian-Dionysian

In connection with the conceptual couple instrumental-expressive, the terms Apollonian-Dionysian are briefly discussed below.

These two dimensions are at least partially attached to each other and should therefore be possible to combine into a deepened image of the relationship between on the one hand an instrumental-Apollonian outlook and on the other an expressive-Dionysian orientation.

The dualistic terms Apollonian (or 'Apollinian' as Nietzsche's original denomination reads) and Dionysian were originally developed by Nietzsche in his work *The Birth of Tragedy and the Genealogy of Morals* (transl. New York, 1956) and connect on to the Greek deities Apollon and Dionysos. According to Nietzsche, Apollon embodies 'the moderate restriction, freedom from mental excitements, the wise peacefulness ...', ... 'principium individuationis ...', while Dionysos represents the intoxication, 'total selfforgetting', 'reunion between man and man' and between man and nature, whereby the limits to the individual's ego-conception are erased and instincts and emotions will predominate. More recently, Ruth Benedict (*Patterns of Culture*, Boston, 1934) has brought up this division and applied it to the description of three separate cultures. One of these is depicted as Apollonian with marked streaks of control, temperance and on the whole a damping of every form of manifestation, emotional and ceremonious as well as economic. The remaining two cultures are described as Dionysian by Benedict, and here the road to the essentials in life goes through a breaking down of the everyday restrictions and self-control towards strong emotional experiences and intoxication of the senses.

A thorough analysis of the dimension Apollonian-Dionysian in its original Greek context is carried through by Alvin Gouldner in *Enter Plato* (New York, 1965). Gouldner emphasizes, that Apollon had his chief anchorage in aristocratic circles, while Dionysos was the deity of the people. The Dionysian culture flourished above all among poor farmers, slaves and women, who sought oblivion from the daily troubles. Apollonianism on the other hand, was widespread among the leading

male urban inhabitants and comprised, as mentioned above, demands on emotional control, autonomy and rational behavior. Whereas the Dionysian cult devoted itself to the relation between man and man and especially the emotional, intuitive contact, Apollonianism was concentrated on the relationship between man and the divine. The strong emphasis in Apollonianism on restraint and reason, knowledge and science contrasts with the orientation toward a dissolution of precisely those factors in the Dionysian cult. The Apollonian man is reserved and occupied with external, object-directed activity, whereas the Dionysian is relatively passive when it comes to exterior, worldly goals. In a factor analytical study of a number of societies, Gouldner and Peterson (*Notes on Technology and the Moral Order,* New York, 1962) find a strong positive correlation between degree of Apollonianism and technological level. In a comparison between the two dimensions, instrumental-expressive and Apollonian-Dionysian a number of parallel traits appear. The concepts instrumental and Apollonian are both characterized by rationalism, control of emotional impulses and extrovert activeness with long-term aims. The terms expressive and Dionysian both include the following components: emotionally and impulse-governed introverted activity, concentrated on interpersonal relationships. The acts are passive and not accumulative as they constitute purposes in themselves.

Thus the two conceptions can be combined into a new and fuller one: instrumental-Apollonian and expressive-Dionysian, which for the sake of simplicity henceforth will be abbreviated to I-A and E-D, respectively.

I-A and E-D applied to research

In view of the characteristics of research work, research can be described as typically instrumental-Apollonian. The principal factors included in scientific work are: insistence on systematic rational acting, susceptibility to new and original angles of approach and modes of thought, objective critical analysis and on the whole, a typically instrumental behavior with questions and replies. The fewer the elements of expressive-Dionysian acting in research work, the more efficient and objective it becomes. The definition of science excludes in itself impulse behavior.

I-A and E-D applied to the sex roles

Thus, the research role is a direct further development of the male instrumental-Apollonian sex role. Certain factors are stressed more heav-

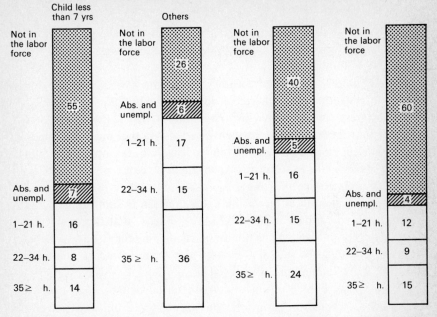

Figure 2. *Married women in age groups and occupation in 1969.* (The figure is taken from the report: *Familj och samhälle,* Stockholm, 1970.)

ily in the research role and the demands increase, but the basic orientation is identical. Therefore, there are no fundamental contradictions between the sex role of man and his role as a researcher, whereas this is the case for woman. The traditional female sex role with its strong emphasis on expressive-Dionysian behavior is in direct contrast to the instrumental-Apollonian research role.

'Male' and 'female' in education and professional spheres

The extent to which the female sex role still is family centered is evident from e.g. the Swedish manpower study performed in the automn of 1969 (Figure 2).

Among married women without children under 7 years of age, only 36 % are gainfully employed 35 hours or more per week in the age group 14–44. In the ages of 45 to 54 and 55 to 64 the corresponding share of gainfully employed is even lower with 24 % and 15 % respectively. The

amounts of married women totally outside of the labor force are for these three groups 26 %, 40 % and 60 % respectively. In the age group 14–44 with children under 7 years of age, the proportion not in the labor force is 55 %. To the majority of married women in the ages 14 to 64, the home thus constitutes the main field of action, whether they have young children or not.

Of the gainfully employed Swedish women in 1965, 73 % were engaged in 25 occupations where, all in all, only 13.6 % of the persons practising were men (The Swedish Population Census, 1965). A detailed examination of the occupations mentioned shows that most of them are within the scope of the traditional female role with its emphasis on nursing, care and service in all forms. Accordingly, women are extremely inhibited in their choice of a profession. When studying the distribution of men and women in different lines of education in senior high school as well as in vocational training school it appears that the penetration of the sex roles in Sweden has not diminished appreciably during the last few years. The girls still dominate in the from of old as 'feminine' classified lines: humanities – social science and social. This marked trend reappears in the choice of university subject and later, when it comes to the choice of a profession after having passed a university degree. Thus, women constitute a majority at the Faculties of Arts, physiotherapy institutes, schools of education and schools of social studies (source: Statistiska Meddelanden, U 1967: 4). Among female university graduates the dominant professional sphere is 'educational work' (Sw. Pop. Census 1960). The traditional sex role pattern concerning choice of subject and of profession is thus valid even for the women who do continue their education beyond senior high school.

The fact that a larger proportion of girls than of boys at every grade level from junior secondary school on do refrain from further education (see e.g. Sysiharju, A-L. in Sosiologia, 4, 1966) is an even more palpable symptom of the social pressure in a traditionally 'feminine' direction. From a study conducted by Kjell Härnqvist (SOU 1963: 15) it is evident, that girls have a better school adaption than boys but considerably lower professional ambitions, for which reason they terminate their education earlier than the less well adapted but higher aiming boys. To cite the American scientist L. E. Tyler: 'Many girls do not strive to live up to their ability, whereas the problem for the boys sometimes is quite the opposite.'

Those girls who all the same do continue toward higher education have initially on the average better marks than the boys, but this dif-

ference is diminished in the course of the education and is partly turned into its opposite at the end of it. Holter states that the most probable explanation is, that as the girl grows up, her educational achievements are more and more influenced by the social image of her role in family and society, which 'may be somewhat discouraging to high intellectual achievement' (Holter, H. in Patai, R., *Women in the Modern World*, New York, 1967).

Certainly an ever growing percentage of women out of each age group is qualifying for a profession, but the aim and direction of the education follows the old pattern and this leads up to a continuous sex segregation in the labor-market with typically 'female' and typically 'male' occupations as a result. Education in itself does not seem to result in any noticeable weakening of the traditional view concerning woman's role and female personality traits either (Bolton, C. & Kammayer, K., *The University Student,* New Haven, 1966).

It is well-known that the 'effemination' of an occupation in turn has consequences for wage conditions and social benefits. The phenomenon is if anything comparable to the situation, which arises as a black family moves into a 'white' housing area in a town in the South. Families in the surrounding houses move, land prices may decline and the 'de-whitening' trend goes on in an ever increasing rate until the now by no means 'fashionable' area is entirely inhabited by less prosperous people from various ethnic minorities, gradually to become slum. In a similar way a profession is successively 'de-masculinized' as it is opened to women and more and more of them are employed. Owing to their lower pretensions and wage claims they constitute a threat to the male manpower. Soon the latter seek more profitable branches with a permanenting of the low-wage situation for the women as a consequence. Accordingly, the sex segregation is not lessened in spite of the fact that women, especially the married ones, have raised their share among the actively employed.

Home and work

Women's deep-rooted expressive-Dionysian role render their relation to the labor-market marginal, and the sex difference in this respect has been established in a number of studies. The one-sided career goal of the female sex role: marriage make most women disinclined to go in for a vocational training and even more so for one that takes many years. This results in a fairly loose and temporary attachment to a more

71

or less routinary work, where the commitment is low and the absence high.

Some of the factors that have been shown to diminish women's disposition to take a job are: little or no training and education, marriage, children and in particular small children, a husband having good income and the wide-spread notion that 'a mother ought to stay at home when the children are young' (irrespective of the fact that real alternatives seldom are at hand). This reply reappears as the predominant one in a number of studies and is presumably to a large extent an aftermath of John Bowlby's (*Maternal Care and Mental Health,* W.H.O., Genève, 1951) and other similar reports concerning the effects of prolonged institutional residence (orphanages and the like) on the mental health of children. Erroneously one concluded from the behavior of these totally deprived children, that severe mental disturbances arise in the child if the mother is not permanently present. Neither the significance of the father, nor the fact that one here deals with a very exposed group without any enduring and warm emotional contacts whatsoever is allowed for. The new-antifeminist currents caused above all by Bowlby's report (which is even published by World Health Organization) are incalculable in their consequences.

That the attitude of man is also traditionally oriented and is of great concern in this connection is evident from i.a. a study by Edmund Dahlström (*Mödrar i hem och förvärvsarbete,* Göteborg, 1959). The majority of the mothers working in the home stated that their husband preferred their remaining at home. Even among the gainfully employed women this was common. Here is also related an American study (Weil, M.W., in *Amer. Soc. Rev.,* 1961: 1), where the most important factor to the wife's professional work turns out to be the husband's attitude. No attempts at interpreting the data are made, but probably both convenience and prestige come into play: partly, the husband wants to be made comfortable and get the ground service done – a gainfully employed wife entails a lowering of standards in this respect. Partly, it is another aspect of the patriarchal male sex role that haunts him: 'shoudn't I be capable of supporting my wife' etc. with an accompanying high prestige associated with 'a wife who does not have to work'. In spite of the fact that Finnish tradition is more pro-feminist than in the remaining Nordic countries, Anna-Liisa Sysiharju (*Equality, home and work,* Mikkelissä, 1960) finds significant differences between male and female students as regards attitudes to married women's gainful work. Thus, the male students are considerably more negative. A result in the same direction

is reported in a later study by Elina Haavio-Mannila (in *Journ. of Marr. and the Family*, 29, 3, 1967) and a more marked conservatism among men in these matters is also established in Jacobson's study of American spouses (in Biddle & Thomas, *Role Theory*, New York, 1961).

As for women's often observed higher absence from work, in no case wholly comparable conditions have been prevalent for men and women, for which reason the conclusions are hardly possible to generalize to any great extent. Bertil Olsson (*Studier i frånvaro från arbetet;* Stockholm 1967) demonstrates in his study, that the total time of absence is the same for men and women. However, the absence pertaining to illness is higher for women than for men, something that largely appears to be due to women's heavier burden of nursing and child care. It has furthermore been established that absence decreases with increasing wage as well as with increasing position in the professional hierarchy, which applies to both sexes. Accordingly, it is not unreasonable to assume that the higher absence noted for women is in part a result of women's generally low wages and low positions on the career ladder. (In Sweden, 80 % of all fulltime employed men between 24 and 64 years of age earned more than 20 000 Swedish crowns in 1965, whereas 70 % of all full-time employed women earned *less* than that sum.) A closely related phenomenon, which is also connected with the E-D female sex role, is the somewhat higher mobility among women, something that, according to a study by Magnus Hedberg (*The Process of Labor Turnover*, Stockholm,1967) to a great extent can be traced back to the age factor. Mobility lessens with advancing age, wherefore women's higher mobility in the labor-market is at least partly explained by their considerably lower average age. The American Public Health Service-investigation in 1960 shows that women in positions of great responsibility have an even lower mobility than men in corresponding positions.

In this connection, the fact that many professional branches need precisely mobile, inexpensive manpower for work of a routine nature and with fluctuating demands on the amount of work should be emphasized. To occupations with temporary heavy stress (e.g. the commercial branches) and protracted more or less inactive periods in between, the low-wage female labor is a necessary condition.

Seen from a longer time perspective women are used as a buffer in the transition between times of prosperity and times of depression. Thus, even here women's mobility and low expectations constitute apparent market economical advantages to the employer.

In a boom with great demand women are stimulated and employed — at the outbreak of a recession they are the first to be layed off. Under trying financial conditions, greater responsibility is shown toward the men than toward the women, irrespective of their individual merits. This is founded on the assumption, that every man is a breadwinner, that women do not occupy this position and that breadwinners, i.e. men, are exposed to greater problems in the event of unemployment. As recently as in 1952, the idea of reintroducing a prohibition of women in government employment was discussed by the English civil servant association. Married women are apparently in many quarters still regarded as 'supported' appendages to a man without the right to act as independent individuals or to assert their own needs even in times of depression. (In Sweden a prohibition of dismissing women on account of marriage or betrothal was introduced as recently as in 1939.)

The policy exemplified above and the conceptions which motivate it naturally enough infect woman and tie her to the notion that her right place is in the home. This leads to the result that her eventual gainful work is halfhearted, short-termed and not taken seriously.

"Justice can mean both 'distribution according to achievement' and 'distribution according to need'. Women seem to a greater extent to uphold the principle of need, whereas men base their justice on achievement and aspects of usefulness and efficiency" . . . "Women undoubtedly would have stronger reasons to fight for raised wages if they applied the same reasoning of justice as their male colleagues. But now women generously take for granted that their need of money is less" (Berner Öste, M. in *Studievägledning till Kvinnors liv och arbete*, Stockholm, 1963).

No wonder when the dusty argument against raised wages for women reading: 'They don't smoke, they don't drink and they don't chase women', is still brought up in the debate, even though it is dressed in a more moderate verbal attire.

We here get on to the circular reasoning that is put into practice when it comes to women and women's professional work, and which have a tendency to result in a self-fulfilling prophecy. Among employers the lower work commitment and higher absence of the female staff is given as a reason for placing them on low-wage posts with few or non-existent possibilities of promotion. Those fixed positions inhibit in turn any occupational ambitions that otherwise might have existed among women, routine work bores them and soon the life of a housewife appears a tempting alternative. They bear children, leave their routine occupations and the employer's prediction is fulfilled. That those pro-

phecies are based on unfounded suppositions and deeprooted ideas of the behavior of men and women respectively, does not render the consequences less real. Employers are utterly unwilling to give women a fair chance, as they are considered all too uncertain as investment objects in regard to long education and high or middle-high positions.

On the whole, there is a strong tendency to disregard individual qualities as regards both men and women. The sex is used as principal criterion of selection without considering, that the basic similarities between men and women are greater than the differences.

"If an individual woman is unsuccessful in a position of responsibility, a man is chosen the next time. A man who does not succeed is allowed to disappear quietly – a woman fails as a representative of her sex" (Thyberg, S. in *Kvinnors liv och arbete,* Stockholm, 1963).

This stereotyped sex role view evidently reinforces the behavioral tendencies already in existence, and makes the reserve of talent and manpower among women even more inaccessible.

In a Swedish study (ed. Jüring, R., *Kvinnobefordran,* Stockholm, 1965) it is demonstrated, that women cannot be treated as a homogeneous group in these respects. Regarding e.g. the attitude to promotion only the married women, women between 27 and 34 years of age and women with children come up to the traditional expectations, whereas the youngest ones, the unmarried, women over 35 years of age and women with higher education are interested in promotion. These groups consider themselves to be held back by i.a. inferior opportunities of promotion compared to men, greater requirements on women than on men for promotion, the husband's negative attitude and deficient self-confidence.

From the above it is clear, that even in those instances when woman tries to get out of the one-sidedly expressive-Dionysian sex role, she encounters difficulties which often result in resignation and a reversion to the prescribed pattern.

Her relatively protest-free returning to the crib, is the consequence of a number of concurrent factors. One of the more subtly operating and therefore perhaps most elusive ones is the recognition or rather non-recognition that criticism of the traditional feminine role usually is met with. The whole gamut of tools for throwing suspicion on the criticism – from Freud's ingenious theory constructions with the penis-envy as a central attribute to be charged women having disturbing occupational ambitions, to the most unsophisticated forms of invalidating through ridicule and contempt – is systematically and often very

efficiently made use of. The tendency to treat the sex role matter as a manifestation of inner conflicts is prevalent. The demands for changes are considered neurotic reactions, which have to be treated in therapy. In order to have the courage and the strength to maintain the criticism in this situation large personal resources are needed. Very few can afford to insist.

The density and thoroughness of the established sex role pattern is demonstrated in i.a. a Norwegian comparison (Brun-Gulbrandsen, S., *Kjoensrolle og asocialitet,* Oslo, 1958) between the educational ideology of a number of housewifes and their verbally depicted behavior in concrete educational situations. Although the majority (95 %) thought, that girls and boys ought to be brought up in the same manner, the percentage of housewifes being positive to equality decreased with increased specification of educational situation. In the same study, it is noted that even at the age of 8 children are wholly in agreement with the traditional sex roles, this tendency being reinforced the older they get. In an American study (Lehman & Witty in Roe, Anne, *The Psychology of Occupations,* New York, 1956) of children between 8 and 18 years of age, a pronounced stronger preference for sedentary and artistic occupations among the girls is observed. Another American study (Tyler, L.E. in Roe, A., 1956, op.cit.), displays clear sex differences in attitudes with occupational connections even at an early elementary school age.

Data indicating an even earlier sex role learning is reported by Ruth Hartley (in Biddle & Thomas, 1961, op.cit.). She finds a marked sex differentiation in regard to behavior as early as the age of 4 and also relates a number of other studies showing a similar result for the ages of 3 to 6.

Patterns of identification

The early socialization of girls to the expressive-Dionysian sex role pattern and of boys to the instrumental-Apollonian one is further strengthened during adolescence and later on in adult age as well. The child acquires the expected role behavior inter alia through imitation and identification. According to Freud, the principal purpose of identification is to reduce frustration and anxiety. Through the internalization of the traits and behavior of another person in his/her personality the individual is able to reach desired goals and settle conflicts. The persons with whom the individual is identifying or borrowing traits from vary during childhood and adolescence and the process continues far into

76

adult age. However, the parents constitute the first and most important models, the son usually learning the male sex role through identification with the father and the daughter correspondingly identifying with the mother in learning her sex role. It is then conceivable, that the fact that an increasing number of married women are gainfully employed would have repercussions on the daughter's behavior toward a more work oriented outlook. Nevertheless, a study by Anna-Liisa Sysiharju (1960, op.cit.) shows, that the mother's own solution in the choice between home and work does not seem to have any noticeable effect on the daughter's attitudes in this respect. Daughters with constantly work-oriented mothers do, however, have a more egalitarian view as regards the relationship between the sexes. This latter result reappears in a Belgian study (de Visscher, P., *Attitudes antiféministes et milieux intellectuels,* Louvain, 1956).

The fact that the mother's degree of commitment to gainful work does not seem to have any palpable influence on the daughter's behavior could probably at least in part be explained by the phenomenon that the wife's employment in itself does not cause any appreciable changes as to the distribution of tasks between the spouses within the home sphere. Thus Elina Haavio-Mannila (*Sex Differentiation in Role Expectations and Performance,* Helsinki, 1967), notes in a study of a number of randomly selected men and women that the traditional division of labor, where the housework is executed by the wife alone still dominates in the majority of families, in spite of the fact that 2/3 of the wives were employed outside the home. A similar result is established in a study by Blood, R.O. and Wolfe, D.M. (in Biddle & Thomas, 1961, op.cit.) as well as in a Swedish survey (Boalt, C., *1 000 husmödrar om hemarbetet,* Stockholm, 1961). The participation of the husband in the domestic work is somewhat greater when the wife is working, it is true, but the increase is negligible and the chief point is, that the traditional role-assignment still remains although a change has taken place outwardly.

According to Bebel, Engels, Kollontaj and other socialistic ideologists the active participation of woman in the labor market would result in a breaking down of the conservative sex role pattern. Data from societies in which the official ideology proclaims a definite repudiation of the old sex roles give, however, another picture. By way of example the gainfully employed wife in the Soviet Union has, as a matter of fact, two jobs, as the husband extremely seldom joins in the housework (see e.g. Stiernlöf, S., *Kvinnor i Sovjet,* Stockholm, 1970), and in the kibbutzes

of Israel the domestic work and child care is almost exclusively performed by women (Johansson, A. in Fredriksson, I., *Könsroller*, Falköping, 1965). Wilensky's comparative study of 34 societies (Wilensky, H. in *Industrial Relations*, 7, 3, 1968) gives a result which indicates, that the educational level of the country explains a larger amount of the variation in woman's situation in the labor market than does the official ideology.

Blood and Hamblin (in Bell & Vogel, 1968, op.cit.) point out in a study of the power structure within the family, that the wife's paid job by no means changes the power allocation within the family. Children of gainfully employed mothers maintain the traditional view of male and female roles according to a survey by Ruth Hartley *(Women in the Modern World,* Boston, 1953). In all of the three studied age groups: 5, 8 and 11 years of age, the children felt that the principal household tasks fall on woman's lot, whereas the role of breadwinner primarily still belongs to man.

From the above it is clear, that children in their sex role learning have few or no possibilities of getting out of the traditional and narrow pattern for men's and women's behavior by means of the identification process.

Mass media

Upon the basic socialization thus accomplished by the family, society later on goes on building in a continous interaction with the family. Especially the mass media play an important role in this, and their generally conservative power is established by Klapper *(The Effects of Mass Communication,* Glencoe, 1960) in his analysis of investigations in that area. The models that are brought out in the mass media, and above all in the weekly press, coincide primarily with the ideology termed the romantic ideological position by Dahlström. In it the roles of men and women are regarded as complementary and divided up into definite functions, which can be depicted as I-A and E-D respectively. The predominant part of the readers of those products are women (the Swedish *VECT-undersökningen 1967*) and the majority of the weekly magazines read contain strong escapistic elements. Other forms of more manifest escape from reality as e.g. alcoholism or drug addiction are socially judged far more severe in regard to women than regarding men. The consumption of weeklies, however, is a socially accepted type of

escapism for women. (A comparison should here be made with the earlier related oblivion-giving function of the Dionysian cult.)

The reactionary approach to men and women in the world of publicity is illustrated by Betty Friedan in her work *The Feminine Mystique* (1965, op.cit.). A retrogression toward a more passive female model with a lower degree of social participation is demonstrated in a French-Canadian survey of a number of annual volumes of ladies' magazines (Valois, J. in *Recherches Sociographiques,* 8, 3, 1967).

Even the new so-called 'emancipated' pornography is as regards the contents extremely reactionary with a consistent division of roles according to sex: man is the subject, active and enterprising; woman is the object, passive and submissive. The subject role coincides with the instrumental-Apollonian behavior — the object role with the expressive-Dionysian one. The background to and the development of this dicotomization of men and women into subject and object is thoroughly analysed by Simone de Beauvoir in the now classical work *Le Deuxième Sexe* (Paris, 1949). Certainly Beauvoir is critical of the prevailing sex roles, but levels as a matter of fact her criticism almost exclusively aginst the female role. The male sex role and with it the male-governed society are considered to be for woman unattainable ideals. To Beauvoir woman's physiology constitutes an inescapable handicap, something it could be only provided that like Beauvoir one starts from man as an absolute model that everything else ought to follow. That man's sex role with its ideal of intellectual giant and emotional dwarf is also inhuman does, as so often is the case, not occur to the writer at all.

The functionalism within the social sciences and psychiatry can be said to represent the scientific correspondence to the romantic complementary sex role approach of the mass media. The romantic component is omitted, but the complementarity remains in terms that depict clearly defined roles for men and women. The division often turns into a matter of course and an ideal state. Here too the categories I-A for men and E-D for women do apply.

The want of female I-A identification objects

Each statistical return of the distribution of men and women in choice of a profession, education, position in the occupational hierarchy and ascendancy in deciding institutions constitute a direct support to the proposition, that female I-A models are almost entirely missing in

society. The whole extent of the consequences of this is hard to estimate, but it is obvious that the want of female I-A identification models considerably obstructs woman's emancipation from the one-sided E-D role ideal. Naturally, the same thing applies to men in the opposite direction. To act the part of pioneer in these respects attracts maybe a few individuals – to the majority the psychological resistence and the social pressure probably exert a strongly conforming influence.

Those women who occupy high positions involving great responsibility in society, which by definition are pronouncedly I-A, are as yet so few in number that they are regarded as exceptions, confirming the rule of woman's unfitness.

"But even if they urged, insisted, fought to help us educate ourselves, even if they talked with yearning of careers that were not open to them, they could not give us an image of what we would be." "We did not want to be like our mothers, and yet what other model did we have?" "It is my thesis that the core of the problem for women today is not sexual but a problem of identity –" (Friedan, Betty, 1965, op.cit.).

The very few women who have succeeded in reaching high positions in society often hold some kind of 'super-womanrole', that is, a position which fundamentally implies a role generalization of the female sex role on a top-level. In a survey of the 2 % of women who are included in a sample of persons with an annual income of $10 000 and upwards, Bird (1969, op.cit.) has grouped them according to type of position in the following categories:
1) *Dynastic Women,* who have reached their position through a man, that is, through being the wife, widow or daughter of the owner of an enterprise; 2) *Women's Women,* who exploit the male dominance in the business world by mediating between business life and women; 3) *Token Women,* who play a P.R.-role for companies etc. as a proof of their freedom from prejudice but without possessing any real power; 4) *Gimmick Women,* who are employed with the aim of surprise in situations where women ordinarily do not exist; 5) *Sex Women,* who are used for the sake of their personal attractive force in business and the like; and finally 6) *Office Wifes and Housekeepers,* who to a large extent consist of chief secretaries etc. As a matter of fact all of these professional categories are nothing else but instances of distensions in various directions of the traditional role of woman.

Also from Alpenfels' (in Cassara, B., *American Women,* Boston, 1962), survey of 400 students in New York it is manifest that a clearly structured I-A model for female occupational behavior is wanting. In

their description of professional women's characteristics 60 different traits were included, traits which taken together give a very diffuse and incoherent picture. For professional men only 20 traits were mentioned, all having some sort of attachment to performance and competence in an instrumental sense. The tendency in the judgement of women's achievements in regard to them unusual positions in the life of work seems to be a paradoxical combination of the notion that a woman who fails is representative of 'women in general', whereas a woman who succeeds is an exception to 'women in general'. This reasoning evidently results in a stagnation of the development toward increased equality, and actually entails that the very few top-women in society are isolated from their own sex and, if anything, identify with the group of male colleagues. At this the feeling of being 'the exception to the rule' is strengthened and the significance of the role as a model is diminished. The beaten track is obliterated.

"The careers of successful women are uncharted. There is not, as there is for men, a clearly marked path, so success goes almost exclusively to individuals who can create their own opportunities" (Bird, 1969, op.cit.).

The fact that despite all this one finds women within pronouncedly I-A occupational areas, probably is in part the effect of a partial cross-sex identification. Results indicating this are related in an Australian study of women pursuing higher education (Dawson, M., *Graduate and Married,* Sydney, 1965). For instance, a significantly higher percentage of the daughters of physicians are themselves intending to be physicians. The professional heritage in regard to other occupations is lower but does nonetheless exist. Thus, the father could serve as a model for a more instrumentally oriented behavior in the daughter − naturally, on the assumption that a positive and durable contact is established to render the transference and internalization in the daughter's personality of I-A values, action dispositions and problem solutions possible. A study carried through by Bandura, Ross & Ross (in Backman & Secord, 1966, op.cit.) of girls and boys in the age of 4 shows, that the imitative behavior of children not necessarily follows the same sex pattern. Two identification theories were tested: 1) *the status envy theory,* identification is effected with an envied adult, who possesses the status of consumer and in this respect is competing with the child; 2) *the power theory,* identification is effected with a powerful, controling person. A special case of the latter theory was tested, namely the secondary reinforcement theory according to which the identification is made with a person who supplies the child with rewards, since the personality traits of

the former are associated with positive experiences and thus get a secondary reward value. The outcome confirms *the power theory* and demonstrates, that reversals in the power relation between the male and the female model cause a cross-sex imitation especially in girls. Even though there is a tendency to avoid the transgression of the sex role barrier, the choice of a model for imitation can consequently be modified by factors in the individual situation. This identification across the sex limit, however, seldom reaches any marked scope, but is confined to isolated situations, since a far-reaching cross-sex imitation is generally counteracted by both parents.

The unisexual character of the identification pattern have repercussions on the tendency to identify in the opposite direction: from older to younger, from teacher to pupil, from superior to subordinate etc. The pronounced protégé system in certain professions provide an illustration to this. Epstein (*Amer. Journ. Soc.,* 75, 6, 1970) mentions a number of factors, which are apt to hamper female promotion on that occasion. The difficulty for the sponsor or the master, who in most cases is a man, to identify the female protégé or disciple with a possible successor to himself is significant. On the other hand, if the disciple is a man, the transference is easier, not least because the sponsor has greater confidence in his work commitment. Another obstacle is, according to Epstein, the woman's remaining role partners, who find it hard to understand and accept her loyalty toward the sponsor. Also, the wife of the latter can be negatively disposed and refuse to approve of the intimate relationship of dependency, which develops between the master and his female disciple. The expectations of the colleagues exert a strong negative pressure against the choice of a disciple, who too much diverges from the characteristics of the group. Accordingly, to be a woman, a negro etc. are considered deviating characteristics, since those are extremely seldom represented in the top positions in the occupational hierarchy.

Internalization of social expectations and attitudes

The charter of female I-A patterns and the generally low and disparaged E-D position that the majority of women occupy all over the world give rise to a phenomenon, which is well-known in regard to oppressed minorities. The expectations that are directed towards the individual will, if they are enough intense and consistent, by degrees be accepted

and incorporated in the individual's self-perception. The process is accelerated when the norm senders are powerful and hold the possibility of exerting influence upon the person's situation. The greater the dependency, the worse the prospects of developing a working solidarity within the repressed group, and the greater the tendency to accept one's position. The stereotyped attitudes that prevail concerning women's characteristics are employed as an explanation to her low social position and is also accepted as such by the women themselves.

That the woman's own gainful work does not necessarily lead to a more feministic outlook is evident from de Visscher's survey of women with a university education. Of these, the gainfully employed were even more anti-feministic than the ones without paid jobs. In actual fact, the stereotypes assume the nature of convenient rationalizations, which conduce to a perpetuation of the situation in question by way of relieving the individual from demands for independent acting.

The internalization of the conception of woman's inferiority engender as a sequel a self-contempt, which is generalized to the entire female species and renders an organized co-operation between women difficult or impossible. In a study by Philip Goldberg (*Transaction,* 5, 5, 1968) women evinced a manifest tendency to belittle articles bearing female pen-names, whereas the same articles were on the whole judged more positively when one declared, that the authors were men. Thus, the women had entirely internalized the present prejudices about the inferiority of their own sex.

Several studies indicate that women, like men, prefer male works managers to female ones. Paradoxically enough this approval of the male value scale seems to be able to lend certain secondary proceeds owing to the fact that one is accepted by and allied with the men in power and in this experiences the satisfaction of being on the 'right' side and therefore is able to look down upon and despise other women. The phenomenon could be seen as a micro-sociological counterpart to the principle 'divide and rule'.

The acceptance of the male value scale is probably also strengthened by the tendency to identify with the one in power, the one who is in control of means of punishment and reward ('the power theory', compare also with Anna Freud's 'identification with the aggressor'). Men have greater influence than women and, accordingly, ought to constitute a target group for identification. Professional women are (like housewives) as we know supremely dependent upon men in dominating positions and consequently have a significant reason to 'take man's

role'. This in turn ought to cause a further estrangement of separate groups of women from each other.

The apperception of the low status of the female sex and the incorporation of society's values and the rationalizations attached to them lead to adaptive difficulties for girls and resentment against their own sex identity. That this is the case, is apparent from Brun-Gulbrandsens survey (in Dahlström, E. et al., 1963, op.cit.), of children and mothers in Oslo. No marked differences between girls and boys is observable at the age of 8 and 11 concerning the desire to change sex. Among the teen-agers, however, only 71 % of the girls choose their own sex, the rest either being undecided or desiring to be boys. As much as 84 % of the boys wanted to be their own sex, while most of the others were uncertain. Not until puberty a greater consciousness of one's own sex role, its social value and its consequences for the personal freedom arises. In an American Gallup poll (Gallup, G., *Gallup Poll,* Princeton, 1955), as much as 31 % of the consulted women turned out to wish that they were men, whereas only 4 % of the men said that once in a while they had wanted to be women. Brenton notes that every poll that at all has included the question: 'Would you rather have been born a member of the opposite sex?' shows considerably more women than men answering this question in the affirmative.

Sex-differentiated assessment of I-A achievements

In the foregoing, women's tendency to value I-A achievements by women significantly lower than the same performances accomplished by men was noted. This behavior reflects the common opinion about the ability of women in tasks, which are traditionally associated with men. In Goldberg's study (1968, op.cit.) the articles presented were shown to be more rigorously judged when they bore female pen-names even in those instances when they treated traditionally 'female' subjects. This indicates, that women's achievements are considered inferior to men's within 'masculine' as well as 'feminine' areas at least within the scope of I-A behavior.

Additional support of the thought that different markings are applied to men and women is given by Jessie Bernard (quoted in Bird, C., 1969, op.cit.). When identical lectures were held by equivalent speakers of different sex, the students manifested more confidence in the male than in the female instructor both in regard to the 'masculine' and the

'feminine' lecture subject. The thus sex differentiated assessments of individuals in I-A contexts implies, that different liminal values are employed for men and women. Should the person judged be of female sex, a greater effort is in actual fact demanded to 'pass' than if the person is a man. The threshold-value is higher for women than for men, and the distance between the two liminal levels probably varies somewhat according to the nature of the occasion. However, direct empirical evidence of this is as yet missing.

It should be observed, that when it comes to the filling of positions in the labor market, frequently no assessment whatsoever is made of female applicants. Sex is considered a primary criterion of selection: "At the appointment to a post, half the basis of recruitment is in principal generally cut off even before attempting to apply individual judgements of selection", ... (Thyberg, S., 1963, op.cit.).

Conflict between I-A and E-D role

The expressive-Dionysian sex role that women are trained for contrasts strongly with the demands being set up for the fulfillment of an efficient professional role. This state of opposition is most pronounced in society's top and eminent positions, which are characterized by demands for traits like efficiency, go-ahead spirit, capacity for taking initiative and the like, that is, traits that are all included in the male sex role but which are regarded as antithetical to the traditionally female sex role pattern. Parsons (1955, op.cit.) describes the modern occupational role as a secondary group relation, whereas the family is an instance of primary group relation. The masculine sex role with its emphasis on external, secondary relationships is directly programmed for the labor market conditions. However, the feminine primary group-oriented role does not provide any preparation whatsoever for the requirements of the life of work. Harriet Holter (in Patai, 1967, op.cit.) puts the matter in this manner:

"Success for women is judged mainly in terms of their marital status, while that of men is measured in terms of occupational performance. This expresses one of the most significant differences between the social and psychological situation of the two sexes. The two life-goals require different personality traits and represent two different social systems. Adjusting to the life-goal of marriage implies cultivation of one's appearance, charm, social relations and 'feminine' qualities, in short, one's attractiveness to the opposite sex. Occupational fitness and abilities come second. Marriage as the life-goal also implies a satisfactory orientation toward the culturally defined concept of 'love' — in our society often

viewed as a somewhat mysterious, irrational, and highly individualistic affair. In a society that stresses rationality, technical advances, and 'universal' values. extreme romantic love can present difficulties, both social and psychological.''

Thus, there is a harmonious concord between internalized sex role and occupational role for men. Both are I-A in nature and do not imply any latent or manifest contradictions that could give birth to conflicts or adaptive troubles. The family centered female role, on the other hand, is poorly adjusted to the requirements of the labor market, and the transition to gainful work is rendered more difficult by this psychic ballast.

'The second sex'

In relation to the male-dominated society, woman constitutes 'the second sex', which is judged by other value scales than the ones applied to men. That man's socialization to man and to an active member of society amalgamate, while woman's socialization to woman goes on apart and without the other horse of the pair: 'member of society' is of course merely a different way of depicting the malegoverned society. Throughout, man's behavior is employed as a templet for the behavior of 'the human being', at which woman gets a marginal position and becomes some kind of second-hand being. This over-confidence in the masculine partly account for the inability of the early women advocates of feminism to assert their feminine individuality against the masculine one. The reverence to the latter was so well-established and the association between manliness and talent, success etc. so definite, that the active women sought to equal men in looks, dress and general appearance. A more obvious mark of the recognition of the myth of man as the intellectually, physically and psychically 'best' endowed is hard to find. The standard put into practice in regard to women is acting on the needs of the maleman in the subject role. Woman as the object is then valued according to markedly 'female' characteristics as e.g. attractive force, charm and beauty, this value scale being used even in typical secondary group relations. Mirra Komarovsky (in *Amer. Journ. Soc.*, 52, 1946) and a few years later Wallin (*Amer. Soc. Rev.*, 15, 2, 1950) demonstrate, that college girls in co-education deliberatly embrace a 'feminine' behavior that is, behaving non-intellectually, for fear of loosing the attention and interest of boys. As late as in 1970, Hauser (*Amer. Journ. Soc.*, 75, 4, 1970) summarizes his study with i.a. the following words:

"For girls, on the other hand, the conditions for success in the two situations are the same. That is, success in the adolescent society and in adult society is based on appeal to men. The educational aspirations of boys are based on the implications of educational achievement for occupational achievement, while those of girls are based on the implications of educational achievement for the attraction of a suitable husband."

You might as well believe that the world has stood still ever since the turning of the century!

However, since the so-called feminine characteristics lack relevancy to I-A occupational roles, they represent, in actual fact, a handicap to the competition for coveted posts. The accentuation of the female traits is a miscalculation in relation to these positions, where only 'male' traits are in demand. In spite of this, women try to attain the feminine characteristics, since they give a compensatory dividend in the form of admiration and esteem on the intraindividual plane.

Crisis of identity

Rita Liljeström (in Fredriksson, I., 1965, op.cit.) has likened woman's situation to the one that, according to James Baldwin, is typical of the emancipated negro:

"Women climb one ladder of 'womanliness' and one equality ladder for human beings. To be a non-man and endeavour to live 'independently of sex' in a male-governed society with the 'double standards' create a psychological situation just as treacherous as the one described by Baldwin."

This implies, by no means, that the men in the malegoverned society are free of conflicts, only that the type of conflict is sex-determined. The conflict that arises in the wake of the clash between on the one hand, the demand for E-D behavior and on the other, the demand for I-A behavior is principally a crisis of identity. Woman's earliest ego-experience is intimately associated with the feminine sex role, and since it is generally well integrated in the personality by the time of the first contact with the life of work, the confrontation with the I-A requirements often comes as a shock. In this situation marriage seems a convenient retreat away from the demands of an adaption to the work role, an adjustment that would, as a matter of fact, necessitate a painful change in the structure of the personality − simply a new identity. Few venture to take the plunge and nobody applauds them if they do, but all the more eagerly they are praised when they choose the role as a mother and wife. Harriet Holter expresses the phenomenon as follows:

"The conflict between family and work is a general phenomenon. Our hypothesis here is that to most women *in addition to* a time conflict there is also a *psychosocial* conflict, which is impossible to settle since it is composed of the fact that the work role in itself to a certain extent is considered unwomanly, especially when one is married and 'supported'. The psychosocial conflict is for women *added to* the time conflict."
(Holter, H. in Dahlström, et al., 1963, op.cit.)

Moreover, Holter considers the sanctions against a behavior being divergent from the female role heavier than the sanctions against departure from the work role. Thus, women are 'punished' through being regarded as unfeminine if they follow a masculine pattern in their professional role. It is here feasible to speak of a two-sided conflict, consisting of on the one hand, the incompatibility between the expectations in the two positions as 'mother-housewife' and as 'gainfully employed', the conflict that is named 'the time conflict' by Holter, and on the other hand the opposition between the ego and the role, that is, the contradictory demands on woman in the two positions as 'human being' and as 'woman' which then would correspond to the psychosocial conflict in Holter's terminology.

Alternative roles in the conflict situation

In the conflict position mentioned above, the individual solution is of course dependent on quite a number of factors, but the alternatives are nevertheless limited. Liljeström (in Holmberg, P. et al., *Kynne eller kön?*, Stockholm, 1966) employs the following grouping of possible solutions: (1) rejection of the sex role in favor of the requirements of the professional role with loss of self-esteem as a consequence; (2) attempt to integrate the contradicting norms of occupation and sex through being professional and feminine at the same time. According to Liljeström, this both-and role results in a dissociation and renders a complete development of personal resources more difficult; (3) the professional role is rejected and the woman entirely concentrates on the sex role, something that does not encounter any obstacles socially; (4) occupational areas which constitute direct prolongations to the traditionally female role are sought. Role generalization is thus rendered possible. Social service occupations and occupations implying decorative tasks are instances of this.

Out of the four alternatives mentioned above, the two latter ones appear to meet with the least resistance and come most handy to judge

from professional intensity and occupational statistics. The first alternative is characteristic of the pronounced career woman, who does not see any compromises in her professional commitment and who also have a good deal fewer compromise possibilities than a man in an equivalent position. To combine a professional career and a family is to the male a selfevident privilege, and is in the present-day society practicable only because the wife handles the necessary ground-service and child care. The both-and role in alternative number two can be said to constitute the psychic counterpart to 'woman's two roles'. Liljeström here stresses the psychic split between two irreconcilable response patterns, while in referring to 'the double role' one is generally aiming at housewifes with an outside job. However, the concepts can be considered complementary, since they represent different aspects of one and the same phenomenon. The consequences are comparable too: the individual's personality is divided and the capability of whole-heartedly concentrating upon and accomplishing a task is hampered. Also, Liljeström (Liljeström, R. *Jämställdhetens villkor,* Stockholm, 1968), advances a somewhat modified schematized picture of woman's alternatives in adjusting to economic and social circumstances (Figure 3).

Myrdal and Klein (1956, op.cit.) argue in favor of a periodic subdivision of woman's life into three phases embracing education, family and gainful work as the settlement of the dilemma. That this division with its strong emphasis on a relatively long period of child care during the perhaps most important phase in the professional career—the developmental stage, thwart every prospect of reaching high and coveted posts is evident.

Myron Brenton (*The American Male,* Greenwich, 1966) takes one step further in time, to the point where the husband starts to conceive the wife's professional career as a threat against his own status. According to Brenton, to accept the thought of the wife's potential higher income and position is an absurdity to most men, and in this situation either of the following things often happens: (1) the woman abandons her career; (2) she continues her gainful work but takes some steps down in the hierarchy so as not to threaten man; (3) she refuses to choose either (1) or (2), the husband collapses and, according to Brenton, frequently becomes an alcoholic; (4) she deserts her husband and gives priority to the professional career.

Sysiharju (1960, op.cit.) quotes Parsons and Kirkpatrick, who both find three alternative behavior patterns in the wife role. Parsons mentions in addition to 'simple domesticy' a 'glamour pattern' as well

Economical adjustment	Approach to the distribution of responsibility within the family	
	Radical	Traditional
Good occupational training, employment that guarantees financial independence	1. Radical pioneer group	2. Marginal to the labor market
Insufficient occupational training, financial dependence	3. Marginal within the family	4. Traditional wife-role

Figure 3. *Liljeström's schematized representation of women's adaption alternatives in socio-economically complex situations.*

as a pattern of 'good companion'. These are in some measure tantamount to Kirkpatrick's three categories: 'wife-and-mother'. 'companion' and 'partner'. The first pattern in both Parsons' and Kirkpatrick's classification is markedly mother-housewife-oriented, whereas the 'glamour pattern' and 'companion' both are based on woman's role as a sexual object. Finally, Parsons' 'good companion' and Kirkpatrick's 'partner', stress a broader cultural spirit of community, founded upon friendship between husband and wife.

The role patterns related above can all be ranked with reference to degree of I-A and E-D disposition. Along the earlier mentioned hypothesized continuum the patterns can be ordered from the most E-D, across some kind of neutral point of equilibrium to the most I-A pattern (see Fig. 4).

Liljeström's first presented alternative behavior patterns then would be ordered as follows: 3, 4, 2 and 1 in the direction of an ever increasing degree of I-A accentuation. The alternatives of the fourfold table gets the following order of precedence: 4, 2, 3 and 1. According to the same principle of classification, Brenton's four alternatives would keep their original relative order, something that also applies to Parsons' and Kirkpatrick's variants.

Certain data (Dahlström, E., 1959, op.cit.), indicate, that the woman's individual adjusting between different alternative behavior is a manifesta-

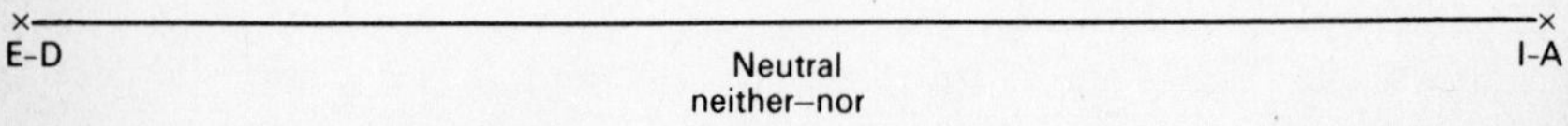

×————————————————————————————×
E-D   Neutral   I-A
           neither—nor

Figure 4. *Hypothetical continuum of degree of E-D (expressive-Dionysian) and I-A (instrumental-Apollonian) accent.*

tion of a more basic orientation. For instance, the housewives appeared as early as school age to have been more bent on nursing occupations than gainfully employed women, who at the same age had been more interested in occupations with longer education and of a more intellectual nature. Hence, to speak of a certainly very rough I-A − E-D typology of behavior in a more profound and personality anchored sense is maybe not entirely unrealistic.

Model

The pattern of acting chosen by the individual represents the result of a more or less conscious weighing of the factors included in the available alternatives. The aim of each separate decision is to maximize the amount of satisfaction, starting out from the given circumstances. Consequently, an optimal adjustment between the various choice factors is sought, thus giving the most significant ones the greatest weight and with that the ability to counterbalance the ones of less importance. Hence, the greater the significance of a choice factor, the larger the distribution required from the remaining factors in order to compensate for the loss of it. Each alternative entails, as is mentioned above, a number of different selection factors, which tend to accompany each other and form a more or less well integrated cluster with positive intracorrelations. On the other hand, a state of opposition prevails between the alternatives, something that finds expression in negative correlations between the clusters, since the alternatives compete for available limited resources in the form of time, interest, money etc. This model is based on Boalt's summation theory, see further e.g. Boalt, G., *The Sociology of Research* (Carbondale, 1968).

The outcome of woman's choice situation is dependent upon a number of psychic, economic, social and practical components, the reciprocal power relation of which varies from one case to the other. At the bottom of this internal order of precedence lies in turn among other things: type of education, personal experiences and growth environment in a broad sense. However, as the one-sided social press in all its forms in combination with the want of female models counteracts choice of I-A behavior alternatives, in actual fact only a very small and severely selected group of women will make use of this part of the continuum. On the other hand, this probably means that they have to dispense with the more E-D accented response patterns. In compliance with this way of looking at things, the I-A professional role must consequently be able to outbalance

91

the E-D sex role and compensate for losses in self-evaluation and social (and then not least male) esteem. In the extreme case (the pronounced career woman) the professional role must give so great a satisfaction that it is even capable of replacing family engagement. Especially in a society where husband and children still are considered as woman's most essential sphere of interest, without which her role as a woman is uncompleted (27 % of the women in Blood & Wolfe's study (*Husbands and wives,* Glencoe 1960) are even of the opinion that a life without children lacks its purpose and meaning, this above all being the case for woman), and where the conception that the never married woman is deficient as to social and personal adaption is so deeply rooted and widespread, that it gets the rank of 'stereotype' and is subjected to scientific investigations (Baker, L. jr., *Journ. of Marr. and the Family,* 30, 3, 1968) — in such a society an unusually high dividend of satisfaction is indeed required from the professional role, if it shall be capable of outweighing the family role.

In the foregoing, a number of factors were referred to that obstruct or preclude woman's simultaneous commitment to husband and children and a demanding professional career. In addition to these factors, of which almost everyone bears reference to the interpersonal plane, factors like: want of day nuseries, scarcity of work opportunities etc. can be mentioned. They are all manifestations of the underlying sex role structure, but since the former group of factors is nearer to the central theme of this study, the latter are mentioned here merely for the sake of completeness.

Presentation of the problem

In a descriptive-exploratory study we thus want to investigate whether female researchers differ from male researchers as regards the adjustment between above all professional role and family role, and if so which shape it assumes. Furthermore, we are interested in any divergences that may exist between the behavior pattern of female researchers and that of a representative sample of prominent women from various occupational spheres. We also want to compare the latter group with an equivalent sample of men as a parallel to the comparison between male and female researchers. In accordance with the related reasoning, a definite order of precedence in regard to degree of compensatory tendency in the role pattern ought to arise between these four samples.

Hypothetical frame of reference

In a previous chapter the hypothesis that the severe and partly incompatible demands of research work give rise to an unusually large distance between the researcher's aspiration level and achievement level was advanced. This in turn leads, according to the presumption, to a compensation pattern in the relationship between the separate role clusters of the individual. The outcome of the comparison between groups of researchers and non-researchers shows a tendency, though not as marked as expected, in the direction of the hypothesis. Starting out from this in addition to the reasoning accounted for in the preceding sections, the female researchers are expected to present a more pronounced compensation pattern than male researchers.

Furthermore, this tendency ought also to manifest itself in a comparison between men and women being randomly selected from Who's Who. However, the difference should be less here, since the group of randomized women reasonably contains a number of persons with role-generalizing occupations (alternative no 4 in Liljeström's first classification), which, unlike the research profession, in some measure harmonize with the E-D sex role and therefore do not create equally strong conflicts but are able to coexist, even if not in harmony, with the family role. Also, the pattern of these two randomly selected heterogeneous groups ought, if anything, approach a unified value pattern rather than the compromise pattern, predicted for the groups of researchers.

We thus expect, that the E-D rule expectations being directed toward woman are so one-sided and narrow as to force her to make a choice without much possibility of compromise if she desires to devote herself to a more exacting professional career. The uncompromising choice results in an artificial polarization in I-A and E-D types of women. Naturally, an absolute dichotomy with a sharp boundary between I-A and E-D is not intended by this, though the distribution is probably strongly oblique in the negative rather than perpendicular (see Fig. 5). (A corre-

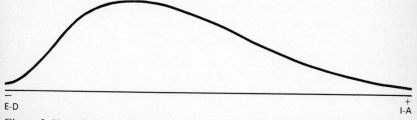

E-D I-A

Figure 5. *Hypothesized distribution of women along the I-A–E-D dimension.*

sponding distribution of men is conceivable, a distribution being even more pronouncedly oblique, now in a positive direction. The more human forms in between are with the present severe sex role norms likely to result in permanent situations of conflict and more or less schizoid response patterns.)

Tentative hypotheses

Role pattern

The pronounced I-A nature of research work ought to result in on the one hand, fewer female than male researchers, and on the other I-A response patterns in those women, who after all enter the research career. The role pattern, divided up into the following three roles: A) research and career role; B) family role, and C) social role, is as for the women likely to contain fewer compromise opportunities and are with that likely to become more compensatory than for the men. Thus, a more intense state of competition between the roles expressed in the amount of negative correlations between the three clusters is above all expected for the female researchers. If the reasoning is correct, the divergence also ought to manifest itself in the comparison between samples of randomly selected men and women.

A ranking of the four groups in question concerning strength in the tendency toward a compensatory pattern should, with increasing degree of compensatory profile, be as follows: (1) representative sample of men, (2) male researchers, (3) representative sample of women, (4) female researchers. In other words, the idea is that sex carries a greater weight than type of occupation when it comes to extorting a choice between different roles in this restricted situation. (Alternatively, research work proves to exert a stronger pressure in this respect than the sex role norms, at which the sample of male researchers is to change place with the representative group of women in the sequence.) The sample of female researchers, however, are dependent on both factors, whereas the representative sample of men in accordance with the argumentation is not affected by either of them, which motivates the hypothetical succession.

Group differences in separate variables. Male and Female researchers

Representation of researchers

As a consequence of the traditional and as yet very vigorous E-D female role, the sample of female researchers ought to be considerably smaller than the corresponding sample among men. Bird (1969, op.cit.) reports a woman representation of 8 % among American scientists in the middle of the 1960ies.

The I-A nature of the research profession and the high prestige connected thereto makes it a typical example of a profession with what Epstein calls 'status-set typing' and that which Merton denominates 'sex-typing'. "Thus I have labeled 'status-set typing' when a class of persons who share a key status (e.g. lawyer) also share other matching statuses (e.g. white, Protestant) and when it is considered appropriate that this be so" (Epstein, C., 1970, op.cit.). "Occupations can be described as 'sex-typed' when a very large majority of those in them are of one sex and when there is an associated normative expectation that this is as it should be" (Merton, R., quoted in Epstein, 1970, op.cit.). The processes behind those phenomena are, according to Epstein, as follows:

"(1) The colleague system of the professions, especially at the upper levels; (2) the sponsor-protégé relationship, which determines access to the highest levels of most professions; (3) the demands of the professions 'inner' structures and its attendant patterns of social interaction which are, under most circumstances, incompatible with the sex-role expectation repertory of even those women engaged in professional careers; and (4) the sex-typing of occupations, which reinforces these processes in linking occupational roles with sex-roles."

At the bottom of these processes lies in turn the old division on 'male' and 'female' occupations.

Position in the occupational hierarchy

The higher up in the occupational hierarchy one gets, the fewer is the number of women in relation to the number of men, and this applies not least to the academic world. Rossi's inventory (Rossi, A., *The Amer. Soc.*, 5, 1, 1970) of women's status at American sociological departments shows that while 42 % of the men with doctor's degrees hold a professorship, the corresponding figure among women with Ph.D.:s is only 16 %. Especially married women are underrepresented. On going through the

number of women in Standard & Poor's Executive Dictionnaire, Bird (in *Exploding the Myths,* Wash., 1967) finds an amount of 1.6 % (33 % of these women are related to a man in the company), a proportion that frequently recurs in inventories of this kind.

Hence, the female researchers should on the average be found on a somewhat lower level than the male ones and also diminish more rapidly than men in number with every upward step in the hierarchy. For natural reasons, the highest academical levels are over-represented in the material from *Vem är det,* and women should here diminish more with ascending level as regards relative amount of the total number.

Area of subject

The first public sphere of work in Sweden where women were admitted was the educational system. Of all the higher studies, those in medicine were first made accessible (1870), while the remaining subjects, with the exception of theology and higher legal education, were not opened to women until some years later. The humanities and medicine could be regarded as extensions of the child educating and caring female role, whereas in particular theology and jurisprudence were associated with 'male' abstract thinking. This approach can be traced even in the society of today, for which reason we expect to find the largest amount of female researchers in the faculties of medicine and of arts, and to find the smallest amount of women in the faculties of law and of theology in the order now mentioned.

Children

Provided the presumption that women aiming at a higher professional career are confronted with a frequently uncompromising either-or choice is correct, the female researchers should on the average have fewer children than the male ones. According to an English study (Gavron, H., *The Captive Wife,* London 1966), children seem to create role problems to a greater extent than matrimony in itself for married women. The higher the woman's academic training, the lower the average number of children, Dawson's study demonstrates (Dawson, 1965, op.cit.).

In a survey carried through by Alice Rossi (quoted in Bird, C., 1969, op.cit.) it is demonstrated, that career oriented women on the average wanted fewer children than women prepared for housework. The rela-

96

tive amount of women with wishes for many children decreases with increased education in the study of Blood and Wolfe. In addition, the average number of children is lower, the more influence the wife has in relation to the husband.

Civil status

A larger amount of the female than of the male researchers should be unmarried. Without specifying his source of information, Brenton notes that statistical surveys show that merely half of all career women marry. More reliable are the figures cited by Moberg (Moberg, S., *Vem blev student och vad blev studenten?,* Lund, 1951) from an American study of women in Who's Who in 1948. 53 % of the women who had passed the Doctor's degree were unmarried, while the corresponding percentage among those with a Master's degree was 66% and for women with a Bachelor's degree, the proportion of unmarried was 38%. In his own study of women included in the Swedish Who's Who of 1945, Moberg found as much as 68 % not married among those with a Ph.D. or a licentiate, 46 % unmarried among women with other academical degrees, 37 % unmarried among the remainder and 40 % not married for the total number of women. Furthermore, data for American women indicate that of those having passed college, 31 % stayed unmarried as against only 13 % for all women in the United States. Marriage mostly (85 % in Sweden) leads to children, and the connection here is so tight that a choice between children and a professional career often is tantamount to a choice between marriage and a professional career. In addition to the strong correlation between children and marriage, factors like the presumptive husband's negative attitude to the woman's strong work commitment and the resulting increased burden of domestic work falling on his lot are likely to raise such obstacles, that the career oriented woman judges marriage as being incompatible with an exacting professional career. To use the words of van den Berghe (*The Amer. Soc., 5,* 4, 1970): "If women expect to win equal status, they will either have to stay single or to fight on two fields" . . . "I am suggesting that the structure of discrimination against women in academia has two institutional loci, namely, the academic system itself and marriage". In Alpenfels survey (in Cassara, B., 1962, op.cit.) of 400 American students, 18 % of the men declared that a woman had to be young and unmarried in order to qualify as gainfully employed.

Marriage début

In her dissertation, Sysiharju confirms the well known negative effect that an early marriage has upon woman's education. The female researchers who marry, should do it at a later point of time than women in general. A comparison with male researchers is also feasible, in spite of the fact that the average age at marriage differ for men and women. This difference is namely relatively constant from year to year and can therefore be utilized as a basic measure for the difference between male and female researchers in this respect. According to the prediction, the distance between the sexes as to age at first marriage should be shorter in the research samples than in the entire population.

Family planning

In line with the earlier conducted argumentation, the birth of the first child also should be postponed longer by female researchers than by male ones. Since women generally become mothers at an earlier age than men become fathers, the age at first parenthood of the person concerned can't be used, but the amount of family planning should be measured by the distance between marriage and the arrival of the first child. The chance that any disparity that there may be between men and women is obliterated through the influence of the preceding variable is a disadvantage of this measure. If, namely, the supposition that female researchers marry later than women in general is correct, this phenomenon in itself has a retarding effect upon the point in time of the birth of the first child. Therefore, if the time interval between marriage and first child is short, it does not necessarily imply want of family planning. Marriage could here reflect a preparedness in woman to take the responsibility of a child as well as of the interruption this entails for the professional activity.

As for the birth of a possible second and third child, a concentration in time should be advantageous from the viewpoint of the woman's gainful employment. The closer on to each other the children come, the shorter the woman's inactive work period. The sooner she can return to her paid job, the fewer the negative consequences of her absence should be for her career opportunities. From Dawson's investigation it is evident, that the more continuously the academically trained women were working, the greater was the probability of publication of their products, and the higher their income. Hence, we anticipate a shorter interval between the births of the first and the second child among the sample of female researchers than for the male sample.

Income

Furthermore, the female researchers are expected to have a lower average income than the male researchers, namely if, as predicted, their positions even within this selected group are lower than those of the males. Irrespective of the influence of this factor, the annual income should be lower especially in the case of married research women, since, because of obligations in the home, they do not have equivalent opportunities to remunerative jobs on the side. In addition to this, wages are at their lowest within the branches where the interspersion of women is at its greatest (Epstein, 1970, op.cit.). American data (Rossi, A., 1970, op.cit.) show, that the higher the prestige of the educational institution, the smaller the proportion of women on either of the three top-levels in the academic hierarchy. Possibly, this also applies to Swedish institutions. Dawson's study of female university graduates, moreover, indicates that women with a Doctor's degree did not receive financial recompense on a par with their high academic qualifications. According to Turner (In *Exploding the Myths* 1966, op.cit.) there are two kinds of rewards in gainful work:

(1) intrinsic rewards (which derive from satisfaction with the occupation in itself) and (2) extrinsic rewards (income, neighbourhood, way of life etc.). Turner feels that women expect to satisfy the extrinsic needs through their husbands, whereupon they can devote themselves in piece and quiet to perhaps less profitable but intrinsically rewarding occupations. To men, the striving for economical, educational and professional success compose a single cluster, whereas to women desired standard of living (income) on the one hand, and professional and educational level on the other form two separate clusters. Provided these data are pertinent to the groups studied here, this factor too should be conducive to diminishing the income level of research women in relation to that of men.

Social origin

The emancipation of women in Sweden as well as in many other countries historically originates from the middle classes. Demands for means of support for women other than marriage and industrial work were raised within those classes. In the course of recent years, the debate on sex roles has been most active within higher educated and economically well off strata of society. On the in these respects worst off levels, where 'the choice between home and work' for financial reasons does

not exist, the discussion is almost non-existent. In these lower social strata, the authoritarian attitudes are more prevalent than in higher social strata. Allen (*Amer. Soc. Rev.,* Oct. 1954) and later Sysiharju (1960, op.cit.) demonstrate a co-variation between authoritarian attitudes and traditional attitudes concerning the role of woman.

The connection between continued studies and social extraction is supported in a number of surveys (see e.g. Boalt & Husén *Skolans sociologi,* Stockholm, 1970)–the higher the social origin, the greater the probability on every grade level of continuing toward a higher education, especially when it comes to girls. As for the girls, the lack of educational tradition in the lower social strata is concurrent with the traditional attitudes to the role of women, for which reason girls here have a double ballast. In a Swedish investigation (Härnqvist, K., SOU 1960: 13), the correlation between the father's education and the passing over to senior high school was found to be 0.50 for girls and 0.43 for boys. In regard to the female researchers we anticipate a somewhat higher level of social origin than as regards the male ones, since we expect the latter to be more unfettered by the social heritage. Also, we expect the mothers of female researchers to be gainfully employed to a greater extent than those of the randomly selected women, and also that their occupations are more I-A in nature. This implies, among other things, that a smaller proportion of the former should hold role generalizing professions.

Birthplace and domicile

The regional origin as well as the social one affects the disposition to seek a higher education. Swedish data indicate, that there is a marked difference between relative number of students in different types of domicile (Moberg, S., 1951, op.cit.), the amount being largest in the big towns and smallest in the countryside. Geographical proximity to schools with higher education and the educational tradition in the domicile bound up with it, evidently play an important part in the choice between pursuing the studies or not. Several investigations (see e.g. Dawson, 1965, op.cit.) confirm the hypothesis, that girls are more dependent on type of domicile for their studies than are boys. Thus, boys generally pass over to higher education more frequently than girls, the sex difference being most remarkable in small towns and in the country. This phenomenon is probably linked to the generally more liberal outlook one finds in big cities. The disparity should above all have reference

to place of birth, since the institutions of research usually are concentrated to big towns and university towns, which limits the possible variation of domicile in our sample.

Regional origin expressed in birthplace and type of present domicile should thus exert a greater influence upon women than upon men, and we anticipate a larger amount among the female than among the male researchers to be born and to live in big cities and university towns. The proportion of agreements with the proposition that 'women oughtn't hold leading positions' is, for instance, higher in the country and among men than in the towns and among women (Haavio-Mannila, E., in *Scandinavian Pol. Studies,* Oslo, 5, 1970). Women in the cities are also more willing to interact with men and are more apt to identify with men than with women, something that does not apply to women in the countryside.

Social activities

The fact that gainfully working women as a consequence of the uneven distribution of tasks in the home have less leisure time than men, necessarily pares their social engagement. However, Haavio-Mannila *(Sex Differentiation in Role Expectations and Performance,* Helsinki, 1967) demonstrates that Finnish wives with a paid job in comparison with the housewives were more frequently affiliated to an organization, which in accordance with our reasoning can be interpreted as a manifestation of a generally more I-A orientation. Furthermore, the study shows, that most registered organizations were male and that the proportion of men in the committees was larger than the corresponding proportion in the body of members. The men were especially engaged in political organizations as well as professional and athletic associations, while the women's interest was concentrated upon charitable institutions and religious and cultural organizations. Data for more exclusive clubs are missing, but presumably, clubs having special entrance requirements and high prestige value are mostly male. Women's reduced spare time in relation to men should manifest itself among the researchers too, in so far as the former more seldom than the latter should be members of a club or engaged in any spare time occupation outside of home.

Relationship between age and occupational position as well as productivity

Roe cites in her work *The Psychology of Occupations* (1956, op.cit.) a survey of 266 faculty members with a Doctor's degree. The outcome

indicates, that the educational cycle and early publishing were significantly related to both quantity and quality of what was produced, and also that previous achievements constituted the best predictor for present activities. In an American (Andersson & Goodenough, 1935, quoted in Roe, op.cit.) study of the productivity of male and female psychologists, the average age at the publication début was found to be the same for both sexes. On the other hand, there are clear sex differences as to the number of annually published pages, which is higher for men, and increased publishing with advancing age, something that also applies to men to a greater extent. However, men reach their peak of publication as early as in the age of 35 to 40, whereupon the number of pages per year decreases, while women reach their peak considerably later, namely between 50 and 55 years of age. Even when one acts on a broader sample of academical professions, women's quantitative performance seems to be lower than that of men, and so we hypothesize, that the group of female researchers partly has a higher average age at the defence of the doctor's thesis, partly has been offered a chair at a more advanced age than men and finally, on the average has fewer published pieces of work than the group of male researchers. Whether even the whole of the female research group comprises a greater proportion of older people, appears hard to predict since two opposed trends are in evidence here. On the one hand, relatively more women have sought a higher education in the course of the last few decades, on the other, they marry earlier and earlier and in increasing numbers. To quote from Viola Klein (in Patai, 1967, op.cit.):

"With the virtual disappearance of the generation of educated spinsters able and willing to devote their lives to their careers, it is a moot point whether women will ever again reach such exalted positions" (namely, as ministers).

Participation in the academic world

Women's generally lower turn-out in organizations is illustrated in a number of surveys, among them Sysiharju's and Haavio-Mannila's (1960, 1967 resp., op.cit.). However, the difference between the sexes decreases with increased education, and Haavio-Mannila shows that 70 % of the women with a university degree and 77 % of the men with an equivalent training are members of some association as against 28 % for women and 68 % for men in the sample having only an elementary school training. This applies to associations and organizations in which the person concerned can seek entrance, and furthermore, the percen-

102

tages bear reference to membership, not positions of trust. The majority of the latter are held by men, something that should apply even more to prestige-loaded learned societies and academies with special entrance requirements. Here, the effect of what Epstein denominates 'status-set-typing' and what Bernard names 'sexism' (Bernard, Jessie, Sexism and discrimination. *The Amer. Soc.,* Vol. 5, no. 4) become expecially pronounced, for which reason we here anticipate a lower participation among female researchers. Bernard defines 'sexism' as follows:

"Sexism has many parallels with racism. It is the naive, unconscious, taken-for-granted, assumed unexamined acceptance by sociologists of the idea that, let us say, sociology as developed by men is the one and only sociology worth researching, that the topics men sociologists are concerned about – especially power, mobility, conflict – are the only topics worth paying attention to."
"Women would contaminate sociology, they would degrade it, they would give it a bad name among fellow scientists, they would lower its standards."

International activities

The dichotomization of men's and women's activities in extroverted for men and introverted for women, that has been learnt through the socialization process, also should be traceable in the degree of commitment outside the boundaries of one's own country. Jessie Bernard (Bernard, J., *Academic Women,* 1964) finds in a comparison between male and female college professors a marked tendency for the men to publish articles in journals 'outside' their own branch more frequently than the women. Thus, men seem to make use of a wider field of action in choice of a subject than do women – there remains to be seen, whether this concerns the spacial sense too. In addition to the fact, that the female sex role, unlike the male one, is inner-directed, the female researchers' possible international work is likely to be impeded by the patriarchal sex role attitudes, being even more prevalent in most countries outside Sweden and especially outside Scandinavia. The geographical mobility should also be more damped in female than in male researchers as a result of the family's greater demands for the presence of the wife-and-mother than of the husband-and-father.

Public functions appointments etc.

In a similar, yet less pronounced, way as in regard to learned societies and the like, we assume, that status-set-typing, sexism and sex-typing

of top-positions, contemporaneously with the demands of the family, contribute to keep the amount of official functions of all kinds lower among female than among male researchers.

Group differences in separate variables. Representative samples of men and women

When it comes to the representative group of men and women drawn from *Vem är det,* we expect to find sex differences with the same direction as between male and female researchers in the variables. However, the disparity ought to be smaller between the representative samples, especially as to variables attached to the family role, since the women to a not inconsiderable extent can be expected to occupy sex role generalizing professions with E-D elements. According to our reasoning, these occupations provide better opportunities for the co-existence of professional role and family role than do the markedly I-A research profession and principally cover the following areas: care in all forms, pedagogical work and decorative tasks (as well in the sense of *being decorative* as in the sense of *decorate,* create artistic products).

Summary

The testing of the hypotheses is thus to be split up in three sections: the first bearing upon the allocation of resources among the roles in variable matrices for each one of the four groups studied and the compensatory force of separate variables connected thereto; the second referring to differences between the groups rendered in averages, proportions and percentage distributions for certain variables; finally, data are analyzed by means of factor analysis.

CHAPTER 8

Design of study

Since the present study of sex role sociology is a direct extension of the research sociological analysis treated in previous chapters, and as the role pattern of each sample here too is expected to be distributed on the three role clusters: A) career and research role, B) family role and C) social role, the same sources of information were utilized. These are: *the Swedish Who's Who* in two different variants *(Vem är det* and *Vem är vem)* published in 1969 and 1962–1968, respectively; the Swedish *Taxpayer's Directory 1969;* eight reference books of varying range and finally, various sources of minor importance.

All in all, four samples were randomly selected from *Vem är det,* two of them being drawn from the population of researchers (persons with least a Ph.D.) and two having the entire population in *Vem är det* as a basis of selection. The sample of male researchers embraces 665 persons, while the female researchers only amount to 50 (this being the total number of female top-researchers in *Vem är det*). The two representative samples comprehend 100 men and 100 women, respectively.

Variables

A total number of 43 variables were registered, 35 of which constitute the set of variables being distributed on the hypothetical role clusters. Thus, 24 variables belong to the research and career cluster, while 9 are included in the family cluster and 2 are part of the social cluster. Since most of the following variables are already accounted for in an earlier chapter, only the newcomers and alterations in the composition of the clusters will be commented upon in detail. For a detailed description of the remaining variables see pages 23–26.

A. Research and career variables

Two of the variables in this cluster are exchanged, namely 'university loyalty I and II', the substitute of which are 'birthplace' and 'private

means'. The reason to this is, that to married female researchers, a change of university between two academic grade levels is likely to bear a relation to the husband's change of place of work, while the possible transfer of married male researchers from one university to another is probably relatively independent of the wife's job. Whenever a family changes domicile, it mostly follows the terms of employment of the husband, and woman has to adapt as best she can afterwards. Married female researcher's change of university are thus likely to mirror other factors than the ones being the basis of the assumptions behind the variables 'university loyalty I and II'. A test of the accuracy of this line of thought is feasible in some measure, wherefore the variables are all the same registered and entered among the 'remaining variables'.

1. Family name.
2. Age.
3. Academic position/performance.
4. Social origin
   measured by father's social class in the same manner as related in chapter 2.
5. Place of residence.
6. Birthplace
   using the same six-point scale as in the preceding variable.
7. Private means.
   A successful career on the one hand should promote the founding of a fortune, and on the other it would probably be facilitated by the financially more secure position, that a fortune occasions. With the aid of the Swedish Taypayer's Directory a breaking up of the individuals upon two categories was accomplished: 1) not in the possession of a fortune; 2) in the possession of a fortune. Since the number of people belonging to the first category was estimated to be rather small, a more detailed division was not considered feasible.
   The variables 8–24 in the research and career cluster are identical to the ones with corresponding numbers related in chapter 2.

B. Family variables

7 out of the 9 original variables in the family cluster (see pages 25–26) are equivalent to the variables 27–33 in the present numbering. As their relative position for practical reasons has been altered, however, all of them are enumerated, although only the new and altered ones are

treated in detail. The variable 'educational level of the subject's spouse' was considered less relevant in the present context and was thus excluded from the role pattern. Since the assumptions connected to the variable 'nearness between first and second child' vary according to the sex of the person concerned, and as the comparison between the compensation pattern of men and women accordingly would not be equitable, this variable is excluded from the family cluster and is registered among the 'remaining variables'. In this way, all presumptions advanced can be tested without the variable clusters loosing in comparability between the samples.

25. Marriage disposition.
    The number of marriages contracted by the subject is registered.
26. Marital début.
    Earliness of marriage, measured by the age of the subject at first marriage in an inverted scale. The scale is obtained through a reversal of the signs for all coefficients of the variable in question.
27. Number of children.
28. Nearness between first marriage and first child.
29. Number of years between first academic degree and appointment to full professor.
30. Age at doctor's dissertation.
31. Age at first appointment to full professor.
32. Income.
33. Income of the subject's spouse.

C. Social variables

34. Number of clubs
    enumerated by the subject in *Vem är vem*
35. Number of hobbies
    stated by the person concerned in *Vem är vem*.

Remaining variables

In addition to the variables enumerated above certain informations were registered, intended to be utilized for a more detailed description of the researcher's situation without for that sake being attributable to any of the three role clusters.

36. Area of subject and occupational area.
    For the groups of researchers this variable is coded as follows:
    1) social scientists; 2) researchers in the humanities; 3) researchers in jurisprudence; 4) res. in theology; 5)medical researchers; 6) res. in agriculture, forestry and veterinary medicine; 7) scientists in engineering; 8) res. in business administration; 9) natural scientists.
    The mapping out of the representative samples of men and women embraces the following main categories:
    1) technical work; 2) chemical and physical work; 3) biological work; 4) medical work and work in the health service; 5) pedagogical work; 6) religious work; 7) legal work; 8) literary and artistic work, business administrative and other technical and economical administrative work; 11) researchers.
37. University loyalty I and
38. University loyalty II,
    variables corresponding to 4 and 5 in page 24.
39. Civil status
    coded in 8 categories:
    1) unmarried; 2) married once; 3) widow/widower, not remarried; 4) widow/widower, remarried; 5) divorced, not remarried; 6) divorced, remarried; 7) married 3 times; 8) married 4 times or more.
40. Educational level of the subject's spouse
    (see page 25 for a detailed description).
41. Nearness between first and second child.
    The number of years between their birth is registered.
42. Creativity,
    measured by the number of enumerated patents, inventions, proposed bills, works of art etc.
43. Social origin of the subject's spouse,
    expressed in the father's social class in the some manner as for variable no. 4.

Result of matrix analysis

Every possible correlation between the 35 variables included in the three role clusters was calculated for each one of the four samples studied. At this, Pearson's coefficient of product-moment correlation, r, was utilized.

Female researchers

Table 15 gives the correlation pattern for the group of female researchers. Of the 35 variables, one proved to be irrelevant, namely no 17: number of academic positions, for which there were no values to be noted in this sample. The variable thus is excluded from the subsequent computations in the matrix. The proportion of positive correlations within the research and career cluster is 193 out of 253, that is, 76.29 %. Thus, the variables in this cluster appear to be relatively well integrated, this being the case even after the three sum variables 22, 23 and 24 ('researcher's status', 'general status' and 'academic power') have been excepted. 136 positive correlations out of 190 possible ones, or 71.38 % is then the result. The degree of inner unity in the family cluster is considerably lower, showing 20 positive intracorrelations of 36 conceivable ones – 55.56 %. The sole correlation between the two social variables is negative, for which reason they can't be considered a homogeneous cluster.

The relation between the three role clusters shows the picture of a fairly well demarcated role pattern. Out of all in all 207 correlations between the research and career cluster on the one hand and the family cluster on the other, 132 are negative, giving 63.77 %. If the sum variables 22–24 are left out, the amount is 112 out of 180 or 62.22 % negative correlations. Furthermore, 32 of 46 possible correlations, 69.57 %, between the research-and-career cluster and the social cluster are negative, this share rising to 29 out of 40 or 72.50 % when the sum variables are excluded. However, no state of opposition appears between the social role and the family role, since only 7 out of 18 intercorrelation – 38 % – are negative.

To sum up, a relatively distinct compensation pattern with, in substance, positive correlations within the two central clusters A (above all) and B, as well as a rather great proportion of negative intercorrelations between the three role clusters (with the exception of B–C) appears in the sample of female researchers.

Male researchers

The role pattern of the male researchers is presented in Table 16. Here, the research and career cluster proves to be better integrated than among the female researchers and contains 225 positive correlations out of 276 possible ones, that is 81.52%. On the whole, the disparity remains

Table 15. *Female researchers*

	A. Research and Career cluster													
	1	2	3	4	5	6	7	8	9	10	11	12	13	14
A. Research and career cluster														
1. Family name	■	+.15	.00	+.55	+.05	+.03	+.20	+.06	+.08	−.12	−.18	+.17	+.01	+.17
2. Age		■	+.02	+.07	+.09	−.07	+.40	+.34	+.19	+.61	+.46	+.20	+.50	−.01
3. Academic position			■	−.15	+.25	−.13	+.30	+.09	+.18	+.10	+.28	+.01	+.15	+.13
4. Social origin				■	+.02	+.24	+.07	+.12	−.06	+.07	−.02	+.13	+.16	+.13
5. Place of residence					■	+.30	+.20	+.16	+.19	+.10	+.06	+.30	+.20	+.09
6. Birthplace						■	−.04	+.11	−.22	+.03	+.11	−.06	+.13	+.17
7. Private means							■	+.32	+.16	+.32	+.24	.00	+.02	+.16
8. Status according to encyclopedias								■	+.23	+.79	+.47	−.08	+.38	+.45
9. Space in 'Vem är det'									■	+.06	+.18	+.02	+.23	+.14
10. Number of reference books										■	+.71	−.04	+.59	+.31
11. Academies etc.											■	−.13	+.39	+.34
12. Swedish honorary doctor's degrees												■	−.11	−.06
13. Government committees													■	+.15
14. Memberships in research councils														
15. Enumerated international commissions														
16. Foreign guest professorships														
17. Academic positions														
18. Published works														
19. Name of doctor's thesis given in 'Vem är det'														
20. Distinctions														
21. Foreign honorary doctor's degrees														
22. Researcher's status														
23. General status														
24. Academic power														

B. Family cluster
25. Marriage disposition
26. Marital début
27. Number of children
28. Nearness between marriage and first child
29. Interval between first examination and appointment to full professor
30. Age at doctor's dissertation
31. Age at appointment to full professor
32. Income
33. Income of the subject's spouse

C. Social cluster
34. Membership in clubs
35. Number of hobbies

even as the sum variables 22, 23 and 24 are excluded; cluster A then contains 165 of 210 or 78.57 % positive correlations. Even the unity within the family cluster is somewhat better for the male than for the female researchers, showing 21 out of 36 or 58.33 % positive intracorrelations for the men. Finally, the two social variables are positively related.

When it comes to the state of competition between the variable clusters, it is considerably less pronounced among the male researchers. The amount of negative correlations between the clusters A and B is here 103 of 216 possible −47.69 %−and between the clusters A and C, 27

										B. Family cluster									C. Social cluster	
15	16	17	18	19	20	21	22	23	24	25	26	27	28	29	30	31	32	33	34	35
−.02	−.23	.00	+.15	+.12	+.03	−.02	+.01	+.07	−.07	+.09	+.10	+.02	+.03	+.07	+.07	+.09	+.05	−.20	−.01	+.04
+.44	−.18	.00	+.32	+.12	+.42	+.61	+.54	+.40	+.58	−.19	−.29	−.13	−.32	+.51	+.24	+.43	−.02	−.01	−.09	−.02
+.15	+.30	.00	+.17	−.11	+.33	+.21	+.31	+.21	+.25	−.19	−.11	−.13	−.11	−.12	−.06	−.11	+.06	+.02	−.04	−.04
−.01	−.35	.00	+.12	.00	+.02	−.14	+.04	+.02	+.08	−.02	+.20	+.11	+.16	+.17	−.14	+.10	−.11	+.03	+.10	+.03
−.03	+.27	.00	+.15	−.04	+.09	+.31	+.18	+.23	+.14	−.05	+.03	−.13	−.02	−.27	−.09	−.32	+.02	+.09	−.01	+.05
−.05	+.03	.00	−.02	−.12	−.11	+.16	+.04	−.14	+.12	+.03	+.12	+.03	−.06	+.04	−.33	−.03	−.23	−.21	+.04	−.14
+.20	+.12	.00	−.03	+.17	+.52	+.55	+.18	+.22	+.18	+.06	−.24	−.04	−.15	−.07	+.07	−.05	−.05	−.29	−.08	−.14
+.38	−.07	.00	+.12	+.03	+.44	+.38	+.40	+.52	+.53	−.18	−.23	−.11	−.21	−.05	−.15	+.05	+.01	−.24	−.06	−.16
+.28	−.01	.00	+.18	−.01	+.25	+.09	+.26	+.91	+.27	+.01	−.12	−.18	−.12	−.37	+.54	−.34	+.83	−.33	+.04	−.08
+.56	−.09	.00	+.27	+.07	+.56	+.56	+.65	+.43	+.79	−.23	−.26	−.23	−.56	+.26	−.25	+.32	−.31	−.32	−.03	−.12
+.32	−.08	.00	+.22	−.03	+.70	+.60	+.69	+.39	+.76	−.19	−.13	−.22	−.67	+.20	−.23	+.19	−.15	−.22	+.02	−.16
−.07	−.06	.00	+.26	−.22	−.02	−.06	+.13	−.03	−.13	−.08	+.06	−.20	.00	−.05	.00	−.09	.00	.00	−.05	−.08
+.59	−.10	.00	+.39	+.06	+.13	+.44	+.57	+.55	+.87	−.14	−.28	−.04	−.12	+.34	−.01	+.21	−.03	+.17	+.16	−.10
+.10	−.06	.00	−.09	−.04	+.45	+.19	+.17	+.26	+.31	+.06	+.19	+.09	−.29	−.03	−.09	−.04	−.10	+.04	−.05	−.08
■	+.08	.00	+.38	+.14	+.34	+.24	+.62	+.48	+.69	−.01	−.44	−.18	−.64	+.34	−.05	+.41	−.07	−.16	−.05	−.09
	■	.00	−.07	−.11	+.03	+.09	+.02	−.05	−.08	+.06	+.08	−.12	−.08	−.06	−.19	−.05	−.08	−.05	−.05	−.08
		■	.00	.00	.00	.00	.00	.00	.00	.00	.00	.00	.00	.00	.00	.00	.00	.00	.00	.00
			■	+.12	.00	−.07	+.82	+.28	+.39	−.14	−.31	−.24	−.02	+.20	−.13	+.26	−.10	−.17	+.14	−.09
				■	+.03	−.08	+.07	+.01	+.05	+.20	−.21	+.13	+.56	−.23	−.04	+.10	−.17	+.23	−.03	+.26
					■	+.53	+.44	+.38	+.49	.00	−.07	+.01	−.54	+.06	−.12	+.11	−.11	−.08	−.02	+.03
						■	+.35	+.30	+.58	−.14	−.11	−.14	−.64	+.11	−.09	+.04	−.09	−.16	−.05	−.08
							■	+.48	+.77	−.18	−.33	−.32	−.53	+.28	−.22	+.35	−.15	−.24	+.08	−.17
								■	+.61	−.09	−.21	+.09	−.21	−.24	+.40	−.17	+.64	−.32	+.08	−.13
									■	−.17	−.30	−.16	−.56	+.32	−.13	+.29	−.11	−.09	+.09	−.16
										■	+.25	+.47	+.29	−.41	+.09	−.33	+.02	+.05	−.28	+.28
											■	+.38	−.19	+.16	+.09	−.19	−.07	+.06	.00	+.18
												■	+.48	−.47	+.27	−.47	+.24	+.34	−.15	+.38
													■	−.41	+.01	−.42	+.13	+.33	.00	+.27
														■	−.35	+.92	−.34	−.01	.00	−.29
															■	−.36	+.62	−.30	−.08	+.02
																■	−.48	+.15	+.03	−.25
																	■	−.32	−.01	−.07
																		■	.00	+.63
																			■	−.06
																				■

out of 48 or 56.25 % negative correlations. Just as in the group of female researchers, the family cluster and the social cluster here have a low share of negative intercorrelations: 5 of 18, that is, 27.78 %. The omission of the sum variables 22, 23, and 24 does not change the picture appreciably: the number of negative correlations between the two clusters A and B is 89 out of 189, that is, 47.09 %; between the clusters A and C the proportion is 26 of 42 or 61.91 % negative correlations, which, however, comes a bit closer to the amount for the female researchers.

In order to increase the comparability between the groups, the amount

Table 16. *Male researchers*

	1	2	3	4	5	6	7	8	9	10	11	12	13	14
A. Research and career cluster														
1. Family name	■	+.02	−.04	+.16	+.08	+.09	+.05	+.02	+.06	+.05	−.02	+.06	−.05	−.09
2. Age		■	+.02	+.04	−.04	−.15	+.14	+.12	+.42	+.30	+.47	+.27	+.07	+.10
3. Academic position			■	+.03	−.03	+.08	−.06	+.15	+.10	+.16	+.19	+.05	+.08	+.13
4. Social origin				■	+.07	+.14	+.04	+.03	+.07	+.09	−.01	+.03	+.04	−.01
5. Place of residence					■	+.12	+.02	+.16	+.07	+.10	−.13	−.03	+.02	+.03
6. Birthplace						■	−.02	+.05	−.03	+.01	−.11	−.03	−.04	−.02
7. Private means							■	+.03	+.11	+.06	+.06	+.11	+.04	.00
8. Status according to encyclopedias								■	+.42	+.81	+.23	+.11	+.19	+.12
9. Space in 'Vem är det'									■	+.60	+.43	+.15	+.39	+.11
10. Number of reference books										■	+.37	+.18	+.25	+.15
11. Academies etc.											■	+.28	+.16	+.18
12. Swedish honorary doctor's degrees												■	+.09	+.08
13. Government committees													■	+.21
14. Memberships in research councils														■
15. Enumerated international commissions														
16. Foreign guest professorships														
17. Academic positions														
18. Published works														
19. Name of doctor's thesis given in 'Vem är det'														
20. Distinctions														
21. Foreign honorary doctor's degrees														
22. Researcher's status														
23. General status														
24. Academic power														
B. Family cluster														
25. Marriage disposition														
26. Marital début														
27. Number of children														
28. Nearness between marriage and first child														
29. Interval between first examination and appointment to full professor														
30. Age at doctor's dissertation														
31. Age at appointment to full professor														
32. Income														
33. Income of the subject's spouse														
C. Social cluster														
34. Membership in clubs														
35. Number of hobbies														

of positive and negative correlations, respectively, have also been calculated, leaving out variable 17. The amount of positive correlations within the research and career role for the male researchers then turn out to be 208 of 253 or 82.21 %. Moreover, the amount of negative correlations between the clusters A and B decreases to 95 out of 207, that is, 45.89 %, while the corresponding amount between cluster A and C is slightly raised from the original value to 26 out of 46–56.52 %. Thus, the picture on the whole is the same, whether variable 17 is left out or not.

112

										B. Family cluster									C. Social cluster	
15	16	17	18	19	20	21	22	23	24	25	26	27	28	29	30	31	32	33	34	35
+.05	.00	−.03	+.08	+.03	+.03	+.03	+.06	+.05	−.04	+.03	−.01	−.01	−.01	−.03	−.08	−.06	+.03	+.02	−.02	−.02
+.07	−.05	+.17	+.34	−.15	+.52	+.22	+.47	+.36	+.36	+.16	−.36	.00	+.03	+.41	+.05	+.51	−.11	+.05	+.02	+.01
+.05	+.03	+.10	+.08	−.04	+.07	+.09	+.16	+.12	+.19	+.15	+.05	+.08	+.04	−.27	−.17	−.43	−.02	−.01	−.08	−.10
+.04	+.01	−.01	+.08	+.06	+.09	+.08	+.07	+.08	+.02	−.02	+.02	+.03	−.05	+.04	−.04	.00	−.01	−.03	−.07	+.03
+.05	+.09	−.02	+.01	−.02	−.06	−.01	−.02	+.11	−.05	+.04	+.05	−.12	+.08	−.05	−.03	−.05	+.09	+.10	−.08	−.03
+.03	+.04	−.05	−.04	−.01	−.06	−.07	−.07	+.01	−.09	−.05	+.10	.00	−.02	−.03	−.02	−.07	+.03	.00	−.04	+.12
+.09	+.14	.00	+.05	−.05	+.17	+.01	+.10	+.09	+.09	+.02	−.01	+.09	+.06	+.05	−.05	+.01	+.12	+.04	+.11	+.02
+.18	+.04	+.15	+.35	+.08	+.13	+.11	+.40	+.58	+.31	+.12	+.11	+.04	−.01	−.10	−.17	−.08	+.03	+.18	−.07	−.06
+.31	+.09	+.16	+.73	+.12	+.33	+.34	+.80	+.90	+.57	+.23	+.02	+.06	−.01	+.04	−.18	+.03	−.03	+.26	−.01	−.02
+.21	+.05	+.22	+.55	+.09	+.24	+.21	+.62	+.71	+.44	+.17	+.05	+.06	−.03	−.04	−.26	−.03	+.02	+.23	−.06	−.08
+.14	−.02	+.24	+.25	−.02	+.43	+.38	+.64	+.41	+.77	+.13	−.07	+.09	+.02	+.01	−.22	−.01	−.08	−.01	−.01	−.01
+.05	+.02	+.17	+.09	−.10	+.23	+.30	+.26	+.15	+.25	+.14	−.07	+.07	−.02	−.03	−.10	−.04	.00	+.22	−.02	−.05
+.25	+.05	+.11	+.15	+.01	+.19	+.13	+.25	+.54	+.67	+.09	+.05	+.07	.00	−.12	−.16	−.12	+.16	+.10	+.05	+.05
+.07	+.04	+.13	−.05	−.02	+.07	+.14	+.13	+.15	+.35	+.10	−.01	+.06	+.04	−.02	−.08	−.08	+.17	.00	+.02	−.03
■	+.14	+.07	+.11	−.03	+.12	+.14	+.35	+.30	+.52	+.05	−.02	+.01	+.02	−.05	−.06	−.04	+.48	−.09	+.23	+.04
	■	−.03	.00	+.03	+.04	+.09	+.12	+.09	+.05	+.01	+.06	+.04	+.02	−.07	−.08	−.10	+.02	−.05	−.04	−.02
		■	+.07	+.01	+.15	+.04	+.17	+.17	+.32	−.01	−.09	−.02	+.01	−.11	−.09	−.12	−.02	−.02	+.01	−.03
			■	+.10	+.19	+.20	+.86	+.63	+.26	+.12	.00	+.01	−.03	+.01	−.20	+.03	−.10	+.26	−.05	+.01
				■	−.06	−.05	+.05	+.10	−.02	−.10	+.07	−.07	−.05	−.06	+.10	−.05	−.02	+.09	−.05	+.07
					■	+.28	+.36	+.31	+.40	+.16	−.10	+.09	+.07	+.20	−.07	+.18	+.07	+.01	.00	+.12
						■	+.44	+.29	+.35	+.11	−.02	+.06	.00	−.09	−.13	−.12	−.04	+.32	−.03	−.04
							■	+.72	+.64	+.17	−.03	+.05	−.01	−.02	−.27	−.02	−.05	+.20	−.01	.00
								■	+.62	+.23	+.07	+.08	−.01	−.01	−.22	−.01	+.04	+.23	.00	+.02
									■	+.15	−.04	+.09	+.02	−.08	−.25	−.09	+.10	+.01	+.09	+.03
										■	+.08	+.32	+.10	+.05	−.10	+.05	+.12	+.03	+.03	−.02
											■	+.28	−.10	−.20	−.15	−.21	+.12	+.09	+.03	+.01
												■	+.28	+.04	−.04	+.02	+.15	+.01	+.06	−.03
													■	−.04	−.08	−.01	+.04	.00	+.03	−.04
														■	+.38	+.91	−.01	+.04	+.05	−.02
															■	+.46	−.02	+.04	+.07	+.12
																■	−.06	−.04	+.02	+.02
																	■	−.01	+.30	+.11
																		■	−.04	+.01
																			■	+.18
																				■

To sum it up, the male researchers seem, if anything, to show a compromise pattern with low or no correlations between the principal variable clusters A and B. The anticipated stronger relationship of competition between the roles for the female researchers as compared to the male researchers thus emerges in the correlation matrices. Certainly, the clusters A and B each has a higher degree of integration in the male group, but since the differences are relatively small and the emphasis in the inter-group-comparison is on the relation *between* the variable clusters, the outcome supports our predictions.

113

Table 17. *Representative sample of women*

	1	2	3	4	5	6	7	8	9	10	11	12	13	14
A. Research and career cluster														
1. Family name	■	−.17	+.18	+.16	+.08	+.24	+.13	−.18	−.17	−.18	−.08	.00	−.09	+.08
2. Age		■	+.04	+.09	−.22	−.01	+.22	+.05	+.24	+.10	+.30	.00	+.08	+.07
3. Academic position			■	+.21	−.10	−.12	+.24	+.04	+.33	−.01	+.28	.00	+.21	+.27
4. Social origin				■	+.09	+.22	+.14	+.11	+.16	+.03	+.07	.00	−.16	+.10
5. Place of residence					■	+.16	+.04	+.20	−.02	+.18	−.01	.00	−.12	+.05
6. Birthplace						■	+.08	−.01	−.13	−.08	−.10	.00	−.15	−.10
7. Private means							■	+.13	+.24	+.10	+.24	.00	+.08	+.45
8. Status according to encyclopedias								■	+.44	+.88	+.18	.00	−.04	+.21
9. Space in 'Vem är det'									■	+.47	+.52	.00	+.27	+.44
10. Number of reference books										■	+.30	.00	−.04	+.32
11. Academies etc.											■	.00	+.16	+.59
12. Swedish honorary doctor's degrees												■	.00	.00
13. Government committees													■	+.38
14. Memberships in research councils														■
15. Enumerated international commissions														
16. Foreign guest professorships														
17. Academic positions														
18. Published works														
19. Name of doctor's thesis given in 'Vem är det'														
20. Distinctions														
21. Foreign honorary doctor's degrees														
22. Researcher's status														
23. General status														
24. Academic power														
B. Family cluster														
25. Marriage disposition														
26. Marital début														
27. Number of children														
28. Nearness between marriage and first child														
29. Interval between first examination and appointment to full professor														
30. Age at doctor's dissertation														
31. Age at appointment to full professor														
32. Income														
33. Income of the subject's spouse														
C. Social cluster														
34. Membership in clubs														
35. Number of hobbies														

Representative sample of women

From the correlation matrix for the randomly selected women (Table 17) it is evident, that 3 variables from cluster A, namely 12 (Swedish honorary doctor's degrees), 16 (guest professorships) and 17 (academic positions), as well as 3 variables from cluster B: 29 (number of years between first academic degree and appointment to full professor), 30 (age at doctor's dissertation) and 31 (age at appointment to full professor) are irrelevant to the group in question. For that reason they

114

										B. Family cluster									C. Social cluster	
15	16	17	18	19	20	21	22	23	24	25	26	27	28	29	30	31	32	33	34	35
.00	.00	.00	−.07	+.14	+.30	+.06	−.08	−.26	−.10	+.10	+.02	+.04	+.07	.00	.00	.00	+.02	−.18	−.07	+.12
+.13	.00	.00	+.20	+.01	+.28	+.13	+.28	+.02	+.23	−.28	−.09	−.02	−.06	.00	.00	.00	−.24	+.08	−.07	−.13
+.16	.00	.00	+.02	+.62	+.09	+.32	+.11	+.05	+.32	−.15	−.20	+.29	.00	.00	.00	.00	+.06	+.27	−.03	+.10
+.05	.00	.00	+.22	+.16	+.10	+.07	+.24	+.05	−.06	−.04	−.09	+.14	+.08	.00	.00	.00	−.15	+.24	+.02	−.17
+.03	.00	.00	−.02	−.01	−.08	+.04	−.02	+.06	−.08	+.25	+.09	+.01	−.01	.00	.00	.00	−.04	+.02	−.01	−.01
−.10	.00	.00	+.04	−.03	+.02	−.07	+.01	−.01	−.18	+.15	+.19	+.01	+.06	.00	.00	.00	−.06	−.32	−.11	−.05
+.17	.00	.00	.00	+.21	+.16	+.32	+.09	+.13	+.22	−.08	−.12	+.12	+.02	.00	.00	.00	+.01	−.02	+.16	.00
+.12	.00	.00	+.38	.00	−.02	+.26	+.44	+.60	+.09	+.27	+.08	−.03	−.25	.00	.00	.00	+.08	−.10	+.02	−.18
+.31	.00	.00	+.52	+.14	+.10	+.49	+.68	+.73	+.51	−.03	−.04	+.08	−.14	.00	.00	.00	−.22	−.04	+.23	−.03
+.09	.00	.00	+.41	−.07	+.03	+.38	+.49	+.62	+.15	+.26	+.22	−.02	−.36	.00	.00	.00	−.09	+.01	.00	−.14
+.22	.00	.00	−.05	+.11	+.27	+.73	+.25	+.39	+.66	−.13	−.12	−.12	−.32	.00	.00	.00	−.06	−.06	−.08	−.04
.00	.00	.00	.00	.00	.00	.00	.00	.00	.00	.00	.00	.00	.00	.00	.00	.00	.00	.00	.00	.00
+.21	.00	.00	−.10	−.03	+.02	+.10	−.02	+.24	+.83	−.15	+.08	+.18	.00	.00	.00	.00	+.03	+.32	−.01	+.18
+.22	.00	.00	−.04	−.04	+.23	+.70	+.16	+.38	+.64	+.10	+.01	+.14	−.24	.00	.00	.00	.00	+.18	−.03	−.05
■	.00	.00	−.03	+.08	+.15	+.34	+.14	+.17	+.45	−.19	+.05	−.07	−.07	.00	.00	.00	−.12	−.13	−.05	−.09
	■	.00	.00	.00	.00	.00	.00	.00	.00	.00	.00	.00	.00	.00	.00	.00	.00	.00	.00	.00
		■	.00	.00	.00	.00	.00	.00	.00	.00	.00	.00	.00	.00	.00	.00	.00	.00	.00	.00
			■	+.03	−.15	−.04	+.95	+.30	−.10	+.02	+.10	.00	−.07	.00	.00	.00	−.28	−.02	+.16	−.04
				■	+.03	−.03	+.06	−.03	+.04	−.11	−.42	−.03	+.18	.00	.00	.00	+.07	+.15	−.05	+.10
					■	+.36	−.05	−.01	+.18	+.13	+.13	+.04	−.07	.00	.00	.00	−.10	−.07	−.06	+.04
						■	+.21	+.36	+.51	.00	−.02	−.01	−.35	.00	.00	.00	−.04	−.14	−.02	−.03
							■	+.42	+.14	−.03	+.07	−.04	−.20	.00	.00	.00	−.29	−.05	+.13	−.06
								■	+.40	+.13	+.09	.00	−.19	.00	.00	.00	−.22	−.06	+.15	−.07
									■	−.20	.00	+.06	−.18	.00	.00	.00	−.14	−.16	−.05	+.09
										■	+.34	+.30	−.12	.00	.00	.00	+.23	−.02	−.08	+.03
											■	+.34	−.08	.00	.00	.00	−.03	+.16	+.05	+.19
												■	+.37	.00	.00	.00	+.14	+.51	+.12	+.21
													■	.00	.00	.00	+.04	+.02	+.15	−.02
														■	.00	.00	.00	.00	.00	.00
															■	.00	.00	.00	.00	.00
																■	.00	.00	.00	.00
																	■	−.20	−.22	+.25
																		■	−.13	+.18
																			■	+.03
																				■

arc excluded from the subsequent calculations of proportions. As for the three first-mentioned variables, there were no values at all to be noted, whereas the last-mentioned three each embraced so few values, that during the planning phase it was considered more appropriate to exclude them from the correlation computations.

Cluster A, which in this sample is more adequately denominated 'the professional and career cluster', contains 153 positive intracorrelations in a total of 210–72.86 %. When the sum variables 22–24 are left

115

Table 18. *Representative sample of men*

	1	2	3	4	5	6	7	8	9	10	11	12	13	14
A. Research and career cluster														
1. Family name	■	+.04	−.09	.00	+.08	+.06	+.07	.00	+.09	−.06	−.02	−.09	+.04	−.15
2. Age		■	−.07	−.21	−.12	−.29	+.01	+.18	+.09	+.12	+.34	+.16	+.17	+.18
3. Academic position			■	+.15	+.14	−.04	−.16	+.14	+.27	+.10	+.40	+.16	+.03	+.26
4. Social origin				■	+.02	+.15	+.04	+.16	+.12	+.12	+.05	+.13	+.03	+.07
5. Place of residence					■	+.05	−.16	+.07	+.03	−.07	+.02	+.11	+.03	+.07
6. Birthplace						■	+.07	+.07	.00	.00	−.13	+.12	−.03	−.01
7. Private means							■	+.01	+.04	+.06	−.14	+.06	+.10	+.08
8. Status according to encyclopedias								■	+.55	+.85	+.32	+.27	+.26	+.37
9. Space in 'Vem är det'									■	+.58	+.40	+.38	+.54	+.52
10. Number of reference books										■	+.20	+.36	+.28	+.37
11. Academies etc.											■	+.11	+.14	+.47
12. Swedish honorary doctor's degrees												■	+.22	+.13
13. Government committees													■	+.38
14. Memberships in research councils														■
15. Enumerated international commissions														
16. Foreign guest professorships														
17. Academic positions														
18. Published works														
19. Name of doctor's thesis given in 'Vem är det'														
20. Distinctions														
21. Foreign honorary doctor's degrees														
22. Researcher's status														
23. General status														
24. Academic power														
B. Family cluster														
25. Marriage disposition														
26. Marital début														
27. Number of children														
28. Nearness between marriage and first child														
29. Interval between first examination and appointment to full professor														
30. Age at doctor's dissertation														
31. Age at appointment to full professor														
32. Income														
33. Income of the subject's spouse														
C. Social cluster														
34. Membership in clubs														
35. Number of hobbies														

out, 109 positive correlations out of 253, that is, 71.24 %, remain. The integration is somewhat weaker but still rather good in the family cluster, showing 10 out of 15 or 66.67 % positive intracorrelations. Finally, the correlation between the two social variables is positive but insignificant.

As expected, the relation between the clusters of variables is less competitive for this group of women than for the female researchers and has 67 negative correlations out of 126–53.18 %–between cluster A and B, and 27 negative correlations of totally 42–64.29 %–between cluster A and C. After the exclusion of the variables 22, 23 and 24,

116

										B. Family cluster									C. Social cluster	
15	16	17	18	19	20	21	22	23	24	25	26	27	28	29	30	31	32	33	34	35
+.10	+.07	−.10	−.12	+.13	+.10	−.02	−.06	+.06	+.03	−.11	+.02	−.06	+.08	.00	.00	.00	−.02	+.05	+.04	−.09
−.09	−.20	+.16	+.12	+.09	+.54	+.14	+.21	+.12	+.26	−.08	−.38	−.03	−.07	.00	.00	.00	−.19	−.38	+.08	−.12
+.07	+.26	+.19	+.26	+.41	.00	+.28	+.41	+.21	+.29	−.11	+.01	+.09	+.05	.00	.00	.00	−.04	−.42	−.11	−.13
+.09	+.06	+.07	−.04	−.04	+.10	−.03	+.03	+.10	+.08	−.10	+.20	+.21	+.04	.00	.00	.00	+.06	−.06	+.02	+.08
+.19	+.01	−.03	−.17	.00	−.07	+.02	−.04	.00	+.10	−.33	+.11	−.14	−.15	.00	.00	.00	−.17	−.38	−.16	−.14
+.19	+.09	−.12	−.08	−.05	−.17	−.22	−.06	.00	−.02	−.03	+.20	+.01	−.08	.00	.00	.00	+.04	+.07	.00	.00
+.16	−.05	−.04	−.18	−.15	+.01	−.08	−.15	+.04	+.02	−.11	−.01	−.12	−.05	.00	.00	.00	+.08	−.11	−.06	−.04
+.12	−.07	+.24	+.41	+.15	+.30	+.19	+.48	+.73	+.38	+.28	+.15	+.11	+.07	.00	.00	.00	+.40	+.32	−.02	.00
+.30	+.04	+.15	+.44	+.09	+.27	+.19	+.61	+.92	+.65	+.03	+.19	+.12	+.08	.00	.00	.00	+.21	+.06	+.04	+.07
+.01	−.07	+.09	+.54	+.05	+.16	+.12	+.47	+.75	+.28	+.25	+.15	−.02	+.13	.00	.00	.00	+.40	+.36	−.03	−.06
+.14	+.01	+.71	+.32	+.28	+.50	+.39	+.75	+.37	+.74	−.06	+.02	+.03	−.10	.00	.00	.00	−.01	−.37	.00	+.17
+.04	−.02	−.02	+.09	−.07	+.02	−.03	+.15	+.38	+.19	−.05	.00	+.06	−.14	.00	.00	.00	−.05	−.21	−.07	−.08
+.16	−.09	+.08	+.06	−.09	+.28	+.08	+.18	+.63	+.65	−.13	+.02	+.04	+.15	.00	.00	.00	−.04	−.35	+.08	−.13
+.29	−.03	+.27	+.19	−.01	+.30	+.07	+.49	+.51	+.64	−.07	+.09	−.04	+.04	.00	.00	.00	−.01	−.16	−.04	−.04
■	+.27	−.04	−.06	−.15	+.16	−.07	+.35	+.22	+.56	+.01	+.15	+.26	+.21	.00	.00	.00	.00	−.07	−.02	−.04
	■	−.01	−.06	−.06	−.08	−.03	+.09	−.04	+.07	−.04	+.09	+.19	+.13	.00	.00	.00	−.02	.00	−.06	−.06
		■	+.22	+.25	+.24	+.37	+.48	+.17	+.47	−.03	−.06	−.03	−.12	.00	.00	.00	.00	.00	−.04	+.19
			■	+.19	+.02	+.31	+.79	+.43	+.21	+.22	+.06	−.09	+.08	.00	.00	.00	+.26	+.55	−.05	+.02
				■	+.02	+.14	+.20	+.06	+.07	+.03	−.11	+.04	−.01	.00	.00	.00	+.02	−.23	−.05	+.02
					■	+.16	+.31	+.29	+.51	−.11	+.04	+.08	+.02	.00	.00	.00	−.11	−.27	+.08	+.09
						■	+.40	+.18	+.24	−.05	−.07	−.03	−.06	.00	.00	.00	−.07	.00	+.16	.00
							■	+.55	+.69	+.11	+.09	+.04	+.05	.00	.00	.00	+.21	+.31	−.03	+.07
								■	+.64	+.12	+.18	+.10	+.14	.00	.00	.00	+.25	+.14	+.02	+.06
									■	−.10	+.07	+.13	+.08	.00	.00	.00	−.03	−.40	+.03	+.02
										■	+.08	+.16	−.06	.00	.00	.00	+.49	+.74	−.02	+.06
											■	+.09	−.13	.00	.00	.00	+.15	+.15	+.09	+.07
												■	+.34	.00	.00	.00	−.07	+.19	+.10	+.16
													■	.00	.00	.00	+.32	−.18	+.04	−.07
														■	.00	.00	.00	.00	.00	.00
															■	.00	.00	.00	.00	.00
																■	.00	.00	.00	.00
																	■	+.82	−.62	+.06
																		■	−.02	−.04
																			■	+.04
																				■

the corresponding proportions are 56 out of 108 or 51.85 % and 24 of 36 or 66.67 %, respectively. On the whole, the relationship between cluster B and C is analogous to the two preceding correlation matrices, here showing 4 negative correlations of 12 possible, that is, 33.33 %.

Representative sample of men

Table 18, finally, entails no reduction of the number of variables in cluster A, whereas the family cluster in the planning phase was reduced

from 9 to 6 variables for the sake of comparability. Thus, the omitted variables are the same as for the randomly selected women, namely 29, 30 and 31. As in regard to the research groups, the male group here too manifests a higher degree of integration within each role than does the female one. The relative amount of positive correlations within the professional and career cluster is 205 out of 276 or 74.28 %, while the corresponding share in the family role is 11 out of 15 or 73.33 % for the randomly selected men. This stronger concord within the role clusters remains even after the omission of the variables 12, 16 and 17, which are of no relevance to the female group. At this, 161 correlations of 210–76.67 %–are positive within cluster A. When instead, the three sum variables 22–24 are excluded, however, the proportion of positive correlations drops to 147 of 210–70 %–within the professional and career cluster. The sole correlation within the C cluster is positive.

Also as regards the relationship between the clusters, the tendency here is similar to the one in the research groups, namely a stronger marking of the compensation pattern for the women than for the men. Thus, the relative amount of negative correlations between cluster A and B are lower for the men with 64 out of 144 or 44.44 %. This also applies to the relationship between the clusters A and C, showing 23 negative correlations of 48, which makes 47.92 %. On the contrary, the amount of negative correlations between B and C is larger in the male group, namely 5 of 12 or 41.67 %. The picture remains intact, even when the variables 12, 16 and 17 are omitted. This results in 54 negative correlations out of 126, that is, unaltered 42.86 % between cluster A and cluster B, as well as 18 negative correlations of totally 42–42.86 % –between the clusters A and C.

Order of precedence, all variables included

According to the assumptions advanced, the tendency toward a compensation pattern in the correlation matrices should vary between the groups studied. At this, the greatest weight was attached to the element of competition in between the role clusters, expressed in the proportion of negative correlations. When all the relevant variables are included in the calculations, and the order of rank is based upon the most central value in this connection, namely the share of negative correlations between research/professional and career role on the one hand and family role on the other, the sequence between the samples turns out

Table 19. *Amount of negative and positive correlations, respectively, between as well as within the variable clusters for each one of the four samples. (Varying number of basic variables.) A = research and career cluster, B = family cluster, C = social cluster.*

	Female researchers		Representative sample of women		Male researchers		Representative sample of men	
	n	%	n	%,	n	%	n	%
Amount of negative correlations between								
cluster A and B	132/207	63.77	67/126	53.18	163/216	47.69	64/144	44.44
cluster A and C	32/46	69.57	27/42	64.29	27/48	56.25	23/48	47.92
cluster B and C	7/18	38.00	4/12	33.33	5/18	27.78	5/12	41.67
Amount of positive correlations within								
cluster A	193/253	76.29	153/210	72.86	225/276	81.52	205/276	74.28
cluster B	20/36	55.56	10/15	66.67	21/36	58.33	11/15	73.33

as indicated in Table 19. (The group having the greatest relative amount of negative intercorrelations is put first, the group showing the next greatest amount next, and so on.) As is evident from the table, the order of precedence obtained between the groups concerned agrees as regards strength in the compensation pattern with the predicted one. The sex factor thus seems to exert a greater pressure in the direction toward a choice between separate roles than does type of occupation (here, research versus a randomly selected sample of professions in *Vem är det*).

Both samples of women show a stronger compensation pattern than both of the male groups, with a greater amount of negative correlations between on the one hand the research/professional and career cluster, and on the other the family cluster. This larger share of negative correlations for both of the female samples reappears also in the relationship between cluster A and the social cluster. When it comes to the order of precedence between the groups concerning the proportion of negative correlations between family role and social role (cluster B and C respectively), however, the representative sample of men presents the largest share, while the remaining groups have the same relative order as in the two previous measures of proportions.

The degree of integration within each cluster of variables expressed in share of positive intracorrelations follows another order of rank than the one related above and, furthermore, shows a considerably shorter distance between the extremes in the research and career role (cluster A). For the last-mentioned reason, the succession in the variable

119

in question is less convincing than the corresponding rank order for cluster B, where the group of randomly selected men shows the highest degree of integration, in the next place followed by the sample of randomly selected women, then male researchers and finally, having the lowest degree of integration within the family cluster, the group of female researchers. From a technical point of view, however, the samples are not wholly equivalent, for which reason an attempt at interpreting is not made until complete equivalence is obtained.

Order of precedence using the maximum number of variables in common

To make the groups entirely comparable in regard to relative proportions of negative and positive correlations respectively, evidently, the same variables should be included in all groups. Since Table 19 shows shares of a basic number of variables, which varies from sample to sample, the latter are not wholly comparable. Hence, a compilation of the corresponding relative amounts of negative and positive correlations respectively, follows below, calculated with the maximum number of common variables as a basis. To the research and career cluster they are 21 (the variables 12, 16 and 17 are left out), to the family cluster 6 (after the omission of the variables 29, 30 and 31), while the social cluster remains intact. Here too, the basis of the order of precedence is the principal factor from a compensational point of view, namely the relative amount of negative correlations between research − and − career role and family role (Table 20). The values obtained after the reduction give substantially the same order of rank between the groups in reference to degree of compensation pattern. The breadth of the variation has increased to a difference of 42.06% between the highest and the lowest percentage, and the two female samples still show a stronger tendency toward a compensation pattern (72.22% and 53.18%, respectively) than the two male groups.

However, the relative order between the latter is reversed, so that the representative sample of men now has a greater proportion of negative intercorrelations between cluster A and B than has the sample of male researchers. As to the factor II, 'relative amount of negative correlations between the two clusters A and C', the order of precedence is similar to the one before the reduction of variables, thus completely following the anticipated pattern. Between cluster A and C, finally, tendencies

120

Table 20. *Relative amount of negative and positive correlations, respectively, between as well as within the variable clusters for each one of the four samples (constant number of basic variables). A=research and career role, B=family role, C=social role.*

	Female researchers		Representative sample of women		Representative sample of men		Male researchers	
	n	%	n	%	n	%	n	%
Proportion of negative correlations between								
cluster A and B	91/126	72.22	67/126	53.18	54/126	42.86	28/126	30.16
cluster A and C	28/42	66.67	27/42	64.29	18/42	42.86	22/42	52.38
cluster B and C	4/12	33.33	4/12	33.33	5/12	41.67	4/12	33.33
Proportion of positive correlations within								
cluster A	177/210	84.29	153/210	72.86	161/210	76.67	170/210	80.95
cluster B	12/15	80.00	10/15	66.67	11/15	73.33	12/15	80.00

toward a compensation pattern are lacking altogether as was the case in the preceding table.

The integration within the research/professional and career cluster is here at its strongest among the female researchers, next follows the group of male researchers, then the representative sample of men and last, the representative sample of women. That the researchers here come higher up than the representative groups is at least partly a consequence of the fact, that some variables are mainly attached to the scientific profession. However, the most pronounced research variables have been left out with the reduction, wherefore the objection is somewhat weakened. Moreover, we are principally interested in the relationship between the sexes within each group and not primarily in the relationship between researchers and representative samples.

In the rank order of proportions of positive intracorrelations in the family cluster, the two researcher groups have the same high percentage −80−in the next place followed by the randomly selected men and finally, the sample of randomly selected women.

Remaining matrix variable—nearness between first and second child

Since the variable measuring the time interval between the birth of the first and the second child for reasons earlier accounted for have been omitted from the matrix analysis, a report on its relation to the research and career variables here follows in brief.

121

Research groups

The predictions for male researchers in this variable went in the opposed direction as compared to the expectations connected with the female group. Whereas a continuous dispersion of the children's birth in time was assumed to be advantageous to the professional commitment of the male researchers, the female researchers with their considerably more intensive involvement in child birth and child care were assumed to prefer a concentration of the children's birth over a relatively short space of time. The author's thought was that the shorter the interruption she is forced to make, the fewer the negative consequences for the research career should be and vice versa.

In relation to the male researchers, the interest is thus focused on the proportion of negative correlations between closeness of first and second child and the research role. In absolute figures, this amount is 16/24 or 66.67 %, which gives support to the thought, that longer time periods between the deliveries promote the research work for the men. The tendency remains, although a bit weaker with 13/21, that is, 61.91 % negative correlations, when the three sum variables are left out.

As regards the female researchers, the interest is instead centered around the proportion of positive correlations between closeness of first and second child and research and career role. The computations result in 14 positive correlations out of 23 possible ones, that is 60.87 %. Without the sum variables 22–24 the amount of positive correlations is 12/21–57.14 %. (The proportion of negative correlations in each case is 21.71 % and 19.05 % respectively.) Thus, there is a tendency, though not very pronounced, toward the expected positive relationship between research role and concentration in time of childbearing on the part of the female researchers.

Representative samples

Concerning the representative samples, an analogous sex difference for the relationship between child closeness and career role was anticipated, although less clear in this case. This is supported by the outcome: the male sample shows 18 out of 24 or 75 % negative correlations between child nearness and career cluster. When the sum variables 22, 23 and 24 are excluded, 15 out of 21 or 71.43 % of the negative correlations remain. A somewhat stronger state of opposition than among the researchers thus seems to prevail in this group between professional role and children born close to each other.

To the female sample, the proportion of positive correlations between child closeness and career role is 12 out of 21–57 %. As the sum variables are excluded, the proportion rises to 11/18 or 61 %. (The amount of negative correlations in the two cases is 38 % and 33 %, respectively.) Even here, the expected sex difference in the relationship between professional cluster and nearness of first and second child appears.

Summing up

In regard to the male groups, spacing of the child births with a greater time interval has a promoting influence on the activity in the research and career role, whereas the professional commitment of the female groups, on the contrary is facilitated by a concentration of the child-bearing to a shorter time period.

Summary and discussion of the matrix analysis

For each one of the four groups studied, a matrix was constructed for all correlations between the 35 variables included in the role pattern. These had been distributed in advance into three hypothetical roles: A) research/professional and career cluster (n = 24), B) family cluster (n = 9) and C) social cluster (n = 2). The variables were expected to follow these cluster formations and to show a compensation pattern with negative correlations between the roles (the variable clusters) and positive correlations within each one of them. On the basis of the earlier related modes of thought, certain assumptions were made concerning the influence of sex upon the role relations partly within the research groups, partly within the representative samples of men and women. A hypothetical order of precedence between the groups in reference to tendency toward a compensation pattern was made.

The outcome of the matrix analysis as a whole supports the hypothesis that professional role and family role are more demarcated from each other among the female researchers, and that these roles are in a more pronounced state of opposition than is the case among the male researchers. The integration within the two central clusters of variables, however, seems within the research groups to be somewhat better for the men than for the women. Whether this is bound up with the colleague system in the academic world, with its putting a premium on the male

sex and its system of services and services in return within the accepted inner circle, is evidently impossible to tell from these scanty data.

Similar disparities as between men and women among the researchers reappear between the sexes in the randomly selected groups, but here as anticipated with less force. No real compensation pattern is clearly discernable for these two samples, but the tendency toward such a pattern is nevertheless as expected stronger for the women. Thus, the state of opposition between the roles is more marked in the female group, while the integration within each separate cluster, as among the researchers, is greater for the men. This outcome agrees with the hypothesis, that the role pattern showing the strongest compensation tendency should demonstrate a relatively more pronounced degree of desintegration within the domineering cluster. In accordance with the assumptions made, this is the family cluster, which is expected to be dominated by the research and career cluster given the priority.

As regards the rank order between the four groups after the reduction of variables not in common, the sample of female researchers shows, as anticipated, the most marked compensation pattern. That the randomly selected women should follow next, also accords with the expectations, whereas the location of the male researchers after the randomly selected men does not follow the hypothetical sequence. Consequently, success within the research and career cluster preclude to a greater extent for female than for male researchers family life in the form of marriage (variable 25) and then above all an early one (variable 26), as well as children (variable 27) and especially children being born early in the marriage (variable 28) and with a wide distribution in time between the deliveries (variable 40). Expressed in other terms, female researchers with a heavy professional commitment have to renounce the family role, whereas men engaged in research do not necessarily have to choose either-or but frequently can get both-and. Inversely, a commitment to the family role from women's part results in a shrinking of their research and career role, which then is less sucessful. An analogous family commitment in the group of male researchers, however, can often exist parallel to the career role. Reward in the economical factor as expressed in the subject's own income (var. 32) and income of the subject's spouse (var. 33) decreases for the female researchers, as the reward in the research role increases, whereas these factors seem to accompany each other as for the men.

To sum up, the outcome of the matrix analysis is in all essentials in accordance with the predictions made.

Description

The purpose of this section is to seek a comprehensive picture of the groups studied, their composition and general character with reference to the predictions being accounted for in the section of hypotheses. The succession between the variables in the present section agrees, on the whole, with the one employed in the section of hypotheses. The measures used are, in addition to simple percentages and medians, t-test and z-test for difference of means, z-test for difference of proportions and chi^2-test for contingency in cross tables. Chi-square values have only been computed for the research groups, while the remaining values have been computed even for the representative samples. The related chi^2-values are based upon each variable's collapsed distribution in absolute figures, for which reason the number of degrees of freedom often differ from (k–l)(r–l) in the present tables. Only the relevant distributions and values are presented in the text. The maximum significance level accepted is set at 5 % for both one-tailed and two-tailed tests.

Sex distribution

First of all, the obvious disparity between the number of male and female researchers presented in *Vem är det* should be observed. The total number of male researchers belonging to any of the nine areas related in chapter 7 is, according to our definition : 1 342. When all researchers in *Vem är det* 1969 are included, the number rises to 2 428, of which only 50–2.06 %–are women.

Among the researchers and masters included in the university catalogs of Umeå, Uppsala, Stockholm, Göteborg and Lund for the session 1970/71. 4 % or 117 of all in all 2 660 associate professors, full professors and researchers of equivalent positions are women.

Academic Position

From the distribution in Figure 6 of men and women on different academic educational levels in the year of 1970 it is evident, that the proportion of women decreases conspicuously with every higher level. As expected, the same applies even to the male and female researchers studied (Figure 7). Thus, the relative amount of women decreases with every higher academic level from 24.49 % on the lowest level to 3.96 % on the highest.

125

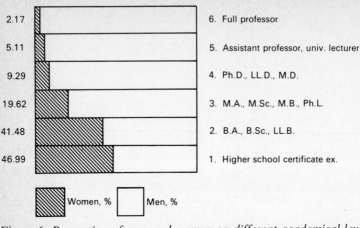

		Level:
2.17		6. Full professor
5.11		5. Assistant professor, univ. lecturer
9.29		4. Ph.D., LL.D., M.D.
19.62		3. M.A., M.Sc., M.B., Ph.L.
41.48		2. B.A., B.Sc., LL.B.
46.99		1. Higher school certificate ex.

Women, %   Men, %

Figure 6. *Proportion of men and women on different academical levels (based upon informations drawn from Swedish university catalogs 1970/71 and statistical data from the Swedish S.C.B. 1970)*

In Figure 8, the total distribtuion in the research samples over different academical levels is presented for each sex separately.

A majority of the men–84 %– are to be found on the academical top level, whereas only 46 % of the women are there. Accordingly, the female researchers in *Vem är det* generally have a lower academic position than the male researchers. A phenomenon which possibly mirrors one or all of the following factors: 1) a desire on the part of the editors of the reference book to include representatives of both sexes, notwithstanding the fact that this entails a lowering of the average professional level among the women; 2) significantly more female full professors

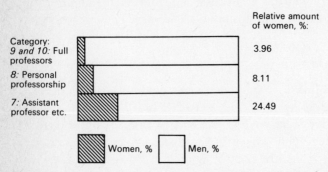

Category:		Relative amount of women, %:
9 and 10: Full professors		3.96
8: Personal professorship		8.11
7: Assistant professor etc.		24.49

Women, %   Men, %

Figure 7. *Distribution of the research samples in the academical hierarchy on the basis of sex. Women ■; men □*

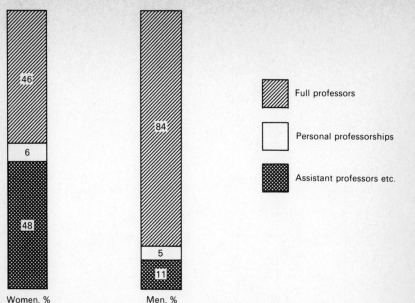

Women, %   Men, %

Figure 8. *Relative distribution on different academical levels within each re-search sample.*

have not answered the inquiry—against this tells the fact, that the total amount of female full professors in Sweden is so small, that a significant number in excess of the 23 represented here hardly can be missing; 3) the more probable case that the threshold value for inclusion in *Vem är det* is the same for men and women as regards eminence, but that women even on the same level of competence as men frequently are to be found on lower positions in the professional hierarchy.

A one-sided significance test of the difference between the proportions of male and female researchers on the academical top level, results in a z-value $=6.33$, which is statistically significant on the 0.00003 % level. When the whole distribution of sex cross-tabulated with academic position is tested, a chi-square value of 56.87 with df $=3$ is obtained, that is, statistical significance on almost the same low level as above. Even in this severely selected material, the male researchers, as expected, occupy significantly higher academic positions than the female ones.

Educational level of representative samples

As for the representative samples of men and women, the relative amount of women decreases more rapidly with every higher educational

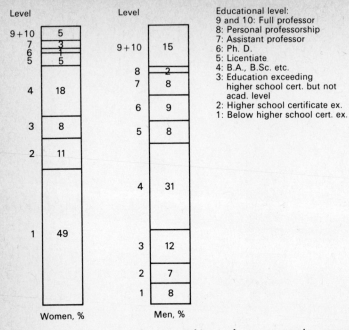

Figure 9. *Relative distribution within each representative sample of different educational levels.*

level than the corresponding proportion among the men (Figure 9).

The median value in the female group lies on level 1, that is, below the 'studentexamen' (higher school certificate) or an equivalent education, while the male median value falls just below level 4, first academical degree (B.A. etc.), which shows a cumulative frequency of 58 %. This indicates, that the women in *Vem är det* are representatives of other professional categories, having lower requirements concerning academic training than in the professions represented by men. A one-sided test of the difference of proportions in regard to relative amounts having a first academic degree or more educational training gives a z-value of 5.86 with significance on the 0.0001 %-level.

Subject sphere of research

The largest proportion of female researchers was anticipated within the humanities and medicine, whereas jurisprudence and theology were assumed to demonstrate the minimum proportions. A summing up of the

128

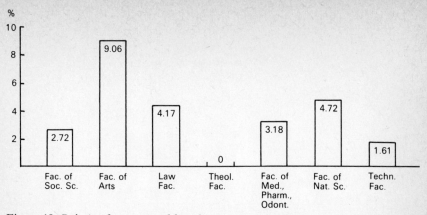

Figure 10. *Relative frequency of female researchers within each separate faculty at the five Swedish universities. (Certain educational institutions outside the universities are, thus, not included.)*

number of female associate professors, full professors and their equivalents at the five Swedish universities within each separate faculty for the session 1970 (Figure 10) results in a distribution being only partly in accord with the expectations. The faculties of arts contain the without comparison highest percentage of female researchers, while the faculties of medicine, unexpectedly, only come fourth.

The 0 % female representation among the thelogians was anticipated, whereas the faculties of law turn out to have a fairly high amount of women from a relative point of view. Consequently, the outcome is, at least in this material, only to 50 % in accordance with the expectations. How then are the female researchers in the sample distributed? Figure 11 shows a distribution pattern, which better agrees with the assumptions

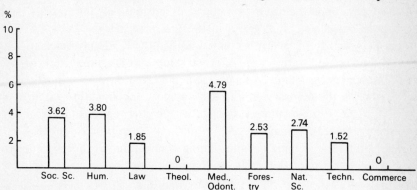

Figure 11. *Proportions of female researchers out of the total number of researchers in Vem är det within each sphere.*

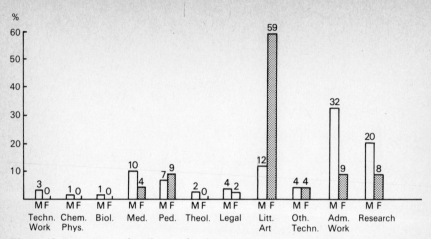

Figure 12. *Percentage distribution for the representative samples on occupational areas within each sex group.*

made: the maximum percentage of female researchers is to be found in the humanities and in medicine, while they are not represented at all among theologians and come sixth as for proportion in jurisprudence. Thus, the selection to *Vem är det* can be said to follow a somewhat more traditional pattern than the one to the universities. A conceivable conclusion is, that female researchers above all excel in traditionally 'female' subjects, partly independent of the amount of basic data.

Occupational areas of representative samples

The occupations being hypothetical extensions of the female sex role (the categories: 4, 5 and 8 in the grouping of professional areas) were assumed to be overrepresented among the randomly selected women as compared to the men. These assumptions are supported concerning the categories 5 and 8 (pedagogical and artistic work, respectively), whereas, on the contrary, the fourth category (occupations within medicine, hygiene and health service) shows a higher representation among the men (Fig. 12). A majority, 59 %, of the women practise professions having a literary, artistic or entertaining connection. Of these, 39 % are doing some form of depicting art (singing, dancing, play-acting etc.) in contrast to creative art (sculpture, painting, writing etc.). Among the men in category 8, only 25 % practise some kind of depicting art. This disparity is interpretable as a manifestation of the object role, that

Table 21. *Relative distribution of civil status in Sweden 1968, divided according to sex*

	Unmarried	Married	Widow/widower	Divorced
Men	47.00	48.00	3.00	2.00
Women	40.48	48.00	8.48	3.00

woman holds in man's world. Man creates works of art, that is, objects, and is himself the subject, whereas woman depicts what others have created and in that way, becomes an object herself. Among the men, category number 10 (general social and business administrative work) accounts for the largest proportion with 32 %, then follows the research category with 20 %

On analyzing the registered professions in detail, as much as 65 % of the men turns out to belong to the top strata of positions within their branch (business managers, full professors etc.). The corresponding proportion among the women is significantly lower—only 13 %.

Judging from these two samples, men gain distinction primarily through achievements in instrumental-Apollonian professional areas, while women's road to the stars by no means crosses that of men, but in the main follows the by and for women well-worn expressive-Dionysian paths.

Civil status

The civil status distribution in Sweden as a whole in 1968 (Table 21) shows the same proportions of married persons among men as among women, but 7 % more unmarried men.

Research groups

In the light of these facts, the difference between male and female researchers as to relative amount of married and unmarried, respectively, look even more interesting (Table 22).

Only 4.7 % of the male researchers are unmarried, while a clear majority, 93 %, are married. The group of female researchers, however,

Table 22. *Percentage civil status distribution of male and female researchers*

	Unmarried	Married	Widow/widower	Divorced
Male researchers	4.7	93.0	2.4	0.2
Female researchers	26.0	60.0	10.0	4.0

Table 23. *Absolute distribution of number of marriages among male and female researchers, respectively*

	Number of marriages					
	0	1	2	3	4	Σ
Male res.	31	562	66	5	1	665
Female res.	13	31	6	0	0	50

chi² = 37.31. df = 2.

contains more than 5 times as large a proportion of unmarried persons −26% − and only 60% married ones. Also, the difference of proportions of divorced is bigger than the corresponding difference in the population as a whole, showing a larger relative amount of divorced women than divorced men. A dichotomous distribution of the research groups according to sex on the categories 'never married'–'married some time', gives a chi-square value of 37.91 with 1 degree of freedom, which is statistically significant far below the 0.1 % level. With that, the assumption that female researchers remain unmarried to a greater extent than male researchers is vigorously supported.

Since the attempt here is to ascertain, whether marriage for the female party clashes with the research role, even the divorced group is of interest. A one-sided significance test of the difference of proportions gives a z-value of −3.80, being statistically significant on the 0.003 % level. Thus, female researchers tend on the one hand, to stay unmarried to a far greater extent than men, and on the other to refrain from remarrying after a divorce more frequently than male researchers. Certainly, even women in general have a lower frequency of remarriage than men, but the disparity is less than among the researchers. That the tendency to remarry is considerably stronger among male as compared to female researchers is also demonstrated in the cross-tabulation of 'number of marriages' with 'sex' (Table 23).

Chi-square for this distribution is 37.31, which with 2 df is significant below 0.1 %. A one-sided test of the difference of means in number of marriages gives a significantly larger number for male researchers on the 0.05 % level (t = 7.0).

Representative samples of men and women

The civil status distribution of the randomly selected samples shows (Table 24), as in regard to the research groups, a considerably larger

Table 24. *Percentage civil status distribution for the representative samples of men and women, respectively*

	Unmarried	Married	Widow/widower	Divorced
Men	4	94	2	0
Women	23	55	13	9

proportion of never married women. As anticipated, the disparity is, however, smaller than among the researchers, depending on the higher percentage of unmarried women among the latter.

The rest of the sex differences all go in the same direction as among the researchers, only more strengthened here. For instance, the relative amounts of widows and divorced are larger in the present group of women at the expense of the proportion married. Possibly, at least the larger proportion of divorced can partly be explained by the great number of artists among the women. According to certain studies (see e.g. Boalt, *Familjesociologi,* 1963) these have a higher frequency of divorce than other occupational categories.

The difference of proportions between men and women in the category 'unmarried' is statistically significant on the 0.003 % level with a one-sided test ($z = 3.80$). A corresponding test of the relative amount of divorced gives a significance of 0.0001 % with $z = 4.5$. Further, the difference of means for men and women as for number of marriages is significant on the 5 % level with a onesided test ($t = 1.9$). Like among the researchers, the tendency to report an existing marriage is high and higher (though not significantly) for women (97.4 %) than for men (96.87 %).

Marital début

From a relative point of view, a later marital début was expected for the female groups and especially for the researchers among them. As a basic measure for the comparison between the average marriage ages of men and women, the arithmetical mean for the differences between the annual average values for men and women is used. The years being relevant to our samples are delimited with the aid of the average ages (59.10 years of age, s =11.8 among male researchers and 57.2 years of age, s=10.8 for female researchers), their standard deviations and a hypothetical minimum age of 20 at first marriage. The relevant period then extends from 1921 to 1960, and the difference of means between

the ages of men and women at first marriage is 2.86 with a deviation of $s = 0.11$ for this time period. (The computations being based upon data from *Statistisk Årsbok.)*

Research groups

Between male and female researchers the corresponding difference (age at first marriage) is merely 0.83, indicating that the assumption concerning a later marital début for research women as compared to women in general is reasonable. If, instead, the average age at first marriage is compared within each sex, and the difference is tested, one gets a z-value of ± 2.55 with a confidence interval of 97.5 % for women, the difference being significant on this level. The corresponding difference for the men falls within the confidence interval and is accordingly, not statistically significant. Even using this measure, the predication of a later entry into marriage for research–commited women, thus, holds true. The marital début of the latter on the one hand, occurs later than among women in general, and on the other, takes place later than among male researchers from a relative point of view (if, namely the population difference serves as a standard).

Representative samples

It is true, that the difference of means for the representative samples as regards age at first marriage, 1.89, falls below the population difference – 2.86 – but nevertheless, as expected, decidedly above the disparity between male and female researchers. Using a confidence interval of 95 %, none of the intra-sex differences are statistically significant. For the men, the difference 0.29 gives a z-value of ± 1.22, while the difference between the randomly selected women and the women in the total population is 1.25 and gives $z \pm 1.45$. Even this group of women thus manifests a tendency toward relatively later marriages than partly, comparable men and partly, women in general.

Comparison within each sex group

Finally, for the sake of completeness, researchers and randomly selected samples within each separate sex should be compared. It then appears, that female researchers on the average marry later, namely at the age

Table 25. *Key table. Average age at first marriage. All samples.*

	Population average for the years 1921–1960	Researchers	Representative samples
Men	28.83	29.62	29.12
Women	25.98	28.69	27.23
Diff.	2.85[a]	0.83	1.89

[a] cp. $M_{(\bar{x}_M - \bar{x}_F) = 2.86}$.

of 28.69, than the randomly selected women, who have an average of 27.23 years of age at first marriage. The difference is 1.46 years. Male researchers have an average age at their marital début of 29.62 as against 29.12 for the group of representative men. Diff. $= 0.50$. Since the samples partly coincide, the differences are not tested. The greater disparity between the female groups could be interpreted as a consequence of the larger discrepancy between them as regards instrumental-Apollonian pressure from the professional role. This is indicated by the grouping of occupations related above, where the two male samples both are characterized as working within generally I-A areas, whereas the female samples differ in this respect, since a clear majority of the randomly selected group is engaged in E-D professional areas (as opposed to the I-A research women) (Table 25).

Children

Research groups

According to the hypothesis, female married researchers should desist from children more often than male researchers, and in case they get children, their number should be smaller. This is, by no means, contradictory to the percentage distribution in Table 26, which demonstrates a significantly larger proportion on the 2.1 % level of female married researchers without children ($z = -2$). Among the not childless, the relative amount with only one child is significantly higher in the female sample

Table 26. *Number of children among male and female researchers.*
Relative amounts (%)

	0	1	2	3	4 or more
Male res.	17.7	8.2	25.4	28.2	20.7
Female res.	32.4	27.0	13.5	10.8	16.2

Table 27. *Number of children among the 'ever married' in the representative samples of men and women. Relative amounts* (%)

	0	1	2	3	4 or more
Men	17.7	2.1	29.2	24.0	27.0
Women	35.1	16.9	22.1	18.2	7.8

with a z-value of -5.0, something that with a one-sided test gives a significance level of about 0.0001%.

A cross tabulation of sex with number of children in absolute figures results in a chi-square value of 22.31, with 4 df being significant below the 0.1 % level. Both links in the hypothesis advanced are, consequently, supported by the outcome.

Representative samples

Here too, the married women were expected to exhibit a larger relative amount of childless persons and on the average fewer children in not childless marriages. Still, the sex difference between the representative groups was assumed to be smaller than between the research samples. The sex difference of proportions (Table 27) in the category of childless is statistically significant on 0.3 % (one-tailed test) with a $z = -2.83$.

Among the not childless, the disparity between the proportions having only one child is significant on the 0.0001 % level ca ($z = -3.83$). In both cases, the differences point in the expected direction with higher proportions of zero- and one-child marriages, respectively, in the female sample. However, the difference of proportions in regard to the category of childless is larger in between the present samples than between the two research groups. As for the category of one-child marriages, the sex difference is, as anticipated, smaller between the former.

All samples

As is evident from the key Table 28, the median value is, as expected, at its minimum among female researchers, next followed by the representa-

Table 28. *Cumulative frequency of number of children among married people in all samples. Relative numbers* (%)

	0	1	2	3	4 or more
Male res.	17.7	25.9	51.3	79.5	100
Female res.	32.4	59.4	72.9	83.7	100
Repr. sample of men	17.7	19.8	49.0	73.0	100
Repr. sample of women	35.1	52.0	74.1	92.3	100

tive sample of women, then by the male researchers and finally, the representative sample of men. This succession apparently coincides with the hypothetical order of precedence advanced in regard to tendency toward compensation profile. This, in turn, is founded on the conception of a higher degree of uncompromisingness for deeply involved professional women in general and research women in particular, as compared to the corresponding male groups. The result accounted for above supports this idea.

Family planning
Nearness between first marriage and first child

Research groups

The percentage distribution (Table 29) of number of years between the entering into marriage and the arrival of the first child shows at a cursory glance a tendency in the direction of the hypothesis, that is, toward a shorter interval between marriage and child for the men.

A one-sided significance test of the difference between relative amounts of families with children, having had a child within 2 years after marriage gives a z-value of 2.33 with a significance level of 1.1 %. Thus, the degree of planned parenthood in this stage is higher among the research women. When it comes to the distribution as a whole and in absolute figures however, the picture is another with a chi-square of only 7.66. With 5 degrees of freedom, this is not significant on an acceptable level (20 % implies a much too strong influence from chance factors). In order to seek a further elucidation of the relation between sex and early family planning, the difference between average number of years elapsed between marriage and first child was tested. The mean is higher for the men, and using a one-sided t-test the difference is statistically significant on the 5 % level ($t = 1.83$). Thus, the picture is differentiated in so far as relatively more female than male researchers get a child in the same year as the entering into marriage, whereas the

Table 29. *Interval in years between marriage and first child among researchers. Relative amounts* (%)

	Same year	1 year	2 years	3 years	4 years	5 years or more
Male res.	6.2	40.8	23.7	13.1	6.0	10.4
Female res.	12.5	20.8	16.7	20.8	12.5	16.8

Table 30. *Interval in years between marriage and first child among representative groups. Relative numbers (%)*

	Same year	1 year	2 years	3 years	4 years	5 years or more
Men	7.9	38.2	25	13.2	9.2	6.5
Women	8.5	27.7	14.9	17.0	14.9	17.0

ones who do not have children immediately postpone the birth of the first child very much longer than do male researchers. However, the predominant feature is the stronger tendency toward planned parenthood among the women.

Representative samples

An analogous tendency toward less closeness between marriage and first child among the women can be traced in the representative samples (Table 30). When the disparity between relative amounts of families in which the first child was born within 2 years after the entering into marriage is tested, the proportion in question appears to be significantly larger among the men. The z-value obtained–2.5–is statistically significant on the 0.6 % level, using a one-sided test.

Accordingly, the sex difference in this respect seems to be larger in the representative samples than among the researchers. Considering the difference of means, which turns out to be significant on the 0.05 % level with one-tailed test and t = −4.72, this view is strengthened. The divergence between the sexes as for degree of planned parenthood calculated with the measure above is thus greater among the representative groups. Whether this can be traced back to a stronger tendency to postpone the birth of the first child among the researchers as a whole remains to be seen. The key table (Table 31) gives a partial answer.

Table 31. *Percentage cumulative frequency distribution and arithmetic means for number of years between marriage and birth of first child. All samples*

	Same year	1 year	2 years	3 years	4 years	5 years or more	M
Male res.	6.2	47.0	70.7	83.8	89.8	100	2.23
Female res.	12.5	33.3	50	70.8	83.3	100	2.96
Repr. sample of men	7.9	46.1	71.1	84.3	93.5	100	2.12
Repr. sample of women	8.5	36.2	51.1	68.1	83	100	3.30

All samples

Since the overall view of this form of planned parenthood, as the preceding analysis shows, is not quite unambiguous, both arithmetic means and cumulative frequencies are accounted for here. The measures present different kinds of information: the arithmetic means indicate a maximum average interval between marriage and first child for the representative sample of women, next follows the female researchers, then the male researchers and finally, the representative sample of men, showing the maximum closeness between marriage and first child. The order of rank is as anticipated except for the women groups, which ought to be reversed to be in line with the assumptions made. On examining the more detailed information given through the cumulative frequencies, however, a difference, although small, is found in the expected direction. Consequently, the median of the randomly selected women falls below that of the female researchers. For the remaining samples, the sequence stays unaltered. Both the female researchers and the representative sample of women thus demonstrate a stronger tendency to defer the birth of the first child and, at least in this stage, plan the parenthood more than the corresponding groups among the men.

Nearness between first and second child

Research groups

As concerns the time interval between birth of first and second child, the expectations were completely opposed for men and women. The male researchers were assumed to desire a dispersion of the children in time and a delay as long as possible before getting a second child. On the contrary, the female researchers, who are more palpably involved in the child bearing, were supposed to prefer giving birth to the children as near to each other as possible, by that minimizing the not professionally active period.

At a cursory examination, Table 32 does not confirm the correctness of the related reasoning. Rather, the tendency seems to be the reverse. The chi-square value of the absolute distribution is only 2.92, which with 5 df is not significant. A test of the difference of means also shows, that the female group has a significantly greater distance between the first two children with $t = -2.75$, being significant on the 1 % level using a two-sided test. Accordingly, the result in this variable is wholly

Table 32. *Percentage distribution of time interval between the birth of the first and second child in each research group, respectively*

	Same year/ 1 year	2 years	3 years	4 years	5 years	6 years or more
Male res.	10.5	33.3	26.2	12.6	7.0	10.3
Female res.	14.3	21.4	21.4	14.3	7.1	21.3

contrary to the expectations. Certainly, the matrix analysis bears out the assumptions, that the research role is in a state of opposition as against the spacing of the deliveries in time, something that implies, that successful research is positively correlated to concentration of the child bearing over a shorter period. However, in the present connection men and women are compared with regard to another aspect of the variable in question, and it is for that reason properly speaking not surprising that the predictions are not fulfilled. Unlike male success in the resarch role, female research success is promoted by pronounced closeness between children, but the female researchers, nonetheless, show a larger average time interval between first and second child than do the male researchers.

Representative samples

Nor with respect to the randomly selected groups are the expectations supported (Table 33). When the difference of means is tested, it turns out to be not significant ($t = -0.85$). In other words, the two groups are similar as regards nearness between children, and the significantly larger dispersion in time, demonstrated by the female researchers in comparison to the male ones, is not discernable in this sample of women.

All samples

The order of precedence among the means shows (Table 34) a highest value for female researchers, next follows the representative group of

Table 33. *Percentage distribution of time interval between first and second child in the representative samples*

	Same year/ 1 year	2 years	3 years	4 years	5 years	6 years or more
Men	11.7	29.9	28.0	18.2	3.9	7.8
Women	13.9	19.4	19.4	22.2	16.7	8.4

140

Table 34. *Percentage cumulative frequency distribution and arithmetical mean for number of years between first and second child. All samples*

	Same year/ 1 year	2 years	3 years	4 years	5 years	6 years or more	M
Male res.	10.5	43.8	70	82.6	89.6	100	3.24
Female res.	14.3	35.7	57.1	71.4	78.5	100	5.0
Repr. sample of men	10.7	41.6	70.2	88.4	92.3	100	4.05
Repr. sample of women	16.7	33.3	52.7	74.9	91.6	100	4.33

women, then male researchers and finally, the representative sample of men. This sequence is against the anticipated, but agrees with the outcome in the preceding variable (distance between marriage and first child) except for the placing of the female samples in relation to one another. The cumulative frequencies also indicate lower median values for both the male groups with the same relative order, whereas the rank order between the female samples is reversed as compared to that of the means. Evidently, it is here a matter of a more general family planning variable, with a stronger tendency all along the line toward spacing among the women as compared to the men.

Income

All samples

Since a splitting up of the research samples into equivalent academical levels is not feasible as a consequence of the slight number of female researchers, a fair comparison between the income standards of the sexes cannot be made. The same applies to the randomly selected samples, where we all too seldom find men and women represented in sufficient numbers in similar professional areas. Still, the income distribution is of interest, and a key table is presented below (Table 35). As can be seen, the representative sample of men comes highest, as measured

Table 35. *Percentage cumulative income distribution, arithmetical means and* s

	Income in Sw. Kr.						
	1– 45 000	46– 60 000	61– 75 000	76– 90 000	90 000–	M	s
Male researchers	1.5	11.3	38.4	66.4	100	90 130	39 720
Female researchers	4.6	22.8	63.3	76.9	100	82 818	61 021
Repr. sample of men	6.1	14.6	42.7	61.0	100	105 768	88 684
Repr. sample of women	29.4	56.8	70.5	86.2	100	60 863	31 907

both by arithmetical mean and median value. As expected, the male researchers come in the next place, but falls clearly below the mean of the
previous group, in spite of the fact, that an even greater majority here
consists of representatives of the top levels (84 % as against 65 % among
the former). Indeed, an expression for the lower financial recompense
given by even the most distinguished research in relation to other comparable exacting professional activities.

In view of the big standard deviations, demonstrated in the income
variable, however, the median is a more reliable measure. The sample of
female researchers even have almost as big a standard deviation as
average income. However, the order of rank between the groups, remains the same, irrespective of the measure utilized. Consistently, the
representative sample of women shows the lowest average income, while
the female researchers come last but one, with a median income of 61–
75 000 Sw. Kr.

Thus, not even in this extremely delimited high-status material, that
individuals in *Vem är det* form, the income distribution is even between
the sexes.

Private means

All samples

We expected female researchers to be more dependent on financial
security to pursue long and expensive studies. No specific assumptions
were made respecting private means among the randomly selected
groups, yet they are presented along with the others in Table 36 for the
sake of completeness.

As anticipated, the proportion with private means is higher among
the female researchers than among the male ones. However, the difference is not statistically significant on an acceptable level (10.6 % with
one-tailed test and z = −1.25). For the representative samples, the relation between the sexes is reversed, but still not significant (z = 1.0).

Table 36. *Percentage distribution of private means in all four samples*

	No private means	Private means
Male researchers	90.7	9.3
Female researchers	86.4	13.6
Repr. sample of men	84.8	14.1
Repr. sample of women	90.9	9.1

The latter lack of significance seems a bit surprising, since the male group to a large extent consists of business managers. However, the element of salaried employees in relation to managers with own businesses has in recent years increased even in this group, something that possibly gives part of the explanation.

A comparison within each separate sex group indicates a higher percentage of female researchers with private means, whereas among the men it is the representative sample that accounts for the highest relative amount of persons with fortunes. This fact is an indication, that women who concentrate on an academical career are more dependent upon exterior financial security than are men, who more can trust to their own intrinsic possibilities, job chances, the colleague-system etc. The idea that academic position can precede private means is consciously ignored here. The probability of a causal connection can, with the ruling salaries of researchers, be considered as exceedingly small.

Social origin

Research samples

According to the predications, the relative amount of female researchers, having a social origin in the upper strata (social group I) should exceed the corresponding proportion among the men (Table 37). This also seems to be the case when examining the percentage distribution, where uncertain cases have been introduced between the two relevant groups.

However, a chi-square test of the corresponding absolute distribution does not give a significant outcome, $\chi^2=4.11$ with 3 df. To a certain extent, the uncertain in-between cases have a leveling effect, but even if they are excluded, chi^2 is not significant, having a value of 2.0 and 2 df. Since the interest here is principally focused upon the proportion coming from the upper social strata (social group I) and not really upon the entire distribution, however, the difference of proportions in this

Table 37. *Percentage distribution of social origin for male and female researchers*

	Social group				
	I	I or II	II	II or III	III
Male researchers	64.3	9.6	21.0	3.8	1.4
Female researchers	77.6	4.1	16.3	2.0	0

Table 38. *Social origin in the representative samples of men and women respectively. Percentage distribution*

	Social group				
	I	I or II	II	II or III	III
Men	61.9	6.2	24.7	2.1	5.2
Women	63.2	8.4	19.0	6.3	3.2

category is more interesting. When the latter is tested, it turns out to be statistically significant on the 2.3 % level, using a one-sided test ($z=2$). Consequently, the more severe sorting out of women from lower social strata in education also makes itself felt on the highest academical level. Female researchers are more dependent upon their social background than are male researchers. Thus, to the former this factor is concurrent with the sex factor in further shrinking the potential proportion of women among researchers.

Representative samples

Among the randomly selected samples, the distribution of social origin (Table 38) shows a relatively regular picture without a significant difference in relative amounts from the upper social strata (social group I). The proportion of women originating from the latter is, however, larger than the corresponding share of men, and the outcome therefore does not contradict the reasoning related above, although it was primarily assumed to apply to the research groups.

All samples

The order of precedence between the group medians (Table 39) demonstrates a maximum proportion from the upper social strata among female researchers, this group thus being more selected than any of the

Table 39. *Percentage cumulative frequency of social origin in all of the four samples*

	Social group				
	I	I or II	II	II or III	III
Male res.	64.3	73.9	94.9	98.7	100
Female res.	77.6	81.7	98.0	100.0	
Repr. sample of men	61.9	68.1	92.8	94.9	100
Repr. sample of women	63.2	71.6	90.6	96.9	100

others in this respect. Next follows the male researchers, who therefore come before the representative sample of women. In regard to social origin, the factor 'research−not research' thus appears to sort out somewhat harder than the sex factor. Between the representative groups, however, the sex factor eliminates the most, showing a greater dependence upon the social heritage among the women. Finally, the not unexpectedly oblique social group distribution in the material as a whole with a maximum representation from the upper social strata should be noted.

Social origin of women, measured by mother's occupation

Unfortunately, it is not possible to trace any relationship between the mother's own social group, if any, and the professional areas of the female samples, since only 4 persons−18 %− out of the research group and 3−3 %−out of the representative sample state, that their mother has an occupation. It is true, that the relative amount of mothers with professions is larger among the research women, something that possibly indicates a higher prevalence of identification patterns on their part, but the number is much too small to render a more detailed analysis possible. A mapping out of the mothers' occupational spheres over various degrees of instrumentality-Apollonianism is thus not feasible. Among the mothers of the female researchers there were 2 elementary-school teachers, 1 Master of Arts and 1 sculptress. Of the randomly selected women's mothers 1 was an elementary-school teacher, 1 a commercial teacher and 1 Bachelor of Arts. If anything comprehensive at all should be said about these small groups. it is to emphasize the strong element of pedagogical professions: 4 out of 7 are teachers and the 5:th has an education with pedagogical orientation. Otherwise, the group contains one person with esthetic professional orientation plus one unidentified university graduate. Thus, 6 out of 7 mothers with clearly sex role generalizing occupations.

Place of birth and domicile

Research samples

As in regard to the social origin, female researchers were also assumed to be more dependent than the male ones upon their regional origin, in

145

Table 40. *Percentage distribution of types of place of birth and domicile for the research groups*

	Country	Towns with less than 100 000 inhab.	University towns	Big cities	Scandinavia except Sweden	Outside Scandinavia
Birthplace						
Male res.	28.3	26.7	7.6	29.8	2.1	5.6
Female res.	20	24	12	28	10	6
Domicile						
Male res.	3.2	2.4	40.2	51.4	1.1	1.8
Female res.	—	4	34	56	—	6

so far as the sorting out among the former should be more severe in smaller places and in the country than in university towns and big cities. The relative distribution in Table 40 is at least partly in the direction of the hypothesis, showing a higher percentage of women born in university towns and a lower percentage from the countryside and smaller towns and places. In respect to the big cities, the outcome points in the opposite direction with a lower relative amoung of persons born there among the women. Neither is the picture unambigous when it comes to domicile. Certainly, women are as expected more concentrated to the big cities, but this is at the expense of the university towns. In the countryside, however, the relative amount of women is unvariedly below that of men.

None of the differences of proportions enumerated above are significant on an acceptable level, but chi-square for the absolute distribution of type of birthplace is 13.34, which, using a one-tailed test and 5 df is significant on the 5 % level. Chi^2 for domicile is not significant (chi^2 = 4.09, df = 4), neither was it expected to be. The elimination of women on the road to higher education is more severe in the smaller cities and this is manifested also in the research material.

Representative samples

The reasoning above is not directly relevant to the two randomly selected samples, but the greater dependence upon geographical nearness to career opportunities for the women should make itself felt even in other occupational domains. The importance of the university towns is likely to disappear in the present group of women.

The main sex difference regarding birthplace (Table 41) is found in the proportion born in the country, the difference being statistically

146

Table 41. *Percentage distribution of type of place of birth and domicile in the representative samples*

	Country	Towns with less than 100 000 inhab.	University towns	Big cities	Scandinavia except Sweden	Outside Scandinavia
Birthplace						
Men	31	21	5	38	2	3
Women	18	18	2	47	—	5
Domicile						
Men	7	22	12	56	—	3
Women	1	11	8	78	—	2

significant on a 1.4 % level (one-sided test and $z = 2.0$). Furthermore, women are more often than men born in a big city, but the disparity here is not significant ($z = 1.29$).

Even as concerns domicile, women's greater regional dependence is manifested, the difference of proportions in amount of big-city-dwellers being significant on a 0.01 % level (one-sided test, $z = 3.14$).

To summarize, both the female researchers and the randomly selected women from Vem är det manifest a greater geographical restraint than do the men in comparable groups. Also the regional factor, especially as expressed in the degree of centrality of the birthplace, thus, conduce to keep the female representation far below the male one as to size.

Social acitivities

Research samples

The assumed lower social activity level of the female researchers, measured in club membership and leisure time interests, is in evidence in the latter case but not in the former. The female researchers show slightly more activity within clubs and the like with 4 % associated as against 3 % among the men. The disparity is above all concentrated to membership in several clubs, (0.8 % for men and 2 % for women), whereas the percentages associated to only one club is almost identical for the sexes. Possibly, the higher activity in clubs for the research women constitutes a compensation for their slight family commitment. The difference of means in club membership is not statistically secured: $t = -0.02$. Neither does a chi^2-test of the absolute distribution give significance: chi$^2 = 0.15$ with 1 df.

Representative samples

The randomly selected samples show all along the line the expected tendency toward both more frequent club activity and more hobbies among the men. To the former variable, the difference of means is t = 2.5, being significant on the 1 % level with a one-sided test, and to the latter variable t = 1.55, not being statistically guaranteed. Consequently, men are more externally socially active than the women, something that in regard to the present group is likely to be associated to the connection between career and status club, that can be traced in some of the professional categories to which particularly the men belong. In these instances, 'The Club' functions as a forum for the inner circle, where women are not admitted. To this factor are of course also added the earlier enumerated ones, forming the basis of the prediction.

A comparison between male researchers and non-researchers shows a markedly higher average social activity among the latter in both variables. On the contrary, the female groups are equally active in these matters, something that indicates that the sex factor as well as the factor 'research–not research' is of import in this connection.

Age

All samples

Both samples of researchers turn out to be younger on the average than the two representative samples, something that holds true both when measured by arithmetical means and medians. Evidently, the research career is more rapid than other comparable careers and results in recognition at a younger age than do other professions. This applies, even though the female random sample contains a relatively strong representation from occupational spheres connected to show business, where success often is gained at an early age, since youth in itself here is a positive value. Maybe the acknowledgement takes a longer time for women–in other words a kind of sex-bound tardiness.

As for the rest, both female researchers and the randomly selected women are younger (M = 57.2 and M = 60.72 years of age, respectively) than their counterparts among the men (M = 59.1 and M = 61.94, respectively), the differences of means not being statistically secured with t = 1.15 and t = 0.67, respectively. Concerning the representative female group, the sex difference is presumably explicable by the fact, that youth is one of the criterions of success as regards women, but not

Table 42. *Percentage cumulative distribution and arithmetical mean of age at doctor's dissertation and appointment to full professor in the research groups*

	Age at doctor's dissertation							
	20–29	30–32	33–35	36–38	39–41	42–44	45–	M
Male res.	20.6	48.3	73.1	86.6	92.8	98.2	100	33.35
Female res.	2.3	20.9	44.2	62.8	72.1	79.1	100	39.47

	Age at appointment to full professor							
	20–36	37–39	40–42	43–45	46–48	49–51	52–	M
Male res.	22.3	41.0	55.9	71.4	80.1	86.4	100	42.58
Female res.	15.4	30.8	46.2	53.9	69.3	73.2	100	44.69

in regard to men, who, indeed, 'mature' with the course of time and become more valuable the older and the more experienced they are. The estimation of 'youth' is also strongest in professions connected with the stage, where relatively more women than men belong. The age disparity between male and female researchers, however slight, can be traced back to the on the average lower academic positions of the latter. Should this factor really be of importance, however, the female researchers would be much younger than they actually are.

Age at doctor's dissertation and appointment to full professor

Since the present two variables as well as the following ones lack relevance to the two representative samples, they are only accounted for regarding the research groups (Table 42).

The displacement upwards in the ages for the female sample in relation to the male one is clearly noticeable in both variables. Especially prominent is the disparity regarding age at doctor's dissertation, where as much as 48 % of the men fall below the 32-years-of-age line as against merely 20.9 % among the women. At the age of 44, 21 % of the female researchers had not yet defended their doctor's thesis as compared to 12 % among the men. The difference of means is significant on the 0.05 % level, using a one-sided test and a t-value of −6.58. Chi² for the collapsed frequency distribution is 53.91, being statistically secured with 4 df on the 0.1 % level.

Even the average age at appointment to full professor for female professors exceeds that of the male professors. Thus, 80 % of the men were appointed before the age of 48, whereas the corresponding proportion for female professors is 69.3 %. The difference of means is not

Table 43. *Percentage cumulative distribution and arithmetic mean for time interval between first academic degree and appointment to full professor in the research groups*

| | Number of years | | | | | |
	1–11	12–17	18–23	24–29	30–	M
Male res.	13.9	52.7	77.1	91	100	18.66
Female res.	10	35	65	85	100	20.10

secured on an acceptable level $-t = -1.32$. A significance test of the total distribution using chi-square, however, gives statistical significance on the 5 % level with $\chi^2 = 14.15$ and 6 df.

These two measures of the time lag in the female research career support the hypothesis, that women are exposed to a harder pressure towards engaging in the remaining roles and are, accordingly, not given the opportunity to commit themselves entirely to the exacting research work as much as men. Factors like the secondary role (if any at all) that the professional career is considered to play in woman's role set as well as the academic colleague-system with its status-set-typing and sexism are likely to contribute to the delay of woman's research career.

Number of years between first academic degree and appointment fo full professor

Even this variable shows (Table 43) that the career of the female researchers is more time-consuming than that of the male ones. Thus, more time elapses between the first step and the last for the women. 52.7 % of the men accomplish this career climbing in less than 18 years, while only 35 % of the women reach as far in that same period. This difference, too, is ascribable to the sex varying factors earlier enumerated. The difference of means is too small to be statistically guaranteed $(t=-0.86)$, and this also applies to the chi-square (3.35, df=4). Although the difference is not significant, it points in the direction of the prediction and gives some support to the assumptions made.

Achievements connected to research/professional and career role

Since the variables treated in this section have their direct associations to the research and career role and the assumptions connected with it in common, they are presented in compound tables over closely related variables with brief commentaries on significance levels etc.

150

Status-connected variables

Research samples

Table 44 accounts for three variables with a more or less direct connection to the status dimension. To be included in one or more reference books is a public recognition of the competence and social status of the person concerned, and the inclusion in itself gives prestige, thus increasing the total amount of status of the person in question. As measured by the three variables: 'most prominent reference book', 'number of lines in *Vem är det*' and 'number of reference books giving the name of the subject', the prestige level is without exception higher for the male than for the female researchers. For the variable 'status according to reference books' (measured by the most prominent reference book giving the name of the subject), which measures the status quality, the difference of means is secured on the 5 % level with one-tailed test and $t = 1.82$. Chi^2 for this variable is 14.47, being significant on the 2 % level with 2 df.

The variable 'number of lines in *Vem är det*' shows a significant difference of means on the 0.5 % level with $t = 3.0$, as well as a statistically secured $chi^2 = 37.94$ on the 0.1 % level (3 df). The space factor is both a manifestation of actual status, measured by the amount of

Table 44. *Percentage distribution and arithmetical means for status according to reference books (measured by the most prominent reference book giving the name of the subject), number of lines in Vem är det and number of reference books. Research groups*

	Status according to reference books								
	1	2	3	4	5	6	7	8	M
Male res.	47.4	22.9	10.1	3	0.3	7.1	8.9	0.5	2.45
Female res.	74	6	6	—	2	6	4	2	1.94

	Number of lines in Vem är det								M
	1–10	11–15	16–20	21–					
Male res.	14.3	42.1	23	20.1					16.33
Female res.	48	36	10	6					13.24

	Number of ref. books						M
	1	2	3	4	5	6 or more	
Male res.	1.2	46.5	29.7	10.4	5.4	6.9	2.96
Female res.	4.1	71.4	10.2	4.1	2	8.1	2.54

Table 45. *Percentage distribution and arithmetic means for three status variables in the representative samples*

	Status according to reference books							
	1	2	3	4	5	6	7	M
Men	69	8	7	—	—	7	9	2.13
Women	47	24	10	4	2	9	4	2.33

	Number of lines in Vem är det							
	1–10	11–15	16–20	21–				M
Men	24	45	21	10				13.75
Women	42	44	12	2				11.65

	Number of reference books					
	2	3	4	5	6 or more	M
Men	69	13	8	2	8	2.74
Women	46	30	11	7	6	3.02

relevant research data, and of an individual striving for status by means of stating as many facts as possible. This status-seeking activity within the career cluster harmonizes with the male sex role, though not with the female one, something that, in addition to the real status component, is likely to be at the bottom of the sex difference.

Finally, a test of the difference of means in 'status quantity' = 'number of reference books' results in a $t = 2.21$ with statistical significance on the 2.5 % level. $Chi^2 = 16.92$; with 5 df this is secured on 1 %.

The larger total status quantity of male researchers is likely to be partly dependent upon their higher academic position. However, since the correlations between the three status variables on the one hand, and academical position on the other (see the matrices) without exception are low both among the men and among the women, this factor probably does not explain more than a slight proportion of the sex variation in status.

Representative samples

Except in respect to space in *Vem är det* (number of lines), the relationship between the sexes in Table 45 is reversed as compared to the research groups. Thus, women's average status as measured in 'status according to reference books' and 'number of reference books' exceeds

that of men. However, the differences of means are not statistically secured ($t = 0.71$ and $t = -1.40$, respectively). The slightly higher status that after all goes to the female group can probably be traced back to the professional representatives in this sample having a more popular kind of fame, namely the children of Thalia etc. On the other hand, the difference of means for 'number of lines in *Vem är det*' is secured on the 0.05 % level ($t = 3.39$). Since in this case the male group shows the highest mean value, the outcome gives support to the predictions.

When comparing all samples to each other, the female researchers turn out to possess the least amount of status both in the variable status quality (status according to reference books) and status quantity (number of reference books). In the space factor (number of lines in *Vem är det*) female researchers are lowest except for one sample. The I-A career is definitely not the right and accepted road for women to seek status upon! For male researchers it fits perfectly – this group tops the rank list of status in everything except number of reference books, where they are surpassed by the randomly selected women.

Membership in learned societies and the like, number of government committees etc., membership in research councils and academic positions

Research samples

All variables in this section show distributions and sex differences in the direction predicted, the male researchers demonstrating a larger number of memberships in learned societies, higher participation in government committees etc., more memberships in research councils as well as a larger number of academic positions. For the last-mentioned variable, there are no female holders at all in the material. The differences of means are statistically significant for all variables except 'number of government committees and the like', for which, on the other hand, the chi-square value is statistically secured. Moreover, chi^2 is significant for 'membership in learned societies', but not for 'membership in research councils' and 'academic positions'.

To sum up, male researchers have a far greater success than female researchers in all of the four variables enumerated. Their correlations with academic position are relatively low, for which reason the factor mentioned cannot explain the large disparities. The correlation coeffi-

cients are, with the exception of 'membership in research councils', lower for the male researchers. Consequently, the women seem to be more dependent upon their exterior position to obtain the same rewards as the men in regard to career measured by the variables above.

Representative samples

Examining the distribution of the four achievement variables for the representative groups, one finds higher values for the male sample all along the line. However, only the difference of means for 'membership in learned societies and the like' is statistically significant on an acceptable level. As concerns participation in government comittees, the activity in the female group is concentrated to a few extremely active women. A smaller proportion have served on 1 or 2 commissions, whereas the absolute majority is not engaged in committees at all (79 % as against 60 % among the men). The sex differences point in the direction predicted.

International activity

Research samples

International work was assumed to be closer to the male extrovert sex role than to the female introvert one. In fact, male researchers show a higher level of international activity with on the average more international assignments and guest professorships, respectively. The differences of means are not statistically secured, but chi^2 for international assignments is significant on the 1 % level. Guest professorships in the female group are principally concentrated on a small minority of women (4 % of them have 2, while only 2 % have 1). It is true, that the sex disparities are not as pronounced as anticipated, but all the same, they point in the right direction. The female researchers are more dependent upon academic position for their international activity than are the men, something that is evidenced by the higher positive correlations between those variables among women (they are extremely low for the men. See the matrices concerned).

Representative samples

The sex differences in amount of international work among the randomly selected samples point in the direction predicted with a higher

154

activity level among the men. The means in number of international assignments differ significantly, whereas this is not the case concerning number of guest professorships, where the female group is not represented at all.

Published works

Research samples

The level of productivity measured by number of published works (Table 46) is higher among the male researchers both on the average (significant difference of means) and as for the distribution as a whole (significant chi-square value). Publication intensity is employed in several studies as the principal criterion of research success, the men in the present material thus being definitely more successful than the women. It is not possible to explain the disparity by means of the relationship between academic position and publication quantity, since the correlation here is low and lower for male (0.08) than for female researchers (0.17). The stronger dependence between career position and publishing in the female group coincides with the stronger association between the first-mentioned variable and various career variables noted in several earlier instances. Possibly, it indicates the presence of Merton's sex-typing and Epstein's colleague-system. Men are rewarded in the various factors relatively independent of where their research position is located within the upper research strata, whereas research success for the women is dependent upon their academic level in the hierarchy. It is as though women were not entrusted with publishing, memberships in academies and learned societies, appointments to president and dean etc., unless they prove their competence in exterior position first. Whereas the success cycle for the male researchers seems to be a spiral interaction business with smooth transitions, that of the female researchers appears

Table 46. *Percentage distribution, arithmetic means and significance tests for number of published works in the research samples*

	Number of published works					
	0	1	2–3	4–5	6 or more	M
Male res.	7.1	43.2	13.2	11.0	25.8	4.03
Female res.	12.0	62.0	14.0	2.0	10.0	2.12

chi² = 10.90, df = 3, sign. level = 2 %.
M-diff. = 1.91, t = 2.73, sign. level = 0.5 %.

to have a step-by-step structure, requiring a high initial achievement to start. Thus, more seems to be required of the female researchers as compared to the male ones for the same amount of success in the research role.

The outcome of the American study earlier related, showing a rising publication frequency with increasing age for the women, and a publishing curve more like an upside-down U for the men, does not reappear in the present study, judging from the correlation between age and number of published works, which for female researchers is 0.32 and for males 0.34.

Representative samples
The female group contains 12 % writers, whereas among the males, writers only represent 1 %. Accordingly, the average publication frequency of women in this sample exceeds that of men, the difference not being statistically secured.

In a comparison between the distributions of all the samples, the male researchers turn out to have the maximum mean of publication, in spite of the strong element of writers in the group of randomly selected women.

Creativity

All samples
Creativity as measured in number of inventions, patents, bills, works of art etc. shows a higher arithmetic mean for male researchers as compared to female ones. The difference is not significant, but chi^2 is statistically secured for the distribution as a whole. However, the direction of the difference established through chi^2 is contrary to the one between the means, that is, the female group shows more creativity. In other words, the variable is hard to interpret, the reason to it being the wide distribution upwards on the scale among the men. Certainly, the group of female researchers contains a larger proportion of persons with only a few markings, but this fact is balanced through the wider distribution among the male researchers, demonstrating as much as 1.4 % with 12 marks or more (no female researcher exceeds 7 individual marks). Creativity measured in this way is thus comparatively more common among female researchers, whereas among the male ones it is

concentrated on a few all the more creative persons. In view of the high percentage of artists included in the representative sample of women, their high degree of creativity ($M = 2.50$ as against $M = 0.34$ for the men) is explainable and needs no further comment.

Distinctions

All samples

The sex difference points both among researchers and in the representative samples in the direction predicted and gives significant values as well in regard to chi^2 as regarding differences of means. Consequently, men are without exception more rewarded as for distinctions. Like in several earlier career variables, the greater dependence upon professional position among female researchers is manifested here as well. The correlation between academic position and number of distinctions are 0.33 for the latter, whereas for the male researchers it is as low as 0.07.

From a total point of view, both of the male samples exceed both of the female groups, the representative sample of men showing a maximum of distinctions.

Swedish and foreign honorary doctor's degrees and name on dotor's thesis given in Vem är det

Research samples

Both Swedish and foreign honorary doctor's degrees fall more frequently to male than to female researchers, while the proportion of names of doctor's degrees given in *Vem är det* is equivalent for the two samples. None of the differences are statistically secured, but the direction is all along the line as anticipated, and is thus at least not contrary to our assumptions. The correlations between academic position and number of Swedish and foreign honorary doctor's degrees, respectively, are positive and weak but stronger for the female group in the latter variable. In respect to name of doctor's thesis given in *Vem är det*, the correlation is negative for both men and women (-0.04 and -0.11, respectively), something that possibly indicates, that the variable constitutes an 'intra-compensation' factor. The lower the academic position, the greater the need to present compensating achievements.

Representative samples

In view of the sex-differentiated distribution of professions, being prevalent in the representative samples, it is no surprise, that the men without exception exceed the women in number of both Swedish and foreign honorary doctor's degrees as well as in frequency of names of doctor's thesis given in *Vem är det*. Only the last-mentioned sex difference is statistically secured (2.5 % level).

Sum variables

Research samples

Each one of the sum variables represents, as mentioned earlier, a summary of the most relevant variables in respect to: researcher's status, general status and academic power and can, accordingly, be considered as survey variables to the career factors enumerated above. As is evident from Table 47, this summing-up gives a clearer picture of the

Table 47. *Percentage distribution, arithmetic means and significance test for amount of researcher's status, general status and academic power in the research samples*

	Researcher's status total of points					
	0	1	2–9	10–19	20–	M
Male res.	3.31	15.19	56.39	18.8	6.32	7.18
Female res.	10	10	48	8	2	3.76

chi² = 18.58, df = 4, sign. level = 0.1 %. M-diff. = 3.42, t = 3.55, sign. level = below 0.05 %.

	General status total of points					
	0–19	20–29	30–39	40–49	50–	M
Male res.	45.11	34.14	12.78	4.81	3.16	23.42
Female res.	70	22	2	—	6	19.08

chi² = 16.23, df = 4, sign. level = 1 %. M-diff. = 4.34, t = 2.86, sign. level = 0.5 %.

	Academic power total of points				
	0	1	2–9	10–	M
Male res.	26.33	2.71	60.45	10.53	4.15
Female res.	54	2	38	6	2.50

chi² = 17.62, df = 3, sign. level = 0.1 %. M-diff. = 1.65, t = 2.66, sign. level = 0.5 %.

158

Table 48. *Arithmetic means and t-test for the variables researcher's status, general status and academic power. Representative samples*

	M	Difference of means	t	Significande level
Researcher's status				
Men	4.17	0.19	0.24	not sign.
Women	3.98			
General status				
Men	20.34	−0.09	0.08	not sign.
Women	20.43			
Academic power				
Men	3.22	1.56	2.94	0.5
Women	1.66			

sex disparities with strengthened differences and a generally lower statistical level of significance, both in regard to chi^2- and t-test.

Only a few brief comments will be made, since the picture is clear with sex differences all along the line pointing in the direction predicted. The largest gap between male and female researchers is found in researcher's status with a t-value of 3.53 and a level of significance in the chi-square test as low as 0.1 %. Next in size of sex difference follows academic power, also with a chi-square significant on 0.1 %. Indeed, the sex disparity in general status is statistically secured too, but on a somewhat higher level than the previous ones. Prestige in the research world and amount of academic power are both more closely attached to the inner academic circle (the colleague system) and are of greater relevance to the career role than is the broader and more popular kind of prestige, that the variable 'general status' expresses. Possibly, the somewhat greater sex differences in the two first-mentioned variables are signs of the presence of the male colleague-system.

Representative samples
Since the variables 'researcher's status' and 'academic power' are less relevant to the representative samples, and as all of the variables included in them already have been accounted for in the foregoing, only a brief summing-up of the sum variables is presented here (Table 48).

The outcome shows higher values for the men all along the line with a significant difference of means for academic power but not for the two other variables.

On examining all of the four samples it appears, that the representative groups possess higher general status than female researchers but not higher than the male ones. On the other hand, the researchers rather naturally demonstrate higher values in regard to researcher's status and academic power. An exception to this are the female researchers, who even have lower academic power than the representative sample of men. Moreover, the randomly selected women have a higher average researcher's status than the female researchers, something that appears curious but can be attributed to the variable 'published works', which is indeed a central factor in researcher's status.

University loyalty I and II

As the variables 'university loyalty I and II' lack importance to the randomly selected samples, data are only presented for the research groups (Table 49). Female researchers show a markedly lower degree of both kinds of university loyalty as measured by change of university between on the one hand, first academic degree and licentiate's degree and on the other, between licentiate's degree and doctor's dissertation.

In the foregoing, a change of university has been interpreted as a disturbing factor in the career pattern, since a transfer interrupts old already established contacts between researchers and results in a comparatively long transitory period with an establishment of new contacts necessary to the research work. Moreover, a change can be interpreted as a symptom of disturbances in the collaboration between researcher and

Table 49. *Percentage distribution of university loyalty I and II in the research samples*

	Change between passing of degrees	No change between passing of degrees
University for first acad. degree and lic. degree		
Male researchers	12.7	87.3
Female researchers	27.3	72.7
University for lic. degree and doctor's degree		
Male researchers	8.5	91.5
Female researchers	23.3	76.7

institution. It is possible, that the lower degree of university loyalty among the women plays a part in their being less successful in the research role. However, to this is added an earlier mentioned factor of significance to female researchers: the wife is expected to move with her husband wherever his job may take him. The reversed case appears absurd to most people and is also, in view of the prevailing sex role norms and labor market conditions, hard to realize in practice. A large part of the greater disposition to move between examination levels among female researchers should thus be possible to trace back to this 'co-moving' factor. Naturally, this does not prevent the possible disturbing consequences of the change for the research career from remaining active. Once again the traditional sex roles place obstacles in woman's way.

Educational level of subject's spouse

The fact that women's marriage partners have higher average education than those of the men is of course a triviality in the light of the prevailing sex role structure. However, it is of a certain interest, that female researchers mostly (59.5 % as against 12.9 % among the representative sample of women) marry researchers. At least the sympathy with the hardships of the research role ought to be greater among spouses, who themselves carry on research. Maybe it promotes a reduction of the pressure exerted upon the woman from her E-D sex role.

Male researchers also more frequently than the remaining sample of their own sex marry partners with a university education: 27.1 % of their wives have at least a first academic degree (B.A. etc.). The corresponding proportion in the representative sample of men is merely 7.3 %. Part of the explanation is to be found in the fact, that the universities also function as marriage markets. In addition, the wife of the researcher does not, like e.g. the wife of the business manager or the diplomat, occupy an established side role as a representation wife. To the researcher, this kind of social contacts and activities lack importance, for which reason his wife, at least in that respect, is free to seek a professional role of her own, independent of the husband.

Social origin of the subject's spouse

69.3 % of the wives of the male researchers come from the upper social strata, this sample showing the highest average social origin of the

spouses. The corresponding proportions in the remaining samples is in a downward sequence: representative sample of men (64.1 %), representative sample of women (62.5 %) and finally, the female researchers with only 46 % of the spouses coming from the upper social strata (measured by father's occupation). Men form their own destiny, their social background is probably less important in the marriage market than is that of women, who seldom belong to a social group themselves, but do so through a man—the father in childhood, the husband in adult age. The present samples of women both consist of eminent professional people, but the representative sample still marry men from the upper social strata to a far greater extent than do the research women.

The sex difference among the researchers in relative amount of spouses coming from the upper social strata is statistically secured on the 1.2 % level with a two-tailed test and z = 2.56. For the representative samples, this same difference is not significant with a z-value of 1.00.

Summary and discussion of descriptive section

A detailed analysis of most of the 43 registered variables was performed for male and female researchers, respectively, as well as for the representative samples of men and women. The interest was chiefly concentrated on sex disparities between the two research groups, the representative samples serving as objects of comparison in that respect. Chi-square, z- and t-test for differences of means and z for significance test of differences of proportions were used. Highest acceptable level was set at 5 %.

A summing-up of the principal results shows *statistically secured sex differences in the direction predicted* for the following variables in the research samples: 3) academic position (higher for men), 4) social origin (larger proportion coming from the upper social strata among the female researchers), 6) birthplace (female researchers more often born in university towns), 8) status according to reference books —higher for male researchers), 9) space in *Vem är det* (greater for men), 11) membership in learned societies and 13) number of government committees as well as 14) membership in research councils, 15) international assignments, 17) number of academic positions, 18) published works, 20) distinctions (the seven last-mentioned variables are all characterized by a significantly larger relative amount for male researchers, something that cannot be explained by their higher average academic posi-

tion, since most correlations here are slight for the men), 22) researcher's status, 23) general status, 24) academic power, 42) creativity (a larger amount of the four preceding variables for male researchers), 25) marriage disposition (lower for female researchers), 26) marital début (later among female than among male researchers in relation to the national average difference between the sexes for the relevant years), 27) children (larger proportion of childless, larger proportion with only one child and a lower average number of children among female researchers), 28) nearness between first marriage and first child (lower relative amount of children within 2 years after the marriage for female researchers), 30) age at doctor's dissertation and 31) age at appointment to full professor (these two variables both show a significantly higher age for the female researchers), 39) civil status (larger proportion unmarried and divorced—not remarried among the female researchers), 40) educational level of subject's spouse (lower in the male group—female researchers to a large extent marry researchers), 43) social origin of subject's spouse (higher for male researchers). Total sum = 26 variables.

Not statistical significance but sex differences in the direction predicted was established in the research samples for the following variables: 1) family name (proportion of nobility larger among female researchers), 7) private means (more frequent among the women), 12) Swedish honorary doctor's degrees, 16) guest professorships, 19) name of doctor's thesis given in *Vem är det,* 21) foreign honorary doctor's degree (the four last-mentioned variables showing higher values for male researchers), 29) number of years between first academic degree and appointment to full professor (longer time period for women), 32) income (higher for male researchers), 35) hobbies (more wide-spread among male researchers), 36) area of subject —this variable was not tested for significance but shows the predicted higher concentration of women in comparatively more E-D colored areas), 37) university loyalty I and 38) university loyalty II (these two variables show the anticipated greater university loyalty among men). Total sum: 11 variables.

Results in the research samples pointing in *another direction than the one predicted:* the variables 34) club membership (is rather more common among female than among male researchers) and 41) nearness between first and second child (the time interval is somewhat longer for the female group). Total sum: 2 variables.

For the representative samples the following variables show a *signi-*

163

ficant sex difference in the direction predicted: 3) educational level (higher in the male sample), 5) domicile (larger relative amount of women in the big cities), 6) birthplace (fewer women born in the countryside etc.), 9) space in *Vem är det* (less for women), 11) membership in learned societies, 15) international assignments, 19) name of doctor's thesis given in *Vem är det,* 20) distinctions, 24) academic power (all of the last-mentioned 5 variables indicate a larger number/larger amount for the male sample), 27) children (significantly larger proportion of childless and of persons with only one child in the female sample), 28) nearness between first marriage and first child (larger proportion of men with children within two years of the marriage), 32) income (significantly higher for the men), 34) membership in clubs (more rare among the women), 36) occupational area (larger porportion in the top strata and in markedly I-A occupations among the men), 39) civil status (larger relative amounts unmarried and divorced in the female sample). Total sum: 15 variables.

A not statistically secured sex difference but a difference in the direction predicted was established for the representative samples in the following variables: 1) family name (larger proportion nobility among the women), 4) social origin (larger relative amount of women from the upper social strata), 12) Swedish honorary doctor's degrees, 13) government committees, 14) membership in research councils, 16) guest professorships, 17) number of academic positions, 21) foreign honorary doctor's degrees, 22) researcher's status (the preceding 7 variables are all characterized by a larger proportion/larger number for the male group), 26) marital début (comparatively later among the women), 35) hobbies (more unusaul in the female group). Total sum: 11 variables.

For the representative samples, *a sex difference in another direction than the one predicted* was established for the following variables: 7) private means (more frequent among the men), 8) status according to reference books (higher for the female sample), 10) status quantity measured in number of reference books (more in the female group), 18) published works (fewer in the male sample), 23) general status (higher for the women), 41) nearness between first and second child (longer time interval for the women), 42) creativity (higher in the female sample). Total sum: 7 variables.

As is evident from the survey above, the outcome is in accordance with most of the predictions and gives thus support to the main part of the hypotheses advanced. The agreement between theory and empiricism

164

is especially good in the research samples, whereas the representative samples, as expected, show a somewhat less pronounced picture in regard to sex differences. For the most part, this can be traced back to the higher proportion of writers in the female group, something that unexpectedly raises the values at least in the variables 18, 23 and 42.

Judging from the result, the sample of research women is more severely selected than the sample of male researchers. It is as though men and women would pass through a number of filters with sex-bound quotas of admittance: one filter is called 'social origin', another 'family name', a third 'birthplace', a fourth 'civil status', a fifth 'marital début', a sixth 'children' and so on. Each one of these filters checks more women than men on the road to research success. The outcome of this section indicates that women, in order to be successful, are more dependent upon external and from the individual himself uninfluencable factors like social background, regional origin etc. than are men.

The hypothetical polarization of women in on the one hand, principally I-A oriented ones and on the other E-D oriented women is further supported by the result of the descriptive section. Thus, even as a total group, the female researchers show a considerably lower family commitment than do both women in general and the male researchers. The uncompromisingness in the female researchers' situation in regard to E-D and I-A role thus, seems to apply not only to the most successful ones (even if the state of opposition is most pronounced here), but also to the group as a whole.

Factor analysis

Certainly, the outcome of the matrix analysis is relatively satisfying, on the whole supporting the hypotheses advanced, but a further examination was considered essential, and to this end the method of factor analysis was chosen. A brief account of procedure and result is given below. Since the number of variables in the role pattern is large and unwieldy, the factor analysis is well adapted for the task from a practical point of view. The role pattern in the matrix, based upon the hypotheses advanced, initially fixed the role affiliation of the separate variables, which, accordingly, were both figuratively and literally speaking attached to a definite role before the analysis of the outcome was carried through. In the factor analysis the procedure is in a way reversed: the expectations in regard to the outcome are the same as earlier, it is true,

165

but whereas the matrix analysis implied a testing of the data's agreement with the hypothesis, the factor analysis is rather a test of the hypothesis' agreement with the data. The distinction is maybe not as subtle as it may appear at first sight.

The varimax method was adapted, and all the variables forming part of the role pattern were included with the exception of the following variables: 12 (number of Swedish honorary doctor's degrees), 17 (number of academic positions), 34 (club membership) and the three sum variables 22, 23 and 24. The three first-mentioned variables were left out, as the risk of zero-division in the program was regarded as imminent. Because of their special complex nature, the sum variables proved technically impossible to include in the analysis. Being of principal interest, only the research samples were analysed. The factors extracted are treated in order of precedence according to decreasing capacity of explanation. Since the main interest in this analysis is concentrated to the female researchers, the male sample serving a purpose of comparison, only the factor matrix of the former is examined in detail, while that of the latter is summarily treated.

When six factors has been extracted from the unrotated factor matrix of the female researchers, the residuals are comparatively large with only 64 % of the variance accounted for. Using as much as 29 variables, however, the large number of factors is explainable and scarcely unexpected.

The first factor accords with the research and career cluster in the matrix analysis and shows high positive factor loadings in pronounced research variables and negative loadings in most of the family variables. When this domineering I-A factor has been extracted, the picture is less clear, but the outcome is in substance concordant with the expectations. Factor number two appears to be a downright 'success'-factor with its strongest positive loadings in the variables 'space in *Vem är det*' (+0.83) and 'income' (+0.74) and negative factor loadings in two of the variables measuring length of career ('number of years between first academic degree and appointment to full professor' = −0.70, and 'age at appointment to full professor' = −0.71). The third factor can be described as E-D, since it contains high positive loadings in above all the variables 'number of children' (+0.52), 'nearness between first marriage and first child' (+0.45), 'marriage disposition' (+0.29) and 'income of subject's spouse' (+0.61). Only 'social origin' (+0.40) and 'name of doctors's thesis given in *Vem är det*' (+0.61) from the research cluster indicate positive factor loadings ⩾0.40. Even in the

matrix analysis, the last-mentioned variable came out as an internal compensation variable within the career cluster.

The remaining three variables account for a diminishing part of the total variance. Hence, they are only treated in brief. Factor four is interpreted as a time-factor in the career, showing negative factor loadings in most of the research variables and a positive loading for the variable 'age at doctor's dissertation' ($+0.41$). The fifth factor expresses, if anything, social background with high positive loadings in the variables 'family name' ($+0.56$) and 'social origin' ($+0.64$). Factor six, finally, covers a large part of the variance in the variables 'domicile' ($+0.51$) and 'birthplace' ($+0.51$) and is thus to be considered a regional factor.

For the male researchers, the picture is different, showing less marked factors and larger residuals. Indeed, the first factor is possible to interpret as a research and career factor, but as for the rest, the factors are, as anticipated, more pronounced for the female researchers. Even this very cursory examination of the unrotated factor matrix for the male researchers thus gives support to the reasoning earlier related.

Summary of factor analysis

A factor analysis using the varimax-method was performed for the group of male and female researchers, respectively. The three first extracted factors in the unrotated matrix are for the female researchers characterized as: I) I-A factor, II) success factor and III) E-D factor. The corresponding factor matrix for the male researchers contains less marked and therefore more difficult variables to interpret. Possibly, a rotation of the matrix is necessary to make more fundamental variables, if any, stand out in this sample. However, the analysis is not further developed in the present context, since even the unrotated factor matrix for the female researchers shows an outcome in the direction predicted.

Summary and discussion

At the basis of the view of the research process adopted in the present study is Boalt's summation theory, the compensation model of which is applied to male and female researchers, respectively. A correlation matrix of 35 variables, distributed on three hypothetical role clusters: A) research and career role, B) family role and C) social role, was constructed for each one of the samples studied, whereupon the possible occurrence of a sex-differentiated allocation of resources in the role structure was inquired into.

For the maximum number of available female researchers in *Vem är det* (the Swedish *Who's Who*)—that is, 50—all in all 45 variables were registered on the basis of information obtained in various reference books recently published. An identical set of variables was registered for the sample of male researchers, consisting of nine randomly selected samples from various research fields making a total of 665 persons. Furthermore, two representative samples of 100 women and 100 men were randomly selected from *Vem är det* to serve as material of comparison.

The result is treated in three sections: a) matrix analysis, 2) description and 3) factor analysis. The outcome of the three sections point, with rather few exceptions in occasional variables, in the direction predicted and consequently, supports the thought that female researchers are exposed to considerably stronger tensions between the various roles than are the male researchers, something that results in a more pronounced compensation role profile for the female group. The sex disparity is also manifested in the comparison between the representative samples of men and women but is here, as expected, somewhat less marked than between the research samples. A strong I-A (instrumental-Apollonian) commitment to the research and career role appears to obstruct or preclude a contemporaneous commitment to the family role for the women. Female researchers marry to a significantly lesser extent than do the male ones, and when they marry, it occurs later than the men from a relative point of view. Moreover, the female researchers have on the average fewer children than the male ones, are more frequently childless and get children later in marriage than do male researchers.

Also, the result indicates, that female researchers are more bound by various forms of acquired status in contrast to achieved status. Thus, both the regional and the socioeconomical dependence is greater among female than among male researchers. This concords with the society at large, where women are judged more by what they *are* than by what they *do*. Successful research is to women often tantamount to a renunciation of rewards related to the family role and the social role. Vice versa, a strong involvement in these latter roles is to women incompatible with research success. The hypothetical polarization of women in I-A and E-D oriented is thus substantiated through the outcome of this study. The generalizability of the result is inevitably restricted by the specific nature of the groups studied, as well as by limitations in the methods adopted. (For a comparison using data from the United States,

see the Appendix prepared by Mr. Stephen Hall.)

However, the outcome of the present study gives cause for a closer reflection upon the consequences, that the exceedingly severe sorting out among the women is likely to have for research. The overwhelming over-representation of male researchers with a probable concomitant over-emphasizing of problems centered around power relations, conflict, competition etc. pares the breadth of our knowledge in areas character-ized as 'feminine' and treating interpersonal relations.

"And as long as women, in desperate cave-woman style, devote their whole lives to narrow domesticity, first in school-girl dreaming and searching for roles which make them appealingly ignorant, then as mothers and then as grand-mothers, our scientific activity will remain one-sided, with an overemphasis on power and an underemphasis on human values." (Mead, M., *American Women*, Boston, 1962.)

The absence of female models and the fact, that the permit to in-fluencial and high positions in society is named instrumentality presum-ably lead to the few women, who all the same succeed in pursuing an exacting professional career, being assimilated by the male world and adopting their values and outlook. An identification with the only avail-able model – the male one – and an imitation of the domineering pattern of behavior is likely to be the result. Probably, this identification is necessary for the woman to be at all tolerated and even more so for her to be accepted on high instrumental positions.

"Women scholars are not taken seriously and cannot look forward to a normal professional career . . . because they are outside the prestige system entirely. Being outside the prestige system, they cannot hurt . . . or be a threat to men." (Caplow, T. & McGee, R. J., *The Academic Market-place*, New York, 1959.) " . . . in the world of 'ideas' women simply do not count". " . . . most men in higher education seem unaware that women are outside the rigid caste system of the academic world. Indeed, men at the top of the intellectual pyramid are constantly reminding women that they are not matching their male colleagues in scholarly research and publication. What they fail to recognize is that the fault may lie, in part, in the discrimination that comes, – not because women are newcomers to the academic world, not because as women they have low status – but because women have simply never been inside". (Alpenfels, E. J., *American Women*, Boston, 1962.)

From i.a. a study of assaultive crimes in 48 societies (Bacon & Barry, *Journ. of Abnormal and Soc. Psychology*, 1963, 4) it is evident, that the imitation of the male behavior pattern among women in the lower social strata, where female identification patterns are hardly lacking, is not very marked. In spite of the introduction of woman suffrage and a larger

active female participation in the labor market etc., the proportion of female violent deeds remains low in the United States and other western countries. In the social anthropological material societies with a larger amount of female influence and responsibility than is customary do not show any apparent tendencies toward a higher degree of criminal aggression among women.

The disparagement of the 'feminine' expressive behavior in almost all societies is, in view of today's society, all the more strange as this behavior is characterized by antiaggressiveness, humanity and lack of destructiveness–that is, precisely those traits which today are more indispensable than ever. Since subdued minorities gradually tend to accept and internalize the conceptions and expectations directed toward them, women in a misogyne society will integrate with their personality and their behavior the opinion, that they are weak, insufficient, incapable of logical reasoning, unable to lead and to organize etc. The internalization justifies and 'explains' her subordinate position and serves the purpose of rationalization. The consequence is, that woman experiences herself as the chief agent of frustration. In accordance with the theory of self-aggression (Berkowitz, L., *Aggression. A social psychological analysis,* New York, 1963) women in this position should exhibit more aggressiveness against their own sex and also against their own self. A testing of the theory in a comparative study of cultures with varying degree of misogyny and a contemporaneous investigation of the relationship between the social aggressiveness of women and their identification with the traditional sex role would be of interest but will not be further discussed in this connection.

Thus, woman makes man's value scale her own and generalizes it to other women, which naturally hampers or entirely thwarts the possibilities of creating solidarity between them. Without solidarity toward the group of one's own, thorough changes are hardly feasible. As a further impeding factor operates the defectiveness in woman's identity experience. A genuine affinity can only be built upon the individually experienced identity of many individuals. This identity is based upon a self-experienced strong ego-feeling, in which all of the components of personality have merged into an integrated whole. The socialization of the boy and the man is suited to produce a certainly emotionally incomplete but in other respects strong such a totality of the personality, whereas the education of the girl and the woman is adapted to suppress large parts of the potentialities, by that turning interest, ambition and creative force on to the narrow sphere named Home.

170

Considering the hard sex-determined elimination that is established in this study, it is evident, like in so many other connections, that the real reserve of talent is to be found among the women. The only way to take advantage of it is to cease considering it a 'reserve'. As long as the reserve-mentality is prevalent in regard to one sex, it will be denied the self-realization and the development of inherent talents which is officially granted all individuals irrespective of race, ethnic and social origin, religion and sex, with losses in personal, social, cultural and economical respects as a consequence.

"It is well known that public opinion lags far behind technical and social change. Society at large still cannot tolerate the idea of the mass of women exercising the right to work and to have a family; it still cannot accord to all women what it accepts for sharwomen, actresses and royalty." (Berger, R. and Maizels, J., *Women—Fancy or Free,* Mills and Boon, 1962.)

'The right of gainfully employed women to family and marriage' is since a certain time substituted for the old feminism matchword 'married woman's right to employment'. This exchange of phrases has taken place on the formal level of debate, on the informal one not even the older slogan is in force. The lag is a well-known phenomenon in several contexts but seems to be especially striking in the sex role question, which probably is a consequence of its strong psychological loading and ego-involvement. According to a relatively widespread opinion, now that woman has the vote, formal right to higher official positions etc., the matter has been settled. Unfortunately, this idea is disproved by the actual conditions in society. In certain places even a retrogression has been noted. The phenomenon has especially attracted attention in the United States, where one doctor's degree in six within all subjects was taken by a woman in 1920, whereas women only took one in ten in 1970 (Hunt, M., *Dialogue,* 1970, 3, 4), and where the proportion of gainfully employed women has declined from 50 % in 1930 to below 35 % in 1960 (Alpenfels, 1962, op. cit.). It remains to be seen, what consequences the present educational boom will have for the equality between the sexes. A regenerated glorification in a covert and more subtle form of the trinity: 'Kinder, Küche, Kirche'? A useful rationalization has in fact already been constructed by Patai (Patai, R., *Women in the Modern World,* New York, 1967), who maintains the following:

"In these countries", (United States, Great Britain, Scandinavia, Soviet Russia) "having to a large extent achieved what they wanted, women now are saying in effect: 'Now that we have won the right to take an equal place in a

171

man's world, we prefer to return to the home, to our own places in our women's world. It is good to know that we can play both roles, that we have a right to both worlds, but we shall be satisfied with relatively brief excursions into the world of men before taking up, or after having fulfilled, the role to which nature has predestined us, of being wife, mother and home maker.''

PART FOUR

by Gunnar Boalt

CHAPTER 9

The summation theory tested on the research process

In the previous chapters researchers and non-researchers have been compared. But what is research and why does it affect behavior so much?

Published in 1970 was a study of research behavior by Boalt and Lantz entitled *Universities and Research* using the summation theory already known to the reader. But most of the data came from Sweden and so as usual it must be pointed out: this chapter neither should be considered as something more than a pilot study nor generalized outside the Scandinavian social science field.

It is believed that research has a very high status in the Swedish society because it has laid down a set of values very difficult to attain. This set of values varies with social background, research school, field of science, country, time, etc. Evidently no list can be made of them, not even a complete list of the values important to the author in his own research. Some of these values may influence behavior although it would be hard to believe. Some are too silly to state in print (any researcher can furnish good examples) and some that are enumerated may nevertheless lack all relevance and just remain lofty ideals far above reality. But if the interaction of research values is to be studied, then a number of values possible to measure must be stated even though this set lacks some important values and may contain several unimportant ones.

About 30 values have been used and these divided into three classes: 13 *planning values* taken into consideration already during the planning of research projects; nine *working values* generally coming in before data collection or processing; and six *additional values* brought into action during the hammering out of the reports. The values are:

I. Planning values
   1. Presentation of the hypotheses
   2. Reliability
   3. Validity of independent and dependent variables
   4. Sampling procedure
   5. Generalization of the situation
   6. Integration of the problem with a theory
   7. Investigation's value for theory construction in general
   8. Investigation's value for hypothesis formation in general
   9. Investigation's value for statistical model formation in general
   10. Investigation's value for variable construction in general
   11. Investigation's usefulness to society
   12. Problem's news value
   13. Research orientation's utility from the chairman's point of view

II. Working values
   14. Definitions of variables
   15. Mathematical models
   16. Statistical models
   17. Scaling technique for testing data
   18. Analysis method's value
   19. Mathematical treatment of data
   20. Material's size
   21. Non-response in the material
   22. Fate of hypotheses

III. Additional values
   23. Information additional to planned report
   24. Citation of literature
   25. Value of language
   26. Number of pages
   27. Value of researcher's title
   28. Ability of researcher to disguise deficiencies of the project

IV. Three remaining scales used for our own analysis
   29. Year of publication
   30. Mark given the thesis by the faculty
   31. Sum of scientific value grades on scales 1–29

Most of these 31 scales have been given five steps. The reliability of these scales was tested by Boalt and Erikson who used them independ-

ently on a sample of doctoral theses. The mean reliability turned out to be +.72, probably a little higher as several weaknesses were retrieved with the help of the reliability test.

The interaction of the research values

Even though the set of research values is incomplete and should not be generalized, they are used to test hypotheses about their interaction and also hypotheses based on the summation theory.

Swedish theses are carefully scrutinized by officially appointed opponents and handled by many others. There is very little willingness to understand or excuse weaknesses. This lack of generosity we can neither prove nor explain. Alvin Gouldner has discussed the problem in his introduction to Gunnar Boalt: *The Sociology of Research* (Carbondale, Southern Illinois University Press, 1969). It is, however, bound up with the very strict Swedish rules for research.

It is believed that Swedish researchers are anxious to pay consideration to as many values as possible. But this of course cannot be done as the researchers, alas, discover at the planning stage. They have restricted time and resources and must allocate them, giving priority to the values they deem most important and caring little for those they deem less important or impossible to take care of in the particular case. They find it, for instance, very difficult to give enough time and energy to form a good theory for their project as well as an efficient methodology for sampling, scales, etc. Theorizers tend to give up methodological values and empiricists to give up theoretical values.

Thus if a sample of research projects is studied, some planning values given priority (or no priority) should form a cluster with positive correlations between values from different clusters, thereby demonstrating the allocation patterns. These patterns are formed by values, which can be attained by the same effort or the same resources, forming clusters and competing with the clusters of other values, which need quite different efforts or resources. The researchers try to choose the set of values best suited for their project and consider them important enough to compensate the loss of the remaining values. These clusters of values cannot be identified in advance, but it can be pointed out that the researchers' allocation of energy and resources, always too small for the undertaking, must result in a "compensation pattern" of planning values.

175

Suppose the researcher has made his choice of important planning values and adds a number of impressive working values to make his expected yield of attained values as high as possible. He then starts to collect his data and some of his expectations are quickly destroyed. His interviewers, for instance, come in contact with only 80 % of the sample, while he expects – and needs – at least 95 %. His expectations are always at a maximum, very often reality lets him down and he has to make more of working values and must use refinements of scales or complicated analysis methods. When it comes to writing the report, he can throw in a number of additional values to make a better impression, i.e., a long review of the previous work in the field, more than 200 references, or simply hide some mistakes by an incomplete description of them. The less he gets from his expected values, the more anxious he should be to compensate with additional values, thus creating one or more clusters out of them.

These clearcut clusters can, however, turn up only if all the researchers in our sample have about the same amount of resources available for their project. If some have considerable financing and time at their disposal, they should be able to attain high degrees of many values; if others had very limited resources, they could attain only a few. A mixture of high class projects with low class then must give the impression that all research values tend to follow one another or to form just one large cluster. If the effects of resource allocation on research values is to be demonstrated, samples must be selected so that the projects in each sample have about the same resources, which then can be allocated in different ways. We have done this with four different samples: Swedish doctoral theses up to 1966, theses for Master's degree in sociology at Stockholm University, articles from the Scandinavian journal *Acta Sociologica,* volumes 4–6 (1960–1962) and *The American Sociological Review,* volume 26 (1961).

Let us take the sample of theses for the Master's degree as an example. Each thesis was read and marked according to how far 28 research values were attained. Value 13 is useless in this case as all the candidates were B.A. Then all the intercorrelations were computed and brought together in Table 50.

This matrix certainly fulfills reasonable expectations. There is a decided cluster of empirical research values 1–6, which also includes most working values, but no additional value. There is a theoretical cluster made up of the theoretical research variables 7–10, plus 11 and 19. The remaining six values, five of them additional, can be handled either as

176

three small clusters, each with two values, or as a third cluster with some negative correlations in it.

How are these data to be interpreted? A Master's thesis is either an empirical study trying to pay attention to the statistical and mathematical values or to the theoretical values and in addition consider (as happened) 11 and 19. If too little is obtained from these values, additional values can be added to reduce the risks.

But why is value 13 (school's usefulness), a planning value, included among the additional values in the last clusters? It was included among the planning values because it was felt that Swedish candidates for the Master's degree should be ambitious to side up with their chairman when selecting a theory for their project. The author, as chairman of the Stockholm department, had published the summation theory used in this research. And so, as soon as a thesis was definitely bad, the author tried to save himself by applying the summation theory! Frankly, we had not anticipated this use of it, but there it is where it evidently belongs among the additional values!

The author, however, may excuse himself by pointing out that he tended to give lower marks to the theses presenting additional values. The mark of the thesis is correlated $-.08$ with use of summation theory, $-.12$ with number of pages, $-.24$ with additional information, $-.10$ with translation to foreign language, $-.34$ with number of references and $-.71$ with disguise of defects.

The bad theses first try to compensate lack of merits with the summation theory and with many pages, then by giving additional information nobody has asked for and elegantly wrapping the parcel up in a foreign language or by using a large number of references and trying to disguise the worst deficiencies.

This makes sense, at least in Stockholm. It must be noted that all students but one went for the empirical values, only one for the theoretical. All the data for the theoretical cluster rest on one single thesis, which explains why so many of the correlations for values 7–10 are $+1$ or -1.

The theoretical cluster would not be taken seriously if there was only a single case, but actually there are cases in all four of the samples. It will be kept, but not overrated. The remaining three samples all had an empirical cluster and a theoretical cluster, all of them had one or more additional values forming a small additional cluster of values thrown in at the moment when they were badly needed.

177

The importance of the research values

There is then a general tendency either to go in for empirical research or for theoretical. There is also a general tendency to compensate lack of good values with some additional value as number of references, used for that purpose by three of the four samples. For further information we will try to find out how important each one of the 29 research values are to the four samples of researchers. There are several ways importance can be measured.

1. The marks given to theses for Ph.D. or M.A. are known. The more important a research value is for good marks, the higher correlation it should have with the marks. But unfortunately, articles in journals are not given marks and so this simple technique cannot be used for them.

2. Suppose we were to mark a thesis in our sample, how should we use the data we have about it? The simplest way is to add all the grades the thesis received on our 29 scales. This *grade sum* then can serve as a mark and it is correlated $+.62$ with the marks of Ph.D. theses, acceptable but not very high. We still can use the correlation between grade sum and the grade of each attained value to measure how important each value is. This measure is called *criterion importance,* as grade sum is used as a criterion. But this is not an ideal measure. Suppose for instance that a value was so extremely important that it had to be covered in every report. Then it would give no correlations at all and get a criterion importance of ± 0.

3. If a value is able to compensate for other variables (i.e., translation of a Master's thesis into English substituting for empirical or theoretical values) then we could use the correlations of the language grades with value grades from other clusters to compute a mean correlation. The better a value could compensate values in other clusters, the stronger negative correlations it would have with them. The language value (26) thus has a mean of $-.49$. We intend to use this mean as a measure of importance and call it *interaction weight,* but change the sign of the mean. The language value then gets the interaction weight of $+.49$. Please observe that in this way a value positively correlated with many values in other clusters will get a negative interaction weight. Value 19 (analysis methods) then has $-.24$. But if a value was exceedingly important and present in all reports, it will receive an interaction weight of ± 0.

4. The simplest way to measure importance is, of course, the mean of the grades. If the mean is high, researchers are anxious to attain this value and so it has high importance. How is the scale tested so that it is known whether it is not too generous by giving high grades too easily? We cannot know if it measures generosity or importance or both and so this measure can be used only to compare means of one research value at a time in different samples of reports on researchers.

The last three measures of importance all have some merits, but they certainly measure rather different aspects. All three should be used in an attempt to find out how they behave.

The importance of the values is studied by starting with the values included in the empirical cluster. Value 19 (analysis method) is expected to belong to the empirical values and it does in three cases. But among the M.A. theses it happens to get along better with the theoretical values and so joins that cluster although it still has many positive correlations with the empirical values and is given a low interaction weight. Change of cluster thus has many consequences.

If the four samples are to be compared, let us first have a look at them. The most ambitious set of reports is the Ph.D. theses as they have a mean grade sum 75.7, then comes the sample of M.A. theses with a mean of 65.8, the *American Sociological Review* articles with 60.1, and the *Acta Sociologica* articles with 53.3. But if these four samples actually shared one another's opinions about the importance of each research value, then we would expect that the Ph.D. theses with the top grade sum means also should have the highest means of all research values, as the grade sum is made up of these grades. Then the M.A. theses should come second, the *American Sociological Review* articles' grade means should come third, and the *Acta Sociologica* articles' last.

The values of the empirical cluster, their criterion importance and interaction weights

It is thus expected that all grade means should show the same falling trend as the grade sums, but of course there will be exceptions as soon as the researchers do *not* share one another's opinion about the criterion importance of a particular value. There are four possibilities when this happens:

Table 50. *Intercorrelations between grades of scientific values pertaining to M.A. theses in sociology at the University of Stockholm*

Values etc.	1	2	3	4	5	6	12	14	15	16	17	18
1 Presentation of hypotheses	■	.27	−.12	.52	.75	.21	.39	.30	−.03	1.00	.21	.13
2 Reliability		■	.12	−.52	.52	.35	.03	.45	.03	.02	.79	.82
3 Validity			■	.17	−.41	.50	−.51	.21	.52	.46	.26	.35
4 Sampling				■	.27	−.07	.20	.13	1.00	1.00	−.36	−.23
5 Generalization					■	.07	.46	.32	−.20	−.18	.13	−.00
6 Theory						■	.05	.16	.05	.05	.74	.68
12 News value							■	.70	−.15	−1.00	.27	.33
14 Variables' definition								■	.40	.35	.45	.53
15 Mathematical model									■	.74	.27	.33
16 Statistical model										■	1.00	1.00
17 Scales											■	1.00
18 Scale's actuality												■
20 Mathematical treatment												
21 Material's size												
22 Non-response												
23 Fate of hypotheses												
7 Theory construction												
8 Hypothesis construction												
9 Model construction												
10 Variable construction												
11 Usefulness to society												
19 Analysis method												
13 School's usefulness												
27 Number of pages												
24 Additional information												
26 Language												
25 Number of references												
29 Disguise of defects												
30 Year	.82	.13	.12	.44	.44	−.00	.66	.85	.33	.30	−.11	−.00
31 Mark	.12	.12	.17	−.07	.07	−.27	.52	.62	−.13	1.00	.26	.35
32 Grade sum	.60	.15	.33	.30	.63	.49	.13	.86	.51	1.00	.63	.56
Interaction weight	.21	.05	.24	.10	.10	.22	.36	.04	−.11	−.19	.14	.10

1. If a sample gives an empirical value a grade mean higher than the preceding one, this indicates that the sample attributes more importance to the value.

2. If a sample gives a value the expected grade mean, lower than the preceding one and higher than the following, then the value is given medium importance.

3. If a sample gives a value a grade mean lower than the following, it indicates that the sample attributes low importance to the value.

4. If a sample excludes a value from the empirical cluster, it indicates that the sample considers this value less important than the samples still retaining it.

The data on the mean grades is presented in this order: first, their presence/non-presence in the empirical cluster, then their mean grades in the four samples, their criterion importance and their interaction weights. Cases 1, 3 and 4 have been earmarked as the cases answering to the previous four indications, but case 2 has not been used because it is the most common case.

The general level of importance depends on the interaction patterns

20	21	22	23	7	8	9	10	11	19	13	27	24	26	25	29
.55	− .12	.61	− .04	−1.00	− .31	− .31	− .31	.03	.03	− .12	.03	.09	−1.00	.19	.13
1.00	.12	− .38	.04	−.100	.31	.31	.31	− .31	− .03	.37	.27	− .09	−1.00	.64	− .41
.15	.17	− .12	.07	−1.00	−1.00	−1.00	−1.00	.42	.42	− .08	.15	.08	.18	− .04	.04
− .49	− .17	.64	.49	1.00	− .12	− .12	− .12	.52	.72	− .70	− .23	− .00	− .12	− .42	.42
.49	− .17	.44	.20	−1.00	.12	.12	.12	− .04	.49	− .17	− .04	.30	−1.00	.16	− .16
.67	.24	− .24	.32	−1.00	−1.00	−1.00	−1.00	− .06	− .06	.50	.46	.53	− .25	− .32	.04
.39	.21	− .00	.14	−1.00	−1.00	−1.00	−1.00	−1.00	−1.00	.22	− .03	.21	−1.00	−1.00	− .71
.55	.21	.33	− .13	−1.00	.06	.06	.06	.55	.79	.43	.05	.50	−1.00	− .20	− .81
− .03	.22	.33	1.00	−1.00	.51	.51	.51	− .03	1.00	− .51	.39	− .24	.51	− .32	− .11
1.00	−1.00	1.00	.41	−1.00	.76	.76	.76	− .02	1.00	− .11	1.00	−1.00	−1.00	.10	1.00
1.00	.26	− .11	.36	−1.00	− .06	− .06	− .06	− .30	− .05	.69	− .05	− .22	− .06	− .08	− .47
1.00	.12	− .22	.23	−1.00	− .00	− .00	− .00	− .13	.13	.56	− .13	− .15	− .00	− .00	− .53
■	− .12	.13	.23	−1.00	− .31	− .31	− .31	− .27	.03	.70	.31	− .24	− .31	.19	− .54
	■	.35	.30	−1.00	−1.00	−1.00	−1.00	.12	.15	.17	− .37	− .24	−1.00	− .34	− .24
		■	− .00	−1.00	− .00	− .00	− .00	.13	.61	− .12	.13	.15	−1.00	− .00	.27
			■	−1.00	.12	.12	.12	− .29	.23	− .17	.49	− .64	.12	− .41	.12
				1.00	1.00	1.00	1.00	1.00	1.00	−1.00	−1.00	−1.00	−1.00	−1.00	−1.00
					■	1.00	1.00	1.00	1.00	−1.00	− .31	−1.00	−1.00	.37	− .37
						■	1.00	1.00	1.00	−1.00	− .31	−1.00	−1.00	.37	− .37
							■	1.00	1.00	−1.00	− .31	−.100		.37	− .37
								■	.74	− .12	.03	.48	− .31	− .41	− .19
									■	− .37	.03	.09	− .31	− .64	−1.00
										■	.70	.08	−1.00	− .04	− .24
											■	.09	.19	− .31	.41
												■	.44	− .41	.41
													■	−1.00	1.00
														■	.48
															■
.38	− .35	.22	− .00	−1.00	− .00	− .00	− .00	.61	.38	− .12	.13	.44	−1.00	− .00	− .27
.15	− .08	.12	− .17	−1.00	1.00	1.00	1.00	.42	1.00	− .08	− .12	− .24	−1.00	− .34	− .71
.60	.08	.74	− .07	−1.00	− .18	− .18	− .18	.12	.60	.08	− .15	1.00	− .18	− .24	− .34
.17	.50	.07	.10	1.00	.22	− .18	− .18	− .03	− .24	.16	− .03	.17	.49	.16	.12

and thus varies considerably from one sample to another. To distinguish between high and low importance, the mean criterion importance of the sample has to be used. High importance then would mean criterion importance above the mean of the sample, low importance would be below the mean.

Table 51. *Data on the criterion importance of the empirical cluster for the four samples*

	Ph.D. Importance		M.A. Importance		Am. Soc. Rev. Importance		Acta Importance		Sum Importance	
	< .70	> .70	< .55	> .55	< .80	> .80	< .90	> .90	<	>
1. Higher importance expected	0	0	1	1	0	2	0	0	1	3
2. Medium importance expected	4	8	4	7	6	7	8	9	22	31
3. Lower importance expected	3	1	3	0	0	1	0	0	6	2
4. Cluster changed, low importance	4	0	2	2	4	0	3	0	13	2

< indicates values below the median.
> indicates values above the median.

Table 52. Presence, grade means, criterion importance and interaction weights in the empirical cluster of all four samples

No. Value	Presence in cluster				Mean of grade				Criterion importance				Interaction weights			
	Ph.D.	M.A.	A.S.R.	Acta	Ph.D.	M.A.	A.S.R.	Acta	Ph.D.	M.A.	A.S.R.	Acta	Ph.D.	M.A.	A.S.R.	Acta
1. Presentations of hypotheses	+	+	+	+	2.76	2.75	2.45	2.12	.86	.60	.78	.83	.34	.21	.16	.49
2. Reliability	+	+	+	+	3.38	3.21	2.31	2.14	1.00	.15	.71	.93	.34	.05	.52	.50
3. Validity	+	+	+	+	2.57	2.32	1.47	1.36	.74	.33	.75	1.00	.27	.24	.67	.67
4. Sampling	–	+	+	+	3.10[4]	3.71[1]	2.78	2.18	.09[4]	.30[1]	.96	.91	.11[4]	.10[1]	.24	.62
5. Generalization	+	+	+	+	3.10	2.64	1.15	1.40	.91	.63	.97	.54	.33	.10	.56	.82[1]
6. Theory	+	+	–	+	2.48	2.04[3]	3.42[4]	2.38	.86	.49[3]	.02[1]	.87	.30	.22[3]	.10[4]	.17
11. Usefulness to society	–	–	–	+	2.52[4]	2.11[4]	2.22[1]	1.52	– .36[4]	.12[4]	.32[1]	.54	.18[4]	– .03[4]	.10[1]	– .03
12. News value	+	+	–	+	2.10[3]	2.11[3]	2.25[4]	2.08	.57[3]	.13[3]	– .20[4]	.58	.29[3]	.36[3]	.39[4]	.28
14. Variables' definition	+	+	+	+	3.52	3.36	2.45	2.22	.96	.86	1.00	.93	.21	.04	.31	.55
15. Mathematical model	+	+	–	–	1.81	1.61	1.05[4]	1.00[4]	1.00	.51	±0[4]	±0[4]	.36	– .11	– .18[4]	±0[4]
16. Statistical model	+	+	+	+	1.33	1.32	1.11	1.06	1.00	1.00	1.00	1.00	.37	– .19	– .02	.50
17. Scales	+	+	+	+	2.24	1.93	1.75	1.42	.55	.63	.84	1.00	.32	.14	.48	.62
18. Scale's actuality	+	+	+	+	1.76	1.75	1.53	1.32	.65	.56	.89	1.00	.30	.10	.46	.63
19. Analysis method	+	–	+	+	2.38[3]	2.82[1]	2.40	2.04	.83[3]	.60[3]	.84	.93	.40[3]	– .24[4]	.17	.55
20. Mathematical method	+	+	+	+	2.76	2.71	2.22	1.48	.64	.60	.81	.59	.22	.17	.16	.66
21. Material's size	–	+	+	+	4.14[1]	4.04	2.78	2.76	.62[4]	.08	.74	.86	.32[4]	.50	.27	.54
22. Non-response	+	+	+	+	3.62[3]	4.14[1]	2.31	2.22	.36[3]	.74[4]	.74	.83	.35[3]	.07[1]	.10	.62
23. Fate of hypotheses	+	+	+	+	1.76[3]	2.29[3]	2.78[1]	2.38	.39[3]	– .07[3]	.88[1]	.73	.31[3]	.10[3]	.12[1]	.53
24. Additional information	–	–	–	–	1.38[4]	1.43[4]	1.53	1.20	.57[4]	1.00[4]	.96	1.00	.15[4]	.17[4]	.46	.51[4]
25. References	+	–	–	–	6.48	3.89[4]	4.05[1]	3.26[4]	.62	– .24[4]	– .55[4]	– .25[4]	.37	.16[4]	.52[4]	.11[4]

[1] The mean is higher than the preceding mean.
[2] The mean answers our expectations (should be used for all means without number).
[3] The mean is lower than the following mean.
[4] The value grade has been taken out of the empirical cluster.

Table 53. *Data on the compensation weights of the empirical cluster, summing up four clusters*

	Weights below the median	Weights above
1. Mean too high. Light weights expected.	4	1
2a. Mean all right, importance high. Heavy weights expected.	15	19
2b. Mean all right, importance low. Light weights expected.	12	10
3. Mean too low. Light weights expected.	7	4
4. Value excluded from cluster. Light weights expected.	4	4

We can then compare our expectations of high/low criterion importance with the actual outcome in each sample and then add them together. Table 51 shows the results. Table 52 gives the raw data.

The sum columns certainly validate the expectations as do most of the four samples. The technique to measure criterion importance can be considered valid.

The same technique is used to test the interaction weights and we start with the four possible cases of grade means combinations:

1. If a sample has a mean grade higher than the previous, it indicates that the value is considered important in the sample and that it would be risky to overlook or to substitute with grades of other values. Compensation weight then should be low.

2. If a sample gives a value the expected grade mean, lower than the previous and higher than the following, then the outcome depends on the criterion importance:

a, High criterion importance indicates that the value can be used to compensate other values and so compensation weight should also be high.

b, Low criterion importance indicates that the value cannot be used to compensate other values and then compensation weight should also be low.

3. If a sample gives a value a mean grade lower than the following one, it indicates that the value is paid less attention, which makes it less useful as a compensation and should give it a low compensation weight.

4. If a sample excludes a value from the empirical cluster, it indicates uselessness for compensation purposes and then the compensation weight should be low.

183

Four of the five cases predict low compensation weights. If all five predicted low compensation weights that would make the expectations impossible. Still, four categories out of five expected to give weights below the median, and only one expected to give weights above, do look out of balance. Table 53 shows the results.

The values of the theoretical cluster, their criterion importance and interaction weights

The grade means of the theoretical values are still expected to be highest in the Ph.D. theses, somewhat lower in the M.A. theses, still lower in the articles from *American Sociological Review* and lowest in those from *Acta Sociologica*. The values already studied in the empirical cluster are excluded here in order to avoid repetition. Table 54 shows the data for presence in the cluster, the means of grades, criterion importance, and interaction weights.

We then proceed to the four possible combinations of value means:

1. If a sample gives a theoretical value a grade mean higher than the preceding one, this indicates that the criterion importance should be high.

2. If a sample gives a value the expected grade mean, lower than the preceding one and higher than the following, then the value is given medium importance.

3. If a sample excludes a value from the theoretical cluster, it means that it goes to some other non-empirical cluster, where it should get a similar importance and so a medium criterion importance is expected.

4. If a sample gives a value a grade lower than the following one, this indicates a lower opinion of it and so a low importance is expected.

The data are summed up in Table 55.

Based on the outcome, the criterion importance can be considered valid also for the theoretical cluster.

The next instrument, the interaction weights, and their five possible combinations are presented:

1. If a sample gives a theoretical value a grade mean higher than the preceding one, this indicates that the value can compensate other values and so should have a high compensation weight.

Table 54. *Presence, means of grades, criterion importances and interaction weights in the theoretical cluster of our four samples*

No. Value	Presence in sample				Mean of grade in sample				Criterion importance				Interaction weights			
	Ph.D.	M.A.	Am. Soc. Rev.	Acta	Ph.D.	M.A.	Am. Soc. Rev.	Acta	Ph.D.	M.A.	Am. Soc. Rev.	Acta	Ph.D.	M.A.	Am. Soc. Rev.	Acta
7. Theory construction	+	+	+	+	1.19[3]	1.14[4]	1.15[1]	1.36[1]	-1.00[3]	-1.00[4]	.04[1]	-.40[1]	1.00[3]	1.00[4]	.42[1]	.85[1]
8. Hypothesis construction	+	+	+	+	1.10[4]	1.21[1]	1.15[3]	1.36[1]	-1.00[4]	.18[1]	.04[3]	-.40[1]	1.00[4]	.22[1]	.42[3]	.85[1]
9. Model construction	+	+	+	+	1.10[4]	1.21[1]	1.11[3]	1.24[1]	-1.00[4]	.18[1]	.04[3]	-.40[1]	1.00[4]	.22[1]	.42[3]	.85[1]
10. Variable construction	+	+	+	+	1.19[4]	1.29[1]	1.11[4]	1.12[1]	-1.00[4]	.18[1]	-1.00[4]	.19[1]	1.00[4]	.22[1]	.90[4]	.76[1]
13. School's usefulness	+	-	0	0	1.90[4]	2.04[1]	—	—	.26[4]	.08[1]	—	—	.15[4]	.16[1]	—	—
26. Language	+	-	0	0	3.38[3]	1.18[2]	—	—	.65[3]	.18[2]	—	—	-.12[3]	.49[2]	—	—
27. Number of pages	-	-	+	+	6.48[2]	4.96[2]	2.18[3]	1.76[3]	-.26[2]	-.15[2]	.02[2]	-.01[3]	.15[2]	-.03[2]	.11[3]	.07[3]
28. Title of researcher	0	0	+	+	—	—	2.15[3]	2.88[3]	—	—	.10[3]	.18[3]	—	—	.07[3]	.20[3]
20. Disguise of defects	+	-	+	+	2.67[3]	1.86[2]	1.20[3]	1.04[3]	-.07[3]	-.34[2]	-.28[3]	-.10[3]	.25[3]	-.12[2]	.26[3]	.52[3]

[1] The mean is higher than the preceding mean and so we expect more importance too.
[2] The value is excluded from the theoretical cluster, which probably means that its' importance does not change.
[3] The mean is—as we expect—lower than the preceding and higher than the following. Then we also expect medium importance.
[4] The mean is lower than the following and so we expect lower importance too.

Table 55. *Data on the criterion importance of the theoretical cluster for the four samples*

	Ph.D. Importance		M.A. Importance		Am. Soc. Rev. Importance		Acta Importance		Sum Importance			
	−1.00 ∨	−1.00 ∧	<.18 ∨	>0.17 ∧	0 ∨	0 ∧	−.05 ∨	−.05 ∧	∨	∧	∨	∧
1. We expect an increased importance				4	1	3		1	3	6	3	6
2. Cluster changed, unchanged importance	1		1	2					1	3 ⎫		
3. We expect importance unchanged	1	2			4	1	1	2	6	5 ⎬	7	8
4. We expect a decreased importance	3	1	1		1				5	1	5	1

< indicates values below the median.
> indicates values above the median.

2. If a sample gives a value the expected mean grade, lower than the previous one and higher than the following, then the outcome depends on the criterion importance:

a, High criterion importance indicates that the value is difficult to attain and thus not useful for compensation; therefore a low interaction weight is expected.

b, Low criterion importance indicates that the value is easy to attain but still useful for compensation and so should have a high interaction weight.

Table 56. *Data on the compensation weights of the theoretical cluster, summing up four clusters*

	Weights below the median	Weights above
1. Mean too high. We expect a heavy compensation weight	1	8
2a. Mean all right, importance high. Weight should be light	6	0
2b. Mean all right, importance low. Weight should be heavy	1	4
3. Mean too low. We expect a heavy interaction weight	0	6
4. Values excluded from Cluster. Weight should be light	4	0

3. If a sample gives a value a mean grade lower than the following, it indicates that in the theoretical cluster low grades of this value probably had to be compensated, but also that the value was not very good for compensation purposes. All the same, a high interaction weight is expected.

4. If a sample excludes a value from the theoretical cluster, it probably has some positive correlations with the theoretical values left and so can be expected to have a low weight.

So far only the instruments for measuring the importance of research values have been tested. What have they to say about research values and samples?

In examining the empirical cluster and its 20 values, it is noted that eleven of them belonged to this cluster in all four samples, six in three of them, two in two of them and one turned up only in one sample. There is thus a decided tendency to stick to the cluster.

When comparing the importance and weights in different samples, the median size of them seems to vary from one sample to another. In order to minimize this, we try their rank orders within each sample.

Table 57 gives criterion importance, their rank, interaction weights, and their ranks for all the twenty empirical research values:

The ranks of criterion importance vary far less than the ranks of interaction weights, which can hardly be used in this context. Therefore, high criterion importance is given by all four samples to value 16 (statistical model), 14 (definitions of variables), 18 (actuality of scale). Low criterion importance is granted to 11 (usefulness to society), 12 (news value) and 21 (size of material). The remaining values have mediocre importance.

We then pass to the theoretical cluster and its nine values. Only four of them—7 (theory construction), 8 (hypotheses construction), 9 (model construction) and 10 (variable construction)—belong to this cluster in all four samples, but 29 (disguise of defects) belongs to three of them. There was, however, only one M.A. thesis taking care of these values and only one Ph.D. thesis (written by another researcher). This gives too much influence to chance and so not too much can be expected from the data. However, they are presented in Table 58.

Evidently the four construction values 7–10 tend to form a very fixed kernel of the theoretical cluster, while the remaining values seem to form a fringe. The rank order of criterion importance and interaction weights seem to vary rather little from one sample to another but this

Table 57. *Criterion importance and interaction weights of the values in the empirical cluster of the four samples*

| Value | Criterion importance (criterion: grade sum) | | | | | | | | Interaction weights | | | | | | | |
| | Correlation | | | | Rank order | | | | Mean correlation | | | | Rank order | | | |
	Ph.D.	M.A.	A.S.R.	Acta	Ph.D.	M.A.	A.S.R.	Acta	Ph.D.	M.A.	A.S.R.	Acta	Ph.D.	M.A.	A.S.R.	Acta
1. Presentation																
11. Usefulness of hypothesis	+ .86	+ .60	+ .78	+ .83	5.5	6.5	11	12.5	+ .34	+ .21	+ .16	+ .49	6.5	6	11.5	15
2. Reliability	+1.00	+ .15	+ .71	+ .93	2	13	15	7	+ .34	+ .05	+ .52	+ .50	6.5	14	3	13.5
3. Validity	+ .74	+ .33	+ .75	+1.00	9	11	12	3	+ .27	+ .24	+ .67	+ .67	14	—	1	2
4. Sampling	—	+ .30	+ .96	+ .91	—	12	4.5	9	—	+ .10	+ .24	+ .62	—	10.5	9	6
5. Generalization	+ .91	+ .63	+1.00	+ .54	5	4.5	2	17.5	+ .33	+ .10	+ .56	+ .82	8	10.5	2	1
6. Theory	+ .86	+ .49	—	+ .87	6.5	10	—	10	+ .30	+ .21	—	+ .17	11.5	5	—	17
11. Usefulness to society	—	+ .13	+ .32	+ .54	—	14	16	17.5	—	+ .10	+ .10	- .03	—	2	14.5	18
12. News value	+ .57	—	—	+ .58	13	—	—	16	+ .29	+ .36	—	+ .28	13	—	—	16
14. Variables' definition	+ .96	+ .86	+1.00	+ .93	4	2	2	7	+ .21	+ .34	+ .31	+ .55	15	3	7	8.5
15. Mathematical model	+1.00	+ .51	(+)	(+)	2	9	—	—	+ .36	- .11	(+)	(+)	4	15	—	—
16. Statistical model	+1.00	+1.00	+1.00	+1.00	2	1	2	3	+ .37	- .19	- .02	+ .50	2.5	16	16	13.5
17. Scales	+ .55	+ .63	+ .84	+1.00	1.4	4.5	8.5	3	+ .32	- .14	+ .48	+ .62	9	8	4	6
18. Scales' actuality	+ .55	+ .56	+ .89	+1.00	10	8	6	3	+ .30	+ .10	+ .46	+ .63	11.5	10.5	5.5	4
19. Analysis method	+ .83	—	+ .84	+ .93	8	—	8.5	7	+ .40	—	+ .17	+ .55	1	—	10	8.5
20. Mathematical method	+ .64	+ .60	+ .81	+ .59	11	6.5	10	15	+ .22	+ .17	+ .16	+ .66	15	7	11.5	3
21. Material's size	—	+ .08	+ .74	+ .86	—	15	13.5	11	—	+ .50	+ .27	+ .54	—	1	8	10
22. Non-response	+ .36	+ .74	+ .74	+ .83	16	3	13.5	12.5	+ .35	+ .07	+ .10	+ .62	5	13	14.5	6
23. Fate of hypotheses	+ .39	- .07	+ .88	+ .73	15	16	7	14	+ .31	+ .10	+ .12	+ .53	10	10.5	13	11
24. Additional information	—	—	+ .96	+1.00	—	—	4.5	3	—	—	+ .46	+ .51	—	—	5.5	12
25. References	+ .62	—	—	—	12	—	—	—	+ .37	—	—	—	2.5	—	—	—

Table 58. *Criterion importance and interaction weights of the values in the theoretical cluster of the samples*

No. Value	Criterion importance (criterion grade sum)				Interaction weights			
	Ph.D.	M.A.	Am. Soc. Rev.	Acta	Ph.D.	M.A.	Am. Soc. Rev.	Acta
7. Theory construction	−1.00	−1.00	−.04	−.40	+1.00	+1.00	+.42	+.85
8. Hypothesis construction	−1.00	−.18	−.04	−.40	+1.00	+.22	+.42	+.85
9. Model construction	−1.00	−.18	−.04	−.40	+1.00	−.18	+.42	+.85
10. Variable construction	−1.00	−.13	−1.00	+.19	+1.00	−.18	+.90	+.76
11. Usefulness to society	—	+.12	—	—	—	−.03	—	—
19. Analysis methods	—	+.60	—	—	—	−.24	—	—
27. Number of pages	—	—	+.02	−.01	—	—	+.11	+.07
29. Disguise of defects	−.22	—	−.28	+.10	−.07	—	+.26	+.52

probably is due to the strong ties between the four construction values 7–10, and so has to be disregarded.

The analysis of the theoretical cluster thus is little rewarding in comparison to the study of the empirical cluster, probably because so few theses or reports have paid attention to the theoretical values. There is one last task to perform before we leave our material. An attempt should be made to compare Swedish sociological research patterns with American ones. The most characteristic Swedish sample in our opinion is made up of the 21 Ph.D. theses and the only American sample consists of the articles from the *American Sociological Review,* volume 26. The Swedish Ph.D. theses have to be printed as books and the differences between theses and A.S.R. may be related to the publication form, as well as to the national patterns. The Scandinavian *Acta Sociologica* could be used as a corrective, but the Swedes have no monopoly on this journal.

In general, however, these three samples do not differ very much when the ranks of their empirical research values are compared. There are, however, some exceptions. Value 2 (reliability) seems to be very important in Sweden—rank 2 among the theses, 7 in Acta, but 15 (a very low rank) in A.S.R. Value 23 (the successful outcome of the hypotheses) has a low rank in Sweden—15 in the theses, 14 in Acta, but a much

higher rank, 7, in A.S.R. Value 1 is given a high rank in the Swedish theses, but a low one in A.S.R., as well as in Acta, and so seems to be bound up with book size. Value 5 (generalization of results) is given a very high rank by A.S.R. but a low one in *Acta Sociologica*.

These data suggest that Swedish Ph.D. theses were giving more regard to statistical techniques than American sociologists and as a result have to put on a brave face in front of what happens to their hypotheses and to their chances to generalize their results. The majority of the Swedish values have, however, similar ranks as the American ones. They should, as they have been taken over rather recently.

The conclusions reached look a little meager and probably could have been acquired easier with other techniques. To us, the important point is that we have been able to use the summation theory to study the interaction of scientific values during the research process, where additional values were found to compensate lost planning values. We have tried different ways to measure the importance of these values and got results not at all sensational, rather boring in fact, but indicating that our techniques make sense. Remember, however, that this can be considered a pilot investigation carried out in Sweden and covering the period 1961–66. We are not allowed to generalize our results outside Scandinavia or the 60's. We have not been able to make a good list of the relevant research variables. We have only found that our hypotheses about research work in Sweden did stand an empirical test.

Chapter 10

The summation theory tested on the allocation of resources

We have discussed how researchers allocate their energy and resources to different research values, thereby creating competing clusters of values. Empirical, theoretical, and additional clusters have been studied as they appear in the matrices of intercorrelations between value grades. Can our technique apply to resource allocation which takes place also at the departmental level?

Gunnar Boalt, Herman Lantz, and Erling Ribbing have tried to do so in a book entitled *Resources and Production of University Departments: Sweden and U.S.* Following is a short summary of their results. The theoretical discussion (based on Boalt: *The Sociology of Research,* 1969) went something like this:

A university department has to work out curricula adapted to students as well as to society, give relevant instruction, distribute marks according to students' performance, select the best candidates for graduate work, recruit a good staff, stimulate their teaching, offer them secretarial service, libraries, etc., promote their research, help them to acquire grants, to publish, and eventually make them useful to community and society as experts, advisors, or critics.

Such categories can be considered values that the departments should try to attain or behavior to be measured, i.e., how many students in a department at each level, how many top grades are given, how many M.A. and Ph.D. degrees handed out, how many assistant, associate, and full professors are there, etc. These values often tend to follow one another, hopefully forming clusters, more or less competing for the resources of the university system. What would these clusters look like? Boalt took over an old idea: departments "tend to expand either their production of students or their production of research and few of them succeed in expanding both of them substantially at the same time" (*The Sociology of Research,* 1969, p. 77).

We started with the nine departments of the Social Science faculties at the Swedish universities Stockholm, Uppsala, Lund, Gothenburg, and Umeå. Statistical data on them are seldom available before 1965. We had to concentrate on the actual situation, trying to get a picture of the allocation process and its effects.

The variables used to study the allocation process

All variables, however useful, had to be excluded if a convenient way to measure them could not be found. The 27 variables actually used can be divided into three groups: values pertaining to students, to researchers, and to teachers.

A. Student variables

I. Level of one point (meant to need half a year's study)
1. Number of students new to the department last term.
2. Percentage of new students of all students registered last term in the department.
3. Percentage of students studying for one point receiving one point.
4. Percentage of students, studying for one point, able to get that point in one term.

II. Level of two points (meant to need a full year's study)
5. Number of students having acquired two points last term.
6. Percentage of students registered for two points, who receive these points.
7. Percentage of students, registered at the department, studying for two points.
8. Percentage of students studying for two points able to get them in one year.

III. Level of three or four points (meant to need 1 1/2 and 2 year's study respectively)
9. Number of students having acquired three or four points last term.
10. Percentage of students, registered at the department, studying for three of four points.
11. Percentage of students, registered at the department, studying for three points.

B. Recruitment and performance of the researcher

IV. Economic resources of the department.
  12. Staff salary sum per student. Total salary divided with total student number.

V. Level of studies for M.A.[1]
  13. Number of graduate students registered for M.A. studies at the department.
  14. Percentage of students registered at the department having received a state stipend for M.A.

VI. Level of M.A. studying for Ph.D.[2]
  15. Number of M.A. degrees last year in relation to all students registered at the department.
  16. Number of M.A.'s registered at the department for Ph.D. studies.
  17. Percentage of women among those given M.A. degree at the department.
  18. Percentage of doctoral stipends among all students registered at the department.

VII. Ph.D. level.
  19. Number of dissertations in the department.
  20. Percentage of dissertations among all registered students.
  21. Average mark of the dissertations at the department.

C. Teachers at the department

VIII. Total number of teachers and staff
  22. Number of teachers in relation to all registered students.

IX. Teachers with a commission
  23. Percentage of commissioned teachers who have a Ph.D. with honors.
  24. Number of posts, occupied by Ph.D.'s with honors, in relation to all registered students.
  25. Number of posts with seats in the faculty, in relation to all registered students.

X. Remaining data about the higher staff
  26. Rank of chairman according to his assignments to the state.
  27. Number of full, associate and assistant professors with income above $12 000.

---

[1] This degree, in Sweden labeled fil. lic. is higher than the American M.A. and more close to the American Ph.D.

[2] The Swedish Doctor's Degree is of a higher standard than the American Ph.D.

Table 59. *Rank correlations between 27 department variables from 9 departments in the social science faculty at Stockholm University*

Variables	1	5	7	27	21	23	26	2	3	4	6	8
1. Number of new, registered students	■	+.57	+.40	+.05	+.38	+.42	+.10	+.08	−.23	−.15	−.28	−.15
5. Number of students receiving 2 points		■	+.62	+.17	−.05	+.13	−.19	−.63	−.25	−.33	+.12	+.02
7. Percent students studying for 2 points			■	+.30	+.17	+.04	−.17	−.90	−.33	−.43	−.05	−.13
27. Number of professors having income above 12 000				■	−.33	−.48	+.38	+.03	−.59	−.25	−.48	−.47
21. Average mark of dissertations					■	+.90	+.43	−.12	+.12	−.14	−.29	−.19
23. Percent commissioned teachers with Ph.D.honors						■	+.08	−.03	+.41	+.20	+.14	+.18
26. Rank of chairman acc. to state assignments							■	+.60	+.02	+.15	−.29	−.05
2. Percent new students of all registered								■	+.13	+.45	−.18	−.20
3. Percent students working for 1 point, who receive it									■	+.92	+.80	+.87
4. Percent students for 1 point, receiving it in 1 term										■	+.81	+.80
6. Percent students working for 2 points, who receive it											■	+.95
8. Percent students working for 2 points, receiving it in 1 year												■
9. Number of students having received 3 or 4 points last term												
10. Percent students working for 3 or 4 points												
11. Percent students working for 3 points												
12. Staff salary per student												
13. Number of students registered for M.A. work												
14. Percent of students with stipend for M.A. studies												
15. M.A. degrees in relation to all registered students												
16. Number of M.A:s registered for Ph.D. studies												
17. Percent of women among M.A. degrees 1962–68												
18. Percent of students with stipend for Ph.D. studies												
19. Number of dissertations 1967–68												
20. Percent of dissertations among registered students												
22. Teachers in relation to number of students												
24. Posts occupied by Ph.D. honors												
25. Posts in the faculty												

Most of these variables could be measured for the academic year 1967–68, but for instance the percentages of students receiving their planned point had to be computed back for the academic year 1965–66.

There are some weaknesses in this set of variables. First, several of them cannot be ascertained for the University of Umeå, as it did not get a Social Science faculty until 1965. Second, some of the students' values are constructed in such a way that they cannot form a cluster. Value 2 (percent new students), value 7 (percent students studying for 2 points), and value 10 (percent students working for 3 or 4 points) make up 100 %. If one of them increases, one or two of the others has to decrease.

The interaction between the departmental values

A separate study of each university must be made so that the interaction at the university level can be seen, even though they never have

9	10	11	12	13	14	15	16	17	18	19	20	22	24	25	Weight
−.27	−.05	−.38	−.88	−.03	−.85	−.10	−.01	+.07	−.80	+.02	−.70	−.73	−.73	−.50	.26
−.18	+.05	−.33	−.52	−.08	−.73	−.32	−.20	−.43	−.87	−.12	−.72	−.50	−.83	−.40	.32
−.48	+.20	−.28	−.40	−.42	−.72	−.42	−.51	−.68	−.62	−.36	−.60	−.23	−.45	−.80	.37
−.78	−.58	−.30	−.18	−.83	−.22	−.82	−.60	−.36	−.28	−.23	−.05	−.27	−.12	−.13	.38
−.14	+.10	−.10	−.05	+.33	−.07	+.26	+.37	+.26	+.10	−.21	−.17	−.05	+.31	+.10	−.04
+.27	+.08	−.05	−.23	+.65	−.07	+.55	+.64	+.36	−.03	+.23	−.29	−.18	+.08	+.11	−.03
−.16	−.05	+.40	+.19	−.14	+.21	−.02	+.28	+.82	+.33	−.05	+.40	+.33	+.47	+.33	−.03
+.20	−.50	+.15	+.12	+.29	+.58	+.18	+.38	+.71	+.49	+.41	+.40	.00	+.40	+.68	.36
+.73	+.15	+.58	+.18	+.78	+.40	+.90	+.88	+.57	+.24	+.83	+.65	+.25	+.22	+.07	.35
+.60	−.10	+.61	+.06	+.60	+.40	+.70	+.79	+.57	+.18	+.94	+.75	+.13	+.15	+.08	.29
+.78	+.40	+.53	+.28	+.60	+.17	+.72	+.59	+.14	+.02	+.64	+.37	+.35	−.08	−.17	.17
+.78	+.38	+.60	+.18	+.59	+.12	+.77	+.72	+.54	+.01	+.73	+.43	+.33	−.08	−.22	.18
■	+.43	+.43	+.42	+.78	+.37	+.89	+.75	+.39	+.35	+.56	+.28	+.40	+.15	+.22	.43
	■	+.50	+.43	+.20	−.12	+.35	+.07	+.29	+.07	−.22	−.13	+.60	−.10	−.38	.10
		■	+.52	+.37	+.47	+.50	+.33	+.57	+.30	+.37	+.67	+.62	+.15	+.00	.32
			■	+.12	+.75	+.30	+.07	+.07	+.84	+.19	+.55	+.92	+.67	+.46	.25
				■	+.33	+.90	+.84	+.36	+.16	+.62	+.28	+.03	+.07	+.28	.39
					■	+.40	+.30	+.18	+.84	+.22	+.83	+.55	+.78	+.75	.63
						■	+.88	+.61	+.38	+.27	+.48	+.34	+.29	+.15	.44
							■	+.90	+.21	+.74	+.48	+.13	+.17	+.25	.33
								■	+.25	+.38	+.57	+.43	+.60	+.11	.35
									■	−.05	+.70	+.68	+.94	+.60	.64
										■	+.47	−.18	+.02	+.03	.17
											■	+.53	+.65	+.42	.52
												■	+.60	+.15	.43
													■	+.53	.53

more than nine different departments. If the interaction of the departmental values is to be studied, using correlations between them, we will have only nine cases for each correlation. It would be better to compute them as rank correlations. We have done so and produce as examples of the results the matrices from the Social Science faculties of Stockholm University and Uppsala University (Tables 59 and 60). The other universities show the same pattern. This pattern is shown in the matrix from Stockholm. It has two clearcut clusters. The first includes four values: 1 (number of new students), 5 (number of students receiving 2 points −one full year), 7 (per cent students studying for 2 points), and 27 (number of professors having income above $12 000). The second cluster contains all the remaining 23 values.

The first cluster is considered to be the expected teaching cluster, stressing the number of students, trying to attract large numbers of them (value 1), developing curricula adapted to their interests thereby getting a high percent of students working for a full year at the depart-

Table 60. *Rank correlations between 26 department variables from 9 social science departments at Uppsala University*

Variables	1	3	5	7	11	23	26	2	4	6
1. Number of new, registered students	■	+.94	+.32	+.18	+.47	+.49	+.24	−.23	+.03	−.10
3. Per cent students working for 1 point, who receive it		■	+.60	+.09	+.77	+.60	−.01	−.54	+.60	+.43
5. Number of students working for 2 points, who receive it			■	+.32	+.52	+.55	+.67	−.07	−.23	−.42
7. Per cent students working for 2 points				■	+.29	.00	+.81	−.02	−.36	−.21
11. Per cent students working for 3 points					■	+.53	+.39	+.32	+.50	+.07
23. Per cent commissioned teachers with Ph.D. honors						■	+.48	−.14	+.26	+.27
26. Rank of chairman according to state assignments							■	+.33	−.10	−.29
2. Per cent new students of all registered								■	+.13	−.50
4. Per cent students for 1 point, receiving it in 1 term									■	+.68
6. Per cent students working for 2 points, who receive it										■
8. Per cent students for 2 points, receiving them in 1 year										
9. Number of students having received 3 or 4 point, last term										
10. Per cent students working for 3 or 4 points										
12. Staff salary per student										
13. Number of students registered for M.A. work										
14. Per cent of students with stipend for M.A. studies										
15. M.A. degrees in relation to all students										
16. Number of M.A:s registered for Ph.D. studies										
17. Per cent woman among M.A. degree 1962–68										
18. Per cent of students with stipend for Ph.D. studies										
19. Number of dissertations 1967–68 (doctoral)										
20. Per cent of dissertations among registered students										
21. Average mark of dissertation										
22. Teachers in relation to number of students										
24. Posts occupied by Ph.D. honors										
25. Posts in the faculty										

ment (value 7), as well as a high percent able to acquire these two points (value 5) and eventually present their professors with splendid chances to use the popularity of their subject for their own economic advantage (value 27).

The second cluster is identified with the expected research cluster. Three values (21, 23, and 26) do not quite fit in, but the remaining 20 variables form a closely knit core, the correlations between them high and the correlations with the values of the first cluster negative in 71 out of 80 cases.

If we turn to the Social Science faculty at Uppsala, value 1 (number of new students), together with value 3 (percent students for 1 point who receive it), 5 (number of students working for 2 points and receiving them), 7 (percent students working for 2 points), 11 (percent students working for 3 points), 23 (percent commissioned teachers with Ph.D. honors) and 26 (rank of chairman) form the first cluster, stressing

8	9	10	12	13	14	15	16	17	18	19	20	21	22	24	25	Upps. weight	Sthlm weights
+.42	+.15	+.10	−.68	+.10	−.90	−.59	−.08	−.02	−.83	+.07	−.60	−.32	−.48	−.83	−.83	+.30	+.19
+.77	+.31	+.10	−.71	+.66	−.60	−.09	+.31	+.37	−.54	+.37	−.26	−.63	−.71	−.83	−.66	−.04	−.61
.00	−.07	+.05	−.63	+.08	−.28	−.42	−.43	−.23	−.43	−.43	−.72	+.17	−.58	−.37	−.27	+.28	+.13
−.07	−.79	−.60	−.39	−.36	−.02	−.86	−.78	−.62	−.57	−.79	−.79	−.33	+.71	−.46	−.64	+.45	+.30
+.37	+.14	−.17	−.37	+.20	−.42	−.12	+.02	+.31	−.50	+.09	−.23	−.05	−.20	−.40	−.63	+.05	−.43
+.60	+.61	+.63	−.25	+.43	−.32	−.15	+.29	−.13	+.16	+.33	−.25	+.07	−.49	−.24	−.30	−.07	−.35
+.07	−.40	−.29	−.31	−.38	−.48	−.57	−.48	−.50	−.60	+.15	+.50	+.23	+.19	−.24	−.48	+.20	−.57
−.20	−.25	−.43	+.10	−.58	+.05	+.10	−.34	+.05	−.18	+.15	+.27	+.68	+.50	+.23	+.33	+.05	+.11
+.85	+.37	+.07	+.52	+.27	+.15	+.48	+.72	+.45	+.02	+.31	+.33	−.05	−.17	+.22	−.05	−.04	+.19
+.68	+.40	+.36	+.58	+.67	+.33	+.35	+.79	+.36	+.40	+.15	+.22	−.35	−.15	+.25	+.22	+.03	+.24
■	+.43	+.21	+.40	+.40	−.25	+.10	+.67	+.19	−.27	+.27	.00	−.32	−.03	−.17	−.35	−.12	−.12
	■	+.97	+.04	+.70	+.11	+.40	+.76	+.39	+.17	+.78	+.43	−.01	−.51	+.10	+.15	+.01	+.18
		■	+.05	+.69	+.42	+.29	+.60	+.02	+.21	+.69	+.29	+.11	−.13	+.11	+.33	+.03	+.15
			■	−.02	+.72	+.67	+.52	+.12	+.62	+.12	+.60	+.19	+.62	+.80	+.62	+.48	+.57
				■	+.13	+.20	+.63	+.54	+.38	.42	+.20	−.35	−.57	−.05	+.05	−.04	+.06
					■	+.82	+.32	+.29	+.87	−.02	+.58	+.46	+.20	+.92	+.93	+.43	+.40
						■	+.47	+.43	+.72	+.37	+.83	+.40	+.27	+.85	+.72	+.40	+.62
							■	+.46	+.41	+.59	+.58	−.26	−.06	+.34	+.30	+.16	+.43
								■	+.35	+.35	+.42	−.09	−.23	+.05	+.06	+.12	+.29
									■	+.15	+.68	−.01	+.18	+.77	+.80	+.46	+.61
										■	+.69	−.03	−.04	+.11	−.06	+.03	+.38
											■	+.17	+.40	+.68	+.48	+.34	+.28
												■	+.06	+.46	+.46	+.12	+.16
													■	+.45	+.10	+.29	+.59
														■	+.87	+.50	+.58
															■		+.58

teaching. Three of the four values from the teaching cluster in Stockholm (1, 5, and 7) reappear in Uppsala; but then in Uppsala, new values are added—two from the teachers' values (23 and 26) suggesting that good teachers might attract many students.

The teaching cluster in Uppsala has 20 intercorrelations out of 21 positive, the research cluster has 136 out of 180. The correlations of teaching values with research values should be negative and are negative in 88 cases out of 114.

The remaining universities give similar data and the hypotheses about the different clusters (one labeled teaching and another labeled research) as tested are not confuted by Swedish data.

This, however, does not say much about the allocation problem within the universities and this is the next area to be studied to find out what the data indicate.

197

The allocation of resources to competing departments

Some departments tend to stress teaching and others research. How does their orientation affect their resources? Up to a point a preliminary answer is given by the fact that our measures of resources are all included in the research cluster. The higher authorities thus seem to stack their money on research, but how clearcut is the pattern? Three variables are used as crude measures of resources:

Value 12. Staff salary per student.
Value 22. Number of teachers in relation to number of students.
Value 25. Posts in faculty in relation to number of students.

The best measure of teaching orientation is certainly value 1 (number of students) as it always is a part of the teaching clusters. We can find out the rewards of teaching by finding out the correlations between value 1 on the one hand, and resource values 12, 22, and 25 on the other (Table 61).

The departments with many new students tend to get lower salaries, fewer teachers, or fewer higher staff positions, than the departments with lower numbers of new students (those not oriented toward teaching). However, this does not show that they are deprived resources. The mechanisms for allocating resources are rather complicated and we should take into account at least four:

1. Departments unable to produce good research or secure good resources often go in for teaching. This way an attractive program can be made up in a short time, while it takes many years to create an efficient research staff. Resourceless departments thus stress teaching.

2. The government probably has a special need for economists and statisticians and thus allocates more resources to these departments, stressing research.

Table 61.

Resource variable	Correlation with variable 1 in					
	Stock-holm	Uppsala	Lund	Gothen-burg	Umeå	Mean
12. Staff salary per student	−.88	−.68	−.68	−.93	−.95	−.82
22. Teachers in rel. to students	−.73	−.48	−.45	−.80	−.90	−.66
25. Faculty posts in rel. to students	−.50	−.83	−.82	−.67	−.82	−.73

Table 62. *Correlations between resource variables 12 and 25 and research output values 13, 16, 19, 23*

	Stock-holm	Uppsala	Lund	Gothen-burg	Umeå	Mean
Variables correlated with						
12. Staff Salary						
13. Number of students working for M.A.	+.12	−.02	−.15	+.52	+.03	+.10
16. Number of M.A.'s working for Ph.D.	+.07	+.52	+.35	+.57	+.01	+.30
19. Number of Ph.D. dissertations	−.19	+.12	+.21	+.20	—	+.08
23. Percent commissioned teachers with Ph.D. honors	−.23	−.25	−.14	+.37	+.50	+.05
Variables correlated with						
25. (Posts in the Faculty)						
13. Number of students working for M.A.	+.28	−.04	−.23	+.32	−.05	+.05
16. Number of M.A.'s working for Ph.D.	+.25	+.16	+.62	+.31	+.14	+.30
19. Number of Ph.D. dissertations	+.03	+.03	+.75	+.06	—	+.22
23. Percent commissioned teachers with Ph.D. honors	+.11	−.30	−.05	+.79	+.65	+.24

3. The psychology departments in Sweden accept only a limited low number of students. They then get good resources, as these are measured by our values. They have few students and they stress research.

4. Should the government be willing to allocate more resources to a very successful department, this department certainly was attractive to students before it came to the attention of the authorities. Resources cannot come instantly, but students can. Rapidly changing or expanding departments thus are victims of the allocation lag.

These four mechanisms seem relevant, but even so we have to recognize that departments oriented toward research are allocated more resources. What effect has this allocation policy on research? To study this problem, we relate two resource variables (12 and 25) with four research production values (13, 16, 19, and 23). The correlations are given in Table 62.

The majority of correlations, 27 out of 38, are positive but seldom strong. It seems then as if the allocation policy used on the whole had a reasonable stimulating effect on research-oriented departments.

On the other hand, it must be pointed out that the allocation policy tends to maintain the status quo research output. The departments producing research are rewarded with resources and those unable to

produce do not receive the resources they need for the creation of research teams, etc. The allocation policy may be right, but it should be carefully investigated and its effects studied. This, however, is of little concern to American readers.

The allocation of resources to competing universities

The different departments within each university have been compared and now we turn the table in order to compare the different universities within each Social Science faculty. They include: business administration, economic geography, economics, education, psychology, sociology, statistics, and political science.

It's easy to make the corresponding tables but difficult to predict their outcome. The University of Umeå, however, gives comparatively few data – the Social Science faculty there was organized in 1965 – and so it is excluded from the prediction discussion. Concentration is on the universities of Stockholm, Uppsala, Lund, and Gothenburg, in size order. Size is an important aspect for predicting other aspects of size, in our case such variables as:

Value 1. Number of new registered students.
Value 5. Number of students receiving 2 points.
Value 9. Number of students having received 3 or 4 points.
Value 13. Number of students registered for M.A. work.
Value 16. Number of M.A.'s registered for Ph.D. work.
Value 19. Number of dissertations 1967–68.

All these numbers are expected to be highest in Stockholm, then in Uppsala, Lund, and lowest in Gothenburg. This we call the macro pattern.

How are the remaining variables to be predicted? We could try to stress the negative effects of size: large departments lose contacts, teachers are drowned by students, etc. Value 3 (percent students working for 1 point or receiving 1 point) would be expected to show the highest percent in Gothenburg, lower in Lund, Uppsala, and lowest in Stockholm. We call this the micro pattern.

An alternative view is to stress the traditions of the Swedish universities. Uppsala is an old university, created in medieval times, and Lund is nearly 300 years old, while the universities at Stockholm and Gothenburg were created rather recently. These two new universities are situa-

Table 63. *Output data in the departments of sociology*

Variables	Stock-holm	Upp-sala	Lund	Gothen-burg	Umeå	Pat-tern
1. Number of students	1 987	1 531	1 288	969	416	mac
2. Percent new students	53	46	51	57	56	und
3. Percent students working for 1 point who receive it	39	40	26	31	100	—
4. Percent students working for 1 point who receive it within 1 term	26	18	10	18	—	und
5. Number receiving 2 points	141	140	126	51	0	mac
6. Percent students working for 2 points who receive it	23	27	30	27	—	tra
7. Percent students working for 2 points	29	34	37	28	29	tra
8. Percent students working for 2 points who receive it within 2 terms	16	12	18	18	—	—
9. Number receiving 3–4 points	10	6	7	4	0	—
10. Percent working for 3–4 points who receive it	10.6	6.2	4.4	8.9	—	und
11. Percent working for 3–4 points	3.5	5.7	10.7	4.8	11	tra
12. Staff salary per student	67	82	89	58		tra
13. Number of registered for M.A. studies	23	34	31	12	5	tra
14. Percent students with state stipend for M.A. studies	0.1	1.4	0.6	0.6		tra
15. Percent M.A. degrees	0.90	0.85	0.70	0		mac
16. Number registered for Ph.D. studies	16	8	9	3	1	—
17. Percent women among M.A. degrees	35.3	23.1	33.3	—		—
18. Percent students with state stipend for Ph.D. studies	0.1	0.3	0.2	0.1		tra
19. Number of dissertations	7	1	1	1	2	mac or und
20. Percent dissertations	0.35	0.07	0.01	0.21		und
21. Average mark of dissertations	2.14	2.00	2.00	2.00		mac or und
22. Percent teachers	1.4	1.5	2.4	2.0		—
23. Number of commissioned teachers	3.0	4.0	3.5	2.0		tra
24. Percent Ph.D. honors	0.15	0.26	0.47	0.21		tra
25. Percent posts in faculty	0.25	0.20	0.39	0.21	0.48	—

ted in the two largest cities in Sweden, which may explain their creation. Uppsala and Lund both are situated in cities of more moderate size, up to a point still dominated by their universities. Traditionally, Uppsala and Lund were the important universities having priorities of many kinds. Traditional strength would give a rank order of 1 to Uppsala and Lund and 2 to Stockholm and Gothenburg;–the tradition pattern. But the list of values contains some doubtful items, not very attractive to venerable European universities, for instance, value 3 (percent students

Table 64. *Patterns of sequence for numbers of students on six levels in nine departments, all represented at four universities.* (*Macro pattern*)

	Economic History	Business Admin.	Economic Geography	Economics	Education	Psychology	Sociology	Statistic	Political Science
1. Number of new registered students	tra	mac	und	—	—	—	mac	—	—
5. Number of students receiving 2 points	tra	mac	—	mac	—	und	mac	mac	tra
9. Number of students receiving 3–4 points	—	mic	—	tra	—	—	—	—	—
13. Number of students in M.A. program	—	tra	—	mac	—	—	tra	mac	mac
16. Number of students in Ph.D. program	tra	tra	—	und	—	mac	—	—	tra
19. Number of dissertations	tra	tra	mac	—	mac	—	mac	tra	tra

working for 1 point, half-year). A high percent here automatically brings down value 7, the percent working longer time in a department. Priority should evidently be given to values like 7, not to values like 2, 3, 4, 6, 8, and 17—all of them pertaining to percent data competing with more desirable alternatives. Value 17, for instance, is the percent women among M.A. graduates, a good example on what we call the

Table 65. *Patterns of sequence for nine variables expected to be negatively influenced by the size factor* (*micro pattern*)

	Economic History	Business Admin.	Economic Geography	Economics	Education	Psychology	Sociology	Statistic	Political Science
3. Percent students receiving 1 point	—	—	und	und	und	—	—	tra	und
4. Percent students receiving 1 point in 1 term	tra	—	und	und	und	und	und	tra	und
6. Percent students receiving 2 points	tra	—	und	mac	und	und	tra	—	tra
8. Percent students receiving 2 points in 2 terms	tra	—	und	mac	und	und	—	tra	—
12. Staff salary per student	—	tra	tra	tra	mac	—	tra	—	—
14. Percent students with stipends M.A. program	—	tra	tra	tra	—	—	tra	—	tra
17. Percent women among M.A. degrees	mic	—	mac	—	—	und	—	und	mac
18. Percent students with stipends Ph.D. program	tra	tra	tra	—	—	mac	tra	—	tra
21. Average mark of dissertations	tra	tra	—	—	—	und	mac	—	und

Table 66. *Patterns of sequence for thirteen variables expected to be positively influenced by the tradition factor* (*tradition pattern*)

	Economic History	Business Admin.	Economic Geography	Economics	Education	Psychology	Sociology	Statistic	Political Science
7. Percent students studying for 2 points	—	mac	und	und	—	tra	tra	—	tra
10. Percent students studying for 3–4 points	—	mic	und	—	—	—	und	—	—
11. Percent students studying for 3 points	tra	mic	—	—	und	tra	tra	und	tra
12. Staff salary per student	—	tra	tra	tra	mac	—	tra	—	—
14. Percent students with stipends M.A. program	—	tra	tra	tra	—	—	tra	—	tra
15. Percent M.A. degrees among all students	tra	tra	tra	tra	und	—	mac	—	tra
18. Percent students with stipends Ph.D. program	tra	tra	tra	—	—	mac	tra	—	tra
20. Percent dissertations	—	tra	tra	—	mac	—	und	tra	—
21. Average mark of dissertations	tra	tra	—	—	—	und	mac	—	und
22. Teachers in relation to students	—	—	—	—	—	—	—	—	—
23. Percent commissioned teachers with Ph.D. honors	tra	tra	tra	—	tra	tra	tra	tra	tra
24. Posts occupied by Ph.D. honors	tra	tra	tra	tra	tra	und	tra	—	—
25. Posts in faculty in relation to students	—	tra	tra	tra	—	—	—	und	tra

undesirable pattern. The discussion of the hypotheses is postponed until they can be tested.

The data consist of output results in the departments, the results given for each type of department, and each output value at each university. We thus get nine large tables and present just one, covering the sociological departments (generally showing data for 1967–68). The last column pertains to the four possible patterns for ranking the universities (Table 63).

Nine such tables allow us to test the following hypotheses:

1. Size of the social science faculty will dominate numerical aspects on output. This is called a *macro* pattern, and is defined as the cases where Stockholm output is not below Uppsala, Uppsala output not below Lund, and Gothenburg not above any of the three others. This pattern is expected to be common among the values of numbers (Table 64).

Table 67. *Patterns of sequence for six variables expected to be negatively influenced by the tradition factor (undersirable pattern)*

	Economic History	Business Admin.	Economic Geography	Eco-nomics	Edu-cation	Psych-ology	Soci-ology	Stat-istics	Political Science
2. Percent new students of all registered	und	und	—	—	tra	—	und	—	und
3. Percent students receiving 1 point	—	—	und	und	und	—	—	tra	und
4. Percent students receiving 1 point in 1 term	tra	—	und	und	und	und	und	tra	und
6. Percent students receiving 2 points	tra	—	und	—	und	und	tra	—	tra
8. Percent students receiving 2 points in 2 terms	tra	—	und	—	und	und	—	tra	—
17. Percent women among M.A. graduates	mic	—	und	—	—	und	—	und	mac

The size pattern actually does dominate in these cases (13 out of 30), although the small student number in economic history at Stockholm certainly does not fit the expectations.

2. Small departments should stimulate contacts and communication and this should show among the variables 3, 4, 6, 8, 12, 14, 17, 18, and 21. Here the *micro* pattern is expected. Stockholm should not be above Uppsala, Uppsala not above Lund, and Lund not above Gothenburg. Out of 81 cases, only one produced the micro pattern, thus voiding hypothesis (Table 65).

3. Uppsala and Lund have more status than the newer universities at Stockholm and Gothenburg. The former alumni of the old universities tend to dominate among the civil servants handling university affairs and so they may not only take better care of their students, their students may take better care of them. It is expected that this university tradition is an advantage for values 7, 10, 11, 12, 14, 15, 18, 20, 21, 22, 23, and 24. This tradition pattern is defined as the output of Uppsala or Lund will not be below the output of Stockholm or Gothenburg (Table 66).

The table comes out with so many cases of the tradition pattern that the third hypothesis cannot be confuted.

4. The values Uppsala and Lund can be expected to avoid—values pertaining to high percent of students at low levels or of women at high levels—are called the *undesirable* pattern and it is defined as the outputs of Stockholm or Gothenburg will not be below the output of Uppsala

and Lund. This pattern is expected to hold true for the remaining six values 2, 3, 4, 6, 8, and 17 (Table 67).

The undesirable pattern (undes.) certainly dominates the table and the fourth hypothesis cannot be confuted.

This means then that the numbers of students tend to be highest in Stockholm, but that resources tend to go to the traditional universities of Uppsala and Lund. Up to a point this can be explained as a lag, but the impression is that the handicap of the new universities hardly is less now than ten years ago.

Here we stop. We have demonstrated that the summation theory can be used to study the allocation process at the universities. Departments oriented toward research tend to get more resources than those oriented toward teaching. Old and traditional universities tend to be allocated more resources than new universities. However, only the social science departments at the universities of Stockholm, Uppsala, Lund, and Gothenburg during the period 1967–68 have been studied. Erling Ribbing has found similar tendencies for the faculties of humanities at these universities, but the results can hardly be generalized outside Sweden.

Appendix 1

Swedish youth culture: an analysis of writings 1965–1970

by Herman Lantz, Janice Rienerth, and Marta Herlin

In an earlier section of this book we alluded to the apparent concern of Swedish society for problems of youth culture. In this appendix, the writers wish to report their results of a survey of the literature made of the period 1965–1970. The survey was designed to ascertain the extent of interest in Sweden for the problems of Youth Culture in their society. Swedish society is well equipped to become involved in such concerns. For example, Swedish behavioral science is highly empirical and quantitative. All of the internal requirements for scientific work are present. Considerable technical talent and skill are available. Excellent statistical training for measurement to test and analyze data is also present. While the level of scientific development can represent a positive element in the concern for Youth Culture, an additional factor has to do with the Swedish commitment to the concept of human and social welfare; this would suggest a sensitivity to ongoing problems in the society. From the negative point of view, however, there is considerable reluctance on the part of Swedish people to interfere with the private conduct and behavior of their citizens. There is much value placed on privacy in Swedish society. While a general European trait, Swedish people are neither outgoing or easy to get to know. Their personal lives are their own concerns. Thus, we have a context in which considerable permissiveness appears to be present and considerable reluctance to interfere with behavior which is not socially damaging seems to be the norm. How does such an attitude influence studies regarding youth culture in Sweden?

Procedure

In order to deal with the extent of interest in youth culture in Sweden, publications for ages 15–25 were examined for the period 1965–1970.

We examined sources from the mass media such as weeklies and magazines and we also looked at both professional and semi-professional sources. Professional sources included scientific sociological reports prepared by qualified academic and research personnel designed primarily for a professional audience, semi-professional sources represented other scientific reports, educational, psychological or economic. In order to help with the collection of the data, a schedule was prepared. A copy of the schedule is included with this paper. An inspection of the schedule will show that it was designed to tabulate the source of the material, the content, the methodology, and the significance of the contribution. The examination was laborious, slow and very demanding. Sources on this topic are spread around – not easily located in any central place. In examining these materials for the period in question, one is impressed by several things. First, the data revealed a range of activities including general emancipation of youth, dress, sexual behavior, abortion, drugs, social protest, problems of adaptation, relationship of youth to society, leisure time, traffic accidents, criminal behavior, political behavior, family, education, communication, religion, housing and economic problems. For the period, there was a total of 274 articles in all sources; 100 articles came from professional sources, 64 from semi-professional sources and 110 from mass media. Approximately 50 % of the bigger newspapers were examined. This examination was augmented by using "clipping records." In absolute numbers, the mass-media shows slightly more interest. If one combines both professional and semi-professional sources, this ratio changes. Secondly, since we have no base line in regard to the amount of attention which Swedish youth culture received in earlier periods, we cannot ascertain whether the number 274 indicates an increase or decrease in the amount of space devoted to this topic. Nevertheless, if one remembers that the size and population of Sweden is comparable to an individual state in the United States, such productivity on matters affecting youth culture is rather high.

Thirdly, the trend with respect to sources shows the frequency of the professional and semi-professional articles to be lowest in 1966, 1967 (5, 6 and 6,5) and highest in 1969 and 1970 (38, 19 and 20, 19). Mass media articles are not uniform, but are relatively high (27, 27, 21) in 1968, 1969, and 1970. The high figures for professional and semi-professional sources might suggest the start of a major interest on the part of these groups. However, the fact that all sectors, professional, semi-professional and mass media sources, are implicated in reporting on youth culture suggests that such concern may be rather widely spread

with all sources contributing to the general interest. As one might expect, the most statistical articles are in professional sociological journals; this seems to decrease as one moves to the other sources. Subjects dealing with emancipation of youth, drugs, criminality and violence are equally split on statistical and non-statistical articles. Others such as sex, abortion, adaptation, leisure time, professions, politics, education and certain miscellaneous categories have more statistical articles. Others, such as social system, demonstrations and dress, are mostly nonstatistical. This difference is inclined to be more an indication of where professional interests appear to be since theirs are the most consistently statistical. The highest number of statistical articles appeared in 1969 and the highest number of non-statistical articles in 1966. There appears to be an increase in statistical articles, and a corresponding decrease in non-statistical articles, suggesting once more the possibility that serious attention is beginning to emerge. The majority of the articles were rated as either informative or somewhat informative. Few cases fell into the highly informative or uninformative categories. This could indicate that much of the information, while of interest and value, has not opened up wholly new dimensions that are not in some respects known, at least by the professional.

Fourthly, in 1965 the highest percentage of articles were concerned with the social system, in 1966 with criminality and violence, in 1967, 1968, 1969 with emancipation of youth and in 1970 with the social system. Over time, some topics such as dress, traffic accidents and some miscellaneous topics had only momentary interest; other topics were popular. As time progressed, the range of topics broadened. In professional sociological sources, the five highest number of articles are on emancipation of youth (34), social system (24), drugs (16), sex and abortion (14), and adaptation (10). In semi-professional sources, the range is social system (18), adaptation (14), emancipation of youth (10), criminal behavior (9), and leisure time (6). For the mass media, the range is emancipation of youth (44), social system (26), criminal activity (15), drugs (10), sex and abortion (6). Emancipation of youth (90) and social system (68) have held up as concerns throughout the period; the concern for drugs (30) has a less consistent pattern with a peak year of 18 in 1969, but decreased to 4 in 1970. Criminal behavior and violence (32) shows an uneven pattern although the increase in 1969 and 1970 of 8 and 11 articles may show a new trend.

Conclusions

At the outset, we must recognize that we have assessed the literature for only a brief period of time. We cannot assess any long-term trends; one could conclude more if we knew about publications for earlier periods. One must also keep in mind that publications do not necessarily provide us with a total picture of social interest and concern. We have an insufficient indication of possible changes in interests. Nevertheless, it is important to note that the findings of this report cover virtually all groups of readers in Swedish society. Given the very high rate of literacy in Sweden, one can conclude that no section of the population, regardless of social position or status, remains unaware of what is taking place among Swedish youth. While one would normally expect the popular mass media sources to remain in touch with questions concerning youth, it is of interest that professional interest is also present. Thus, there is one expression of professional involvement with the ongoing problems of the society. How to deal with the problems of Swedish youth culture represents another problem. Sweden is a society undergoing a number of transformations in its social life. This is especially the case in regard to the family, as noted elsewhere in this book. Thus, one finds a situation in which important changes are taking place with regard to *emancipation of youth* and in the relation of youth to the broader society, the most frequently mentioned items. The relationship of these problems to the family is not at all clear. Certainly the problems are greater, that is while the problems of Swedish youth represent the larger problems of Swedish society, it may also be correct to say that in so far as the family is itself going through change, it may not be able to deal with changes among the youth in any orderly way. Moreover, it would appear that in so far as one finds ongoing problems both within the family and significant changes among the youth, effects on other roles, research careers and other would seem to be present. As such, it aggravates both its own difficulties as well as difficulties for youth. While the preoccupation with the general question of emancipation of youth appears to be of major interest, specific concerns about sexual emancipation and abortion may be lessening. If this trend were to continue, it could suggest that the issues of sexual emancipation and abortion are matters that Swedish society has learned to cope with. It is too early to tell as yet.

This is not the case with the question of drugs, the development of which may only be getting underway causing increasing social concern and it may not be the case with criminal behavior and violence, which

209

might be of increasing concern. One can argue that matters of sex and abortion are essentially private matters, although each may have social implications. But in the case of drugs, the social implications are more serious. For example, the addiction to drugs is not reversible in any simple way. Thus, one who is addicted may become both a threat and a burden to society. Crime and violence are likewise phenomena which have significant social implications. One wonders whether the general concern about emancipation of youth represents a fear that such changes may lead to more permanent damage to the social fabric of Swedish society. Perhaps this is the real test of what Swedish society is willing to put up with. So long as the matter is primarily private perhaps one can expect relatively less concern. The matter of drugs and especially violence also carry interesting implications for Swedish society. Each represents *a potential loss of control,* similar to excessive drinking. Such loss of control may constitute a very special problem for people who are in fact rather methodical and predictable. The contrast as represented by loss of control can appear excessively frightening. One may ask whether Sweden can deal with such problems. Swedish social and behavioral science, modeled in the tradition of empirical, quantitative methods is best equipped for fact finding, description and analysis. The model is more one of building a discipline through science and less one of preoccupation with social problems, change and amelioration. On the other hand, funding agencies are apparently divided on these issues, some from the government particularly are concerned with the social problems and questions of relevance for society; other funding agencies are less concerned with these matters. A basic question has to do with the capacity of Swedish social and behavioral scientists to shift their perspective. Assuming such a shift is desirable it might require a change in the conception of professional role and it will require a consistent build-up of scientific data in order that meaningful recommendations for change can be made. These changes in role have still to come about and the data regarding problems of Swedish Youth Culture are still insufficient and too sketchy. Moreover, there is the very real question of whether much can be done under the best circumstances. It may be that among youth interest for assistance with their problems is lacking. Indeed, much of what has been said may only constitute a problem for the older generation with a different set of perceptions. Nevertheless, Swedish society has led the world in many aspects of economic and social change and it is certainly possible if they decided to do so to create imaginative programs concerned with youth culture.

Appendix 2

Researchers in America

by Stephen Hall

Using the Swedish work by Boalt in the previous chapters 2–5 in this book as a model, we have looked to the U.S. to study American researchers. Unfortunately the case of the U.S. presents some severe limitations. A truly comparative study in this instance was impossible. We have instead attempted to test a general hypothesis about American researchers. The hypothesis basically states that scientists tend to pay less attention to their other roles than do non-scientists. (Boalt and Lantz, *Universities and Research,* Ch. 10) Rephrased, we would hypothesize that the scientists pay less attention to values from every day life. Such values would be church membership, marriage, club membership, and number of children. We are suggesting, then, that scientific work would press the researchers hard and force them (if they are successful) to spend less time on the values of every day life.

In order to test this hypothesis we have taken samples of American researchers and non-researchers for comparison. We have attempted to compare the researchers and non-researchers on the basis of the relevant variables available to us. Our greatest difficulty came on this score. We were unfortunately unable to obtain many of the variables used in the Swedish study. In fact, relatively few variables of significance to us could be obtained. The data were collected from *Who's Who in America — 1969,* a source which suffers from similar limitations and biases as the Swedish *Vem är det* which has already been mentioned in the foregoing Swedish study. We will, therefore, not reiterate them here.

The sample we chose as representing researchers and non-researchers is of utmost importance. A random sample of 50 researchers and 50 non-researchers was chosen from *Who's Who in America — 1969.* Both groups were restricted to persons between 50 and 55 years old. The designation "researcher" was reached by a combination of listed occupation and titles of publications of a research nature. For a person to qualify as a researcher he must have either listed his occupation as research (which very few did) or have had at least one publication of a

research nature. Most of those termed researchers by us listed their occupation under one of the following headings: college professor, educator, dean, M.D., or have given a name for a specific academic or research profession, i.e. sociologist, biologist, physicist, virologist. In every case, however, sufficient research work had been done by them to indicate that they were in fact researchers.

The non-researcher sample was randomly selected from those who were clearly not researchers. Their occupations covered a very wide range. Lawyers, military officers, government officials, politicians, clergymen, and executives were some of the categories represented. Teachers or educators were not excluded if they were clearly not researchers.

Our study involved some changes in the variables as mentioned in Boalt and Lantz: *Universities and Research* 1970 (pp. 111–112). They are as follows: (1) Type of name: American type or not, was dropped because it was deemed of no great importance in America, (2) Year of birth was controlled for, so it cannot be used as a variable, (3) Number of years of marriage was not included because it was almost the exact inverse of age at marriage and added no information, (4) Age of the oldest child was not available. Three variables were added: (1) Widowed or divorced (yes-no), (2) Number of publications, (3) Total combined state and federal assignments (although not an entirely independent variable, it was felt to be of sufficient importance to be included). Thus we had a total of 12 variables. It was expected that researchers would have more cases of being widowed or divorced, more publications and less combined state and federal assignments.

The analysis was done by (1) determining the direction of differences (for the 12 variables collected) between the researcher and non-researcher groups, (2) Yule's Q was then calculated and a simple binomial test for significance was made, (3) Yule's Q was then calculated for the intercorrelations of both the researcher and non-researcher groups, (4) matrices for the intercorrelations for both groups were constructed and partitioned for clusters. Although data were collected upon 12 variables, a number of variables were not reported in the matrix because of their small number of cases.

Our test of the basic hypothesis found our directional predictions confirmed for 10 out of 12 variables. The researchers tended to have more divorces and be widowed more frequently, to have less children, to have far more publications, to have fewer assignments for the state govenments but more for the federal government. On this last point, federal assignments, which does not agree with the prediction, if the *total*

number of assignments for both state and federal governments is used then the researchers had less assignments as predicted. We might explain the greater proportion of assignments for the federal governments if we consider that federal research grants might come under such a heading. If the researchers considered this to be the case and recorded it as such for *Who's Who,* then they might well be expected to have more federal assignments. The researchers also tended to have a lower proportion of military commissions, chivalry orders (Legion of Merit), clubs, church memberships, and masonic orders. Particularly great differences were found between researchers and non-researchers for the variables number of publications, number of clubs mentioned and church membership. One other variable, age at first marriage, was opposite to our predictions. The mean age at first marriage for the researchers was 26.54 while for non-researchers it was 26.60.

We then found 10 of 12 variables to conform to our expectations as to the direction of differences. Performing the simple binomial test, we found that this was significant at $< 2\%$ level.

We will now turn to the second aspect of our findings. This involved the researcher and non-researcher matrices. In the researcher matrix three clusters appeared; all formed a decided pattern according to the strength and direction of the correlations, with strong intercorrelations between the variables within each of the clusters and strong negative intra-cluster correlations. Cluster I includes age at marriage, assignments for the state and federal government, and number of children. Cluster II includes number of publications, military commissions, and church membership. Cluster III is made up solely of club membership.

Cluster I can be viewed as a constellation of teaching oriented traits. These traits might well belong among the values of the "old school" of research in which theorizing was viewed as "research". We could consider this constellation of traits, "teaching" traits as distinguished from research traits. The old school "teaching" value complex emphasized the postponing of marriage until academic training was completed and careers were stabilized. Upon the fulfillment of these goals, a large family and perhaps the acceptance of a state or federal assignment became important values. These values, then, suggest a teaching career pattern in quite strong contrast to a research career pattern. The teaching pattern can be viewed as an alternative to a research career.

Our second cluster fits closely the values of a research career. One of these values is an emphasis on the *number* of publications produced. The values of a research career also seem to include an emphasis upon gain-

213

Table 68. *Correlations between researcher and non-researcher groups on 12 variables.*
The signs indicate only the directional agreement or disagreement with predictions

Variable	Q
1. Number of widowed or divorced	+ .36
2. Age at first marriage	− .25
3. Number of children	+ .08
4. Number of publications	+ .99
5. Federal government assignments	− .08
6. State government assignments	+ .59
7. Combined state + federal assignments	+ .07
8. Military commissions	+ .24
9. Legion of Merit	+1.00
10. Masonic orders	+1.00
11. Clubs	+ .62
12. Church membership	+ .72

ing status through military involvement and church allegiance. We are suggesting, then, that cluster I is a teaching cluster while cluster II is a research cluster.

Clubs (cluster III) is an independent cluster and represents a social companionship dimension. Of all the variables in the researcher matrix, this variable seems to involve the strongest compensation pattern. It is clear that the club cluster compensates the teaching and research career clusters. Perhaps the club dimension is a third kind of status variable, representing an alternative means of obtaining status. The club cluster may also represent a pleasure dimension. Since research is frequently a lonely and disappointing task, the need for social companionship is certainly understandable in the sense that it compensates for the lack of success in research.

Of particular interest is the low positive correlation between age at marriage and number of children. This would seem to indicate that at least in a research career, the values number of children and age at marriage are independent. This finding suggests that the control of number of children (planned parenthood) was a value of considerable importance.

To summarize the findings for the research matrix, then, we have noted that the researcher matrix suggests a compensation pattern, particularly cluster III, the club membership cluster. Clusters I and II (the "teaching" and research clusters) reflect clearly different value patterns and a compensation pattern which is clear although somewhat difficult to explain on purely theoretical grounds.

214

Table 69. *Researcher and non-researcher matrices of Q correlations*

A. Researcher matrix

	Variable	1	2	3	4	5	6	7
Cluster I	1. Age at first marriage	■	+.18	+.18	+.32	−.54	−.10	−.24
	2. Assignments for state+fed. gov.		■	+.07	−.57	−.29	−.29	+.69
	3. Number of children			■	−.30	−.40	+.09	−.31
Cluster II	4. Number of publications				■	+.18	+.64	−.28
	5. Military commission					■	+.45	−.31
	6. Church membership						■	+.45
Cluster III	7. Clubs							■

B. Non-researcher matrix

	Variable	1	5	7	3	4	8	9	6
Cluster I	1. Age at first marriage	■	+.18	+.38	−.38	−.18	−.01	−.12	−.17
	5. Military commission		■	+.33	−.01	−.76	−.03	−.34	−.22
	7. Clubs			■	−.38	−.61	−.61	+.52	+.15
Cluster II	3. Number of children				■	+1.0	+.01	+.75	+.01
	4. Number of publications					■	+.28	+.63	+.69
	8. Assignments for state gov.						■	+.62	+.06
	9. Assignments for federal gov.							■	+1.0
	7. Church membership								■

The non-researcher matrix has two clusters. Both formed clearly separate patterns according to the strength and direction of correlations. There were strong positive inter-cluster correlations and strong negative correlations between the variables of the different clusters. Cluster I is made up of the variables: age at marriage, military commission, and clubs. Cluster II includes the variables: number of children, number of publications, assignments for state governments, assignments for the federal government, and church membership.

If we look at clusters I and II, we see that men, successful in general terms (as indicated by their presence in *Who's Who*), have the possibility of achieving children, publications, assignments for the state of

federal government, and church membership. Without these "overt success variables" they can try to compensate for the lack of these signs of general adaptation by using late marriage and/or clubs or a military commission. These compensations might also be the reason responsible for their inability to get church membership, children, publications and governmental assignments.

The variables in cluster I seem to lend themselves to the interpretation that the military variable is indeed an important one. The military career appears to be the overriding career pattern to the exclusion of other career possibilities. A military career pattern includes late marriage and perhaps the compensation of "extra" military career ambitions by membership in one or more clubs. In this sense club membership operates the same as it did in the researcher matrix—as a compensation. Club membership can also be viewed as a value in respect to a military career; it can be the means of obtaining favor at the hands of those of higher rank and thus bettering one's position. In this second respect, clubs seem to again parallel their function in the researcher matrix, i.e. as a means of gaining status.

We should now mention the significance of military commissions and their career relevance. Only one out of the twenty-nine individuals who had military commissions reported a military occupation. This suggests that cluster I does not involve military careers alone. No evidence of a "second" career cluster, however, is evident. We can then, perhaps, assume one or more of the following: (1) the military involvement served as a sufficient interruption to "first" careers to make them unsuccessful and did not allow time for "second" careers, (2) the military became a "second" career (perhaps turned to as a result of an undistinguished "first" career), (3) the military involvement took the time and energy necessary for the development of successful non-military careers. We are not suggesting that a military career is bad, but simply that it is characterized by different criteria of success than is a research career. Indeed, from a military career criteria of success, a distinguished research career would probably appear quite unsuccessful. It is quite probable that a military career results in great personal satisfaction, a variable which we, unfortunately, have no data on. The issue, then, is left to a future comparison of careers and their rewards.

The absence of church membership and children in cluster I can perhaps be explained by the nature of the military system and the fact that late marriage was a value in this cluster. (We have no evidence to suggest planned parenthood in the non-researcher matris.)

One other factor in the non-researcher matrix is of significance. This is the strikingly high negative correlation between number of publications and both military commissions and clubs. This phenomenon greatly enhances the case for qualitative difference between clusters I and II. It also strengthens further the argument that both military involvement and club membership are compensatory variables, compensating for the lack of overt success variables.

Cluster II seems to include many of the overt success variables – children, publications, state and federal favor, and church membership. If we can generalize this picture a little we can see something which we might label the "good citizen" pattern. The "good citizen" has a large family, is successful occupationally, has political affiliation (and perhaps reward) and seeks divine favor. It is with respect to this "good citizen" pattern that cluster I appears as a compensation pattern – compensating for the lack of overt success variables with military and club involvement.

To review then, we have found support for the Summation Theory mainly in its compensation pattern. This has been verified only on a relatively micro level. Had it been possible to include more variables in the study, perhaps a more clear test of the Summation Theory could have been made. As it stands, we have a relatively small scale test of the Summation Theory in regard to career variables. This effort is, unfortunately, not directly comparable to the Swedish work.

To summarize, the original expectation was that researchers would be pressed by their scientific work and therefore, when compared to a sample of non-researchers would have: (1) a larger proportion of widowed and/or divorced, (2) a later age at first marriage, (3) a smaller number of children, (4) a larger number of publications, (5) less state and federal assignments, (6) fewer military commissions, (7) fewer with chivalry orders, and (8) fewer with club membership, church membership and masonic orders. We received support for the predictions in all but two cases. This was significantly different from chance at $< 2 \%$ level. We, then, calculated the inter-correlations for the researcher and non-researcher groups and put them into matrices. In the researcher matrix we found three clusters. They were a teaching oriented cluster, a research cluster and a club cluster. The club cluster was of particular interest as it seemed to compensate for a lack of both research *and* teaching values. This was particularly significant and lends support to the compensation pattern of the Summation Theory. The non-researcher matrix replicated this club phenomenon also. In the non-researcher

217

matrix a "military and club" cluster served as compensation for a "good citizen" cluster which included a number of overt success variables.

As a conclusion, we can say that we have received support for the compensation pattern of the Summation Theory. This compensation pattern was strongly supported by our "club" variable. In general, although we have received some support for the Summation Theory, this support has not been as powerful as we had hoped.

Appendix 3

Correlation matrices in 14 samples

Table 70. *Sample of researchers in humanities*

Variables	A. Research cluster													
	1	2	3	4	5	6	7	8	9	10	11	12	13	14
A. Research cluster														
1. Family name	■	−.04	−.05	−.03	+.10	+.04	−.08	+.08	+.01	+.08	−.10	+.14	−.07	−.03
2. Age		■	+.10	+.01	.00	+.02	−.07	+.14	+.40	+.31	+.49	+.32	+.11	−.01
3. Academic performance			■	−.01	+.05	.00	+.04	+.13	+.13	+.21	+.39	+.09	+.09	+.12
4. University loyalty I				■	+.17	+.12	−.09	−.12	−.06	−.23	−.01	+.06	+.13	+.06
5. University loyalty II					■	+.02	−.16	−.26	−.06	−.26	−.08	+.05	−.06	+.06
6. Father's social class						■	−.06	+.12	+.02	+.16	+.09	+.11	+.09	−.11
7. Place of residence							■	+.26	+.15	+.19	−.16	−.03	+.14	−.05
8. Status according to encyclopedias								■	+.51	+.90	+.23	+.19	+.33	−.13
9. Number of lines									■	+.61	+.48	+.15	+.45	+.01
10. Number of reference books										■	+.36	+.24	+.39	−.11
11. Academies etc.											■	+.12	+.16	−.01
12. Swedish honorary doctor's degrees												■	+.24	−.04
13. Government committees													■	+.08
14. Memberships in research councils														■
15. Enumerated international commissions														
16. Foreign guest professorships														
17. Academic positions														
18. Published works														
19. Name of doctor's thesis given in 'Vem är det'														
20. Distinctions														
21. Foreign honorary doctor's degrees														
22. Researcher's status														
23. General status														
24. Academic power														
B. Family cluster														
25. Number of marriages														
26. Number of children														
27. Educational level of the subject's wife														
28. Number of years between first examination and appointment to full professor														
29. Age at doctor's dissertation														
30. Age at appointment to full professor														
31. Income														
32. Income of the subject's wife														
33. Imminence between first marriage and first child														
34. Imminence between first and second child														
C. Social cluster														
35. Number of clubs														
36. Number of hobbies														

										B. Family cluster										C. Social cluster	
15	16	17	18	19	20	21	22	23	24	25	26	27	28	29	**30**	31	32	33	34	35	36
−.21	+.12	−.02	−.01	+.01	−.01	−.09	−.06	+.03	−.14	+.03	−.10	+.02	+.04	+.11	−.08	−.10	+.29	−.01	−.24	−.01	−.02
+.10	−.17	+.07	+.40	−.27	+.47	+.18	+.52	+.37	+.45	−.12	−.12	−.25	+.26	−.22	+.34	−.15	+.42	+.07	+.16	+.04	+.01
+.10	−.02	+.12	+.09	−.24	+.09	+.14	+.25	+.16	+.37	−.35	+.25	−.17	+.27	−.36	−.52	+.09	−.10	+.05	+.11	−.10	−.30
+.09	+.08	+.06	−.12	−.04	.00	+.06	−.08	−.09	+.05	+.08	+.11	+.11	−.12	−.10	−.29	−.12	+.30	−.13	+.38	+.07	+.12
−.02	−.01	+.06	−.04	+.14	−.32	+.06	−.06	−.14	−.07	−.17	+.18	+.18	+.05	.00	−.10	−.10	+.32	−.10	−.02	+.07	+.06
+.18	−.04	−.13	+.11	−.06	+.15	+.16	+.14	+.07	+.11	+.10	−.02	−.01	−.11	+.01	−.03	−.16	+.05	−.14	−.16	−.06	+.08
+.08	−.04	+.15	.00	−.08	+.20	−.09	−.07	+.20	−.06	−.04	−.13	−.11	−.01	+.01	−.03	+.13	+.58	+.02	+.04	.00	−.03
+.18	−.05	+.12	+.44	−.08	+.22	−.05	+.45	+.73	+.32	−.25	+.25	−.14	−.18	−.28	−.06	+.07	+.28	+.01	−.22	+.01	−.12
+.46	−.02	+.12	+.69	−.12	+.40	+.04	+.77	+.95	+.60	−.43	+.25	−.15	+.13	−.25	+.05	−.03	+.61	+.10	+.11	+.02	−.04
+.26	−.06	+.14	+.53	−.16	+.32	−.03	+.58	+.20	+.45	−.35	+.26	−.19	−.07	−.40	+.08	+.09	+.19	+.08	−.19	−.03	−.11
+.33	−.09	+.20	+.27	−.16	+.31	−.01	+.64	+.46	+.92	−.20	+.17	−.15	−.08	−.33	−.15	−.11	−.31	+.20	+.04	−.09	−.07
+.02	−.05	−.04	+.10	−.20	+.25	−.05	+.16	+.20	+.16	−.07	−.11	−.19	+.10	−.20	+.06	−.23	+.83	−.07	+.03	−.05	−.09
+.42	+.09	−.07	+.07	−.12	+.21	−.08	+.17	+.54	+.48	−.38	+.23	−.17	+.20	−.12	+.11	+.01	+.78	+.14	+.07	+.10	−.05
+.11	+.35	−.03	−.04	−.08	+.01	−.04	+.01	−.03	+.08	.00	+.10	−.08	−.05	−.04	−.07	−.04	+.01	−.07	+.20	−.04	−.07
■	−.01	−.05	+.17	−.09	+.22	−.06	+.36	+.45	+.56	−.20	+.18	−.17	−.01	−.14	+.03	+.04	−.12	+.01	+.14	−.06	+.08
	■	−.04	−.10	−.03	−.09	−.05	−.06	−.03	−.04	.00	−.09	+.05	−.24	+.06	−.14	+.04	.00	+.03	+.08	−.05	−.08
		■	.00	+.05	+.05	−.04	+.07	+.14	+.23	.00	+.05	−.14	−.21	−.15	−.20	−.07	.00	+.13	+.19	−.04	−.07
			■	−.16	+.23	+.16	+.90	+.66	+.26	−.35	+.16	−.13	−.08	−.32	+.09	−.05	−.01	−.08	+.01	−.01	+.09
				■	−.25	−.13	−.21	−.14	−.17	+.17	−.05	+.03	−.06	+.33	−.13	−.06	−.12	+.01	.00	−.03	+.22
					■	+.36	+.34	+.40	+.35	−.17	−.03	−.17	+.21	−.26	+.21	−.04	+.44	+.04	+.28	−.11	−.05
						■	+.14	.00	−.05	−.10	+.09	+.17	−.05	−.01	−.10	+.01	.00	−.24	+.20	−.04	−.01
							■	+.75	+.63	−.37	+.20	−.18	−.11	−.39	+.01	−.09	−.16	+.02	+.66	−.06	+.03
								■	+.61	−.45	+.29	−.18	+.07	−.30	+.05	+.01	+.60	+.10	+.01	+.02	−.07
									■	−.30	+.25	−.21	−.05	−.34	−.11	−.09	+.12	+.21	+.11	−.06	−.07
										■	−.37	+.18	−.06	+.37	−.11	−.27	−.48	−.14	−.06	−.10	+.20
											■	+.07	−.10	−.33	−.14	+.34	−.05	+.20	+.32	+.06	+.05
												■	+.06	−.01	−.11	+.09	−.10	−.31	−.09	+.15	−.14
													■	+.25	+.93	−.03	+.91	−.21	−.05	+.10	−.20
														■	+.22	.00	+.04	−.16	−.21	+.03	+.29
															■	+.16	+.43	−.05	−.07	+.15	+.04
																■	−.29	+.10	−.15	−.01	−.06
																	■	+.25	+.19	.00	−.19
																		■	+.13	−.20	+.09
																			■	−.09	+.14
																				■	−.08
																					■

Table 71. *Sample of teachers, headmasters etc.*

Variables	A. Research cluster													
	1	2	3	4	5	6	7	8	9	10	11	12	13	14
A. Research cluster														
1. Family name	■	−.11	−.01	−.13	−.10	+.29	+.03	+.10	+.16	+.19	+.07	−.14	−.01	+.05
2. Age		■	−.11	+.01	−.18	−.10	−.02	−.20	.00	−.16	−.11	+.23	−.02	−.24
3. Academic performance			■	+.22	+.12	+.11	−.05	−.11	+.04	+.01	+.18	−.19	−.14	−.09
4. University loyalty I				■	−.03	+.16	−.09	+.05	+.06	+.05	−.05	.00	+.04	+.03
5. University loyalty II					■	+.15	−.19	+.04	+.14	+.04	+.07	.00	+.13	+.03
6. Father's social class						■	−.12	−.12	−.02	−.02	+.14	−.23	−.08	+.10
7. Place of residence							■	+.07	+.02	+.08	+.15	+.09	−.01	+.09
8. Status according to encyclopedias								■	+.21	+.83	+.12	−.02	+.02	−.02
9. Number of lines									■	+.29	+.16	−.13	+.42	−.10
10. Number of reference books										■	+.23	−.02	+.09	−.02
11. Academies etc.											■	−.04	−.07	−.04
12. Swedish honorary doctor's degrees												■	−.07	−.01
13. Government committees													■	−.07
14. Memberships in research councils														■
15. Enumerated international commissions														
16. Foreign guest professorships														
17. Academic positions														
18. Published works														
19. Name of doctor's thesis given in 'Vem är det'														
20. Distinctions														
21. Foreign honorary doctor's degrees														
22. Researcher's status														
23. General status														
24. Academic power														

B. Family cluster
25. Number of marriages
26. Number of children
27. Educational level of the subject's wife
28. Number of years between first examination and appointment to full professor
29. Age at doctor's dissertation
30. Age at appointment to full professor
31. Income
32. Income of the subject's wife
33. Imminence between first marriage and first child
34. Imminence between first and second child

C. Social cluster
35. Number of clubs
36. Number of hobbies

		B. Family cluster (25–34)										C. Social cluster (35–36)	

15	16	17	18	19	20	21	22	23	24	25	26	27	28	29	30	31	32	33	34	35	36
+.02	+.05	.00	+.05	.00	.00	.00	+.07	+.13	+.03	+.04	+.11	+.14	.00	+.13	.00	−.13	−.05	+.16	+.16	−.08	+.06
+.03	−.03	.00	−.05	+.05	+.32	.00	−.07	−.04	−.06	−.07	+.09	−.23	.00	+.26	.00	−.36	−.02	+.13	−.03	−.07	−.16
−.11	+.10	.00	−.02	+.55	+.03	.00	.00	−.04	−.09	+.11	−.07	+.22	.00	−.29	.00	+.09	+.20	+.03	+.12	−.12	−.18
−.10	+.03	.00	−.06	+.31	+.04	.00	−.08	+.07	+.01	−.02	+.03	+.10	.00	+.17	.00	−.04	+.51	+.10	+.06	+.10	−.01
+.04	+.03	.00	+.12	−.08	−.08	.00	+.14	+.16	+.15	−.01	−.06	−.03	.00	−.14	.00	−.01	.00	+.11	−.10	−.24	+.06
+.14	−.07	.00	−.10	+.10	−.04	.00	−.02	−.06	+.02	+.03	+.03	−.01	.00	−.16	.00	+.05	.00	+.24	−.02	.00	+.12
+.13	−.02	.00	+.07	−.21	−.05	.00	+.14	+.03	+.09	.00	−.09	+.13	.00	−.19	.00	+.02	+.15	−.01	−.14	−.21	−.30
+.03	−.02	.00	+.41	−.13	−.06	.00	+.40	+.32	+.06	−.02	−.07	+.06	.00	+.03	.00	+.14	−.10	−.26	−.01	−.04	−.06
+.25	+.21	.00	+.53	+.05	−.11	.00	+.57	+.91	+.47	−.20	+.13	+.13	.00	+.34	.00	+.13	−.11	−.01	+.01	−.18	+.10
+.08	−.02	.00	.35	−.03	.02	.00	.39	.40	.18	−.06	−.02	+.14	.00	+.03	.00	+.13	+.03	−.17	−.09	−.01	±.05
.27	−.04	.00	+.04	+.01	+.08	.00	+.38	+.11	+.35	−.08	+.05	+.17	.00	−.12	.00	−.02	+.06	−.14	+.02	−.14	−.06
−.03	−.01	.00	−.06	−.12	+.03	.00	−.04	−.13	−.08	+.02	+.06	−.08	.00	.00	.00	.00	.00	.00	+.12	−.04	−.03
+.20	+.20	.00	−.05	−.18	−.08	.00	−.02	+.73	+.87	−.05	+.09	+.05	.00	+.22	.00	+.10	−.28	+.02	+.03	−.08	+.03
−.03	−.01	.00	−.10	−.12	−.08	.00	−.07	−.11	−.04	+.02	−.01	−.08	.00	.00	.00	−.10	.00	+.15	−.19	−.04	−.03
■	−.03	.00	+.11	−.24	−.02	.00	+.39	+.27	+.53	+.04	+.09	+.03	.00	+.18	.00	−.05	−.34	−.13	−.08	−.09	+.07
	■	.00	+.08	+.08	−.08	.00	+.09	+.22	+.15	+.02	+.14	+.13	.00	+.27	.00	+.12	−.13	.00	+.12	−.04	−.03
		■	.00	.00	.00	.00	.00	.00	.00	.00	.00	.00	.00	.00	.00	.00	.00	.00	.00	.00	.00
			■	−.09	−.22	.00	+.91	+.41	−.01	−.15	−.05	+.03	.00	+.05	.00	−.04	−.28	−.18	−.08	−.22	+.16
				■	−.09	.00	−.13	−.06	−.22	.00	+.02	+.03	.00	+.26	.00	+.03	+.46	+.09	+.11	+.06	−.06
					■	.00	−.18	−.11	−.05	+.12	.00	−.09	.00	−.18	.00	−.06	+.18	−.05	+.03	+.02	−.09
						■	.00	.00	.00	.00	.00	.00	.00	.00	.00	.00	.00	.00	.00	.00	.00
							■	+.45	+.21	−.14	−.01	+.08	.00	+.04	.00	−.05	−.31	−.23	−.08	−.26	+.14
								■	+.72	−.17	+.12	+.13	.00	+.35	.00	+.16	−.19	−.04	+.01	−.16	+.07
									■	−.06	+.12	+.11	.00	+.17	.00	+.06	−.32	−.05	.00	−.15	+.02
										■	−.18	−.09	.00	−.08	.00	−.08	−.17	−.06	−.06	.00	−.11
											■	−.09	.00	+.32	.00	+.09	−.24	+.14	+.46	+.04	+.12
												■	.00	−.08	.00	−.11	+.55	−.10	+.23	+.05	−.01
													■	.00	.00	.00	.00	.00	.00	.00	.00
														■	.00	+.02	+.06	+.17	+.29	+.18	+.31
															■	.00	.00	.00	.00	.00	.00
																■	−.07	−.07	−.21	+.08	+.16
																	■	+.02	+.01	+.24	−.19
																		■	+.04	+.05	−.14
																			■	+.18	−.12
																				■	+.01
																					■

Table 72. *Sample of researchers in theology*

Variables	A. Research cluster													
	1	2	3	4	5	6	7	8	9	10	11	12	13	14
A. Research cluster														
1. Family name	■	+.07	+.22	−.15	+.09	+.22	−.07	+.12	+.10	+.07	−.01	+.06	−.26	+.09
2. Age		■	+.04	+.02	−.42	+.17	−.28	−.09	+.45	+.12	+.26	+.12	+.07	+.04
3. Academic performance			■	+.19	−.08	−.10	−.18	+.23	+.17	+.29	+.21	+.06	+.13	+.08
4. University loyalty I				■	−.11	−.23	−.16	+.22	+.16	+.22	+.24	+.08	+.26	+.11
5. University loyalty II					■	−.10	+.11	+.07	−.21	+.01	−.29	+.05	−.08	+.07
6. Father's social class						■	+.09	−.22	+.02	−.25	−.11	−.07	−.23	+.02
7. Place of residence							■	+.39	−.11	+.10	−.13	−.08	−.26	−.11
8. Status according to encyclopedias								■	+.31	+.79	+.10	−.05	−.16	+.01
9. Number of lines									■	+.54	+.43	+.05	−.02	+.13
10. Number of reference books										■	+.29	−.01	−.07	+.14
11. Academies etc.											■	+.35	+.07	+.40
12. Swedish honorary doctor's degrees												■	+.36	+.70
13. Government committees													■	+.30
14. Memberships in research councils														■
15. Enumerated international commissions														
16. Foreign guest professorships														
17. Academic positions														
18. Published works														
19. Name of doctor's thesis given in 'Vem är det'														
20. Distinctions														
21. Foreign honorary doctor's degrees														
22. Researcher's status														
23. General status														
24. Academic power														
B. Family cluster														
25. Number of marriages														
26. Number of children														
27. Educational level of the subject's wife														
28. Number of years between first examination and appointment to full professor														
29. Age at doctor's dissertation														
30. Age at appointment to full professor														
31. Income														
32. Income of the subject's wife														
33. Imminence between first marriage and first child														
34. Imminence between first and second child														
C. Social cluster														
35. Number of clubs														
36. Number of hobbies														

224

Columns 25–34 fall under the heading **B. Family cluster**; columns 35–36 fall under the heading **C. Social cluster**.

15	16	17	18	19	20	21	22	23	24	25	26	27	28	29	30	31	32	33	34	35	36
+.11	+.09	.00	+.07	−.19	.00	.00	+.09	+.06	−.09	+.18	−.15	−.36	.00	−.21	−.02	−.29	.00	−.17	−.07	.00	−.13
−.13	−.10	+.18	+.49	−.34	+.73	+.46	+.49	+.38	+.18	−.03	−.14	−.23	+.50	−.20	+.30	−.76	−.99	+.07	+.27	.00	−.37
+.10	+.08	+.12	+.05	+.06	+.22	+.13	+.15	+.25	+.26	.00	−.12	−.09	.00	+.08	.00	−.32	.00	+.10	+.06	.00	+.17
+.14	+.11	+.16	+.12	−.07	+.11	−.20	+.18	+.26	+.37	+.34	+.02	−.15	−.07	−.14	−.04	+.13	.00	−.28	−.07	.00	+.02
+.08	+.07	−.29	−.35	+.36	−.54	−.31	−.38	−.18	−.23	.00	−.04	+.22	−.11	+.52	+.21	+.36	.00	+.02	−.28	.00	+.14
+.17	+.14	+.12	−.03	+.08	+.13	+.19	+.01	−.11	−.12	.00	−.24	+.06	−.06	−.20	−.16	−.14	−.63	−.04	−.29	.00	+.01
−.14	+.19	+.12	−.20	.00	−.31	−.08	−.21	−.06	−.26	−.13	−.15	+.11	−.14	+.03	+.01	+.47	.00	−.10	+.10	.00	+.07
+.12	+.33	+.30	+.15	−.15	−.12	+.02	+.19	+.51	+.06	−.15	−.07	+.11	−.19	−.23	−.19	+.28	+.47	+.13	+.23	.00	−.28
+.42	+.04	+.43	+.71	−.05	+.36	+.38	+.81	+.95	+.48	−.23	−.06	−.20	+.13	−.24	−.09	−.30	−.60	+.04	+.37	.00	−.24
+.21	+.17	+.32	+.34	+.02	+.02	+.11	+.42	+.70	+.27	−.30	+.13	+.01	+.08	−.10	−.07	+.19	+.16	+.21	+.19	.00	−.29
−.15	+.07	+.34	+.29	+.08	+.37	+.53	+.69	+.42	+.72	+.11	−.05	−.19	+.13	−.11	−.08	−.10	−.70	+.03	+.20	.00	−.08
−.06	−.05	+.48	−.06	+.10	+.08	+.12	+.12	+.11	+.50	.00	+.03	−.16	.00	+.05	−.09	−.10	.00	−.01	−.16	.00	−.10
+.05	−.04	+.17	−.17	+.04	+.21	−.09	−.10	+.17	+.60	.00	+.15	+.12	+.10	+.11	+.03	−.07	−.34	+.13	+.05	.00	−.01
+.24	+.56	+.29	−.20	−.11	+.11	+.17	+.13	+.20	+.60	.00	+.11	+.04	−.05	+.07	−.14	+.14	−.99	+.10	−.02	.00	−.14
■	+.30	+.36	+.10	+.02	+.04	−.04	+.22	+.41	+.32	.00	−.19	−.05	−.18	−.29	−.19	+.22	−.98	−.25	−.02	.00	−.04
	■	−.10	−.28	−.35	−.01	+.06	−.03	+.11	+.16	.00	−.04	+.29	−.15	−.01	−.15	+.30	−.99	+.15	+.14	.00	−.14
		■	+.18	+.02	+.37	+.36	+.36	+.49	+.56	.00	−.19	−.33	−.15	−.29	−.22	−.08	.00	−.13	−.02	.00	−.20
			■	−.09	+.34	+.17	+.89	+.62	+.22	−.18	+.10	−.38	+.29	−.55	.00	−.35	+.69	+.04	+.41	.00	−.06
				■	−.43	−.04	−.07	−.06	+.08	−.24	−.03	+.09	−.19	+.22	−.20	+.21	+.36	+.04	−.20	.00	+.29
					■	+.62	+.47	+.32	+.42	+.14	−.13	−.17	+.31	−.25	+.16	−.68	−.99	−.11	+.29	.00	−.12
						■	+.43	+.31	+.34	.00	−.35	−.01	−.10	−.04	−.18	−.42	−.99	−.13	+.07	.00	−.21
							■	+.73	+.54	−.10	−.02	−.34	+.21	−.51	−.10	−.30	−.22	+.02	+.43	.00	−.12
								■	+.57	−.25	−.02	−.12	+.10	−.32	−.12	−.20	−.26	+.13	+.36	.00	−.29
									■	+.07	−.04	−.12	+.06	−.14	−.14	−.01	−.10	+.03	+.14	.00	−.10
										■	−.40	−.21	−.13	.00	.00	−.07	.00	−.15	−.14	.00	.00
											■	+.02	−.02	−.05	−.19	+.13	−.99	+.44	+.66	.00	+.33
												■	−.14	+.22	−.10	+.53	+.36	.00	+.09	.00	+.08
													■	+.12	+.86	−.29	−.50	.00	+.10	.00	−.04
														■	+.37	+.09	−.34	+.01	−.43	.00	−.03
															■	−.08	+.16	−.15	−.03	.00	+.22
																■	−.09	−.34	−.12	.00	.00
																	■	−.65	−.36	.00	−.12
																		■	+.19	.00	+.09
																			■		
																				■	.00
																					■

Table 73. *Sample of bishops and deans*

Variables	A. Research cluster													
	1	2	3	4	5	6	7	8	9	10	11	12	13	14
A. Research cluster														
1. Family name	■	−.08	+.02	−.08	+.03	+.30	+.10	+.11	+.18	+.07	+.15	+.06	+.18	.00
2. Age		■	+.34	−.37	+.24	+.08	−.01	+.03	+.51	+.08	+.59	+.27	+.40	.00
3. Academic performance			■	+.03	+.90	+.02	−.30	−.25	+.88	−.35	−.02	−.07	+.69	.00
4. University loyalty I				■	+.03	+.02	−.02	+.01	+.04	−.04	−.48	+.06	−.11	.00
5. University loyalty II					■	−.11	−.44	−.39	+.76	−.49	−.20	−.02	+.63	.00
6. Father's social class						■	−.25	+.36	+.11	+.32	+.33	−.22	+.19	.00
7. Place of residence							■	−.02	−.29	+.14	+.07	+.21	−.33	.00
8. Status according to encyclopedias								■	−.07	+.91	+.26	+.01	−.10	.00
9. Number of lines									■	−.16	+.17	+.16	+.72	.00
10. Number of reference books										■	+.32	+.03	−.17	.00
11. Academies etc.											■	+.17	+.03	.00
12. Swedish honorary doctor's degrees												■	−.15	.00
13. Government committees													■	.00
14. Memberships in research councils														■

15. Enumerated international commissions
16. Foreign guest professorships
17. Academic positions
18. Published works
19. Name of doctor's thesis given in 'Vem är det'
20. Distinctions
21. Foreign honorary doctor's degrees
22. Researcher's status
23. General status
24. Academic power

B. Family cluster
25. Number of marriages
26. Number of children
27. Educational level of the subject's wife
28. Number of years between first examination and appointment to full professor
29. Age at doctor's dissertation
30. Age at appointment to full professor
31. Income
32. Income of the subject's wife
33. Imminence between first marriage and first child
34. Imminence between first and second child

C. Social cluster
35. Number of clubs
36. Number of hobbies

226

										B. Family cluster										C. Social cluster	
15	16	17	18	19	20	21	22	23	24	25	26	27	28	29	30	31	32	33	34	35	36
+.09	+.04	.00	+.30	−.28	+.23	+.08	+.26	+.21	+.21	+.03	.00	+.14	−.44	−.19	−.36	+.05	.00	−.07	−.07	+.20	+.12
+.05	+.21	.00	+.48	−.13	+.63	+.57	+.57	+.52	+.51	−.25	+.33	−.16	−.23	+.23	−.21	+.26	+.06	−.31	−.31	+.01	+.24
−.01	+.03	.00	+.06	−.12	−.11	+.05	+.05	+.81	+.54	−.31	+.91	+.01	−.78	+.04	−.94	+.98	−.73	−.98	−.98	−.08	+.40
+.11	+.06	.00	−.02	−.13	−.54	−.40	−.18	.00	−.20	−.14	+.06	+.16	−.63	−.37	−.48	+.08	.00	−.08	+.97	−.50	−.46
−.17	−.02	.00	−.12	−.29	−.33	−.07	−.16	+.70	+.39	−.40	+.84	+.11	−.78	+.19	−.94	+.91	−.99	−.90	−.07	−.03	+.40
+.21	+.13	.00	+.27	−.03	+.34	+.25	+.33	+.22	+.31	+.03	−.01	−.31	−.05	−.21	+.11	−.01	−.57	+.01	−.90	−.24	+.04
+.02	+.01	.00	−.14	−.24	+.03	+.03	−.06	−.30	−.23	+.12	−.36	−.05	+.57	−.07	+.76	−.37	+.80	+.31	+.31	−.20	−.03
+.17	+.16	.00	+.46	−.02	+.29	+.27	+.45	+.16	+.06	+.03	−.18	−.05	+.51	−.41	+.69	−.24	+.71	+.31	+.31	−.16	−.25
+.09	+.12	.00	+.44	−.17	+.16	+.18	+.39	+.96	+.65	−.40	+.87	+.07	−.86	−.01	−.97	+.86	−.66	−.88	−.86	−.06	+.43
+.13	+.16	.00	+.41	.00	+.29	+.27	+.42	+.07	+.01	+.08	−.31	−.06	+.61	−.31	+.79	−.34	+.71	+.42	+.42	−.17	−.26
+.15	+.12	.00	+.40	+.04	+.66	+.68	+.63	+.22	+.37	+.04	−.12	−.14	+.60	−.06	+.56	−.15	+.90	+.10	+.15	−.17	−.05
−.08	−.04	.00	+.36	−.04	+.24	−.07	+.27	+.10	−.09	−.46	+.13	−.04	.00	−.15	.00	−.09	+.90	+.06	+.07	+.09	+.07
+.33	+.39	.00	+.22	−.23	+.09	+.27	+.28	+.80	+.89	−.14	+.66	+.01	−.99	+.05	−.93	+.67	−.85	−.69	−.66	+.19	+.54
.00	.00	.00	.00	.00	.00	.00	.00	.00	.00	.00	.00	.00	.00	.00	.00	.00	.00	.00	.00	.00	.00
■	+.86	.00	+.29	−.18	+.15	+.53	+.55	+.19	+.61	+.04	−.03	−.14	−.21	−.22	+.05	−.09	.00	+.06	+.06	−.13	−.10
	■	.00	+.32	−.17	+.16	+.63	+.57	+.23	+.60	+.06	.00	−.08	−.21	−.13	+.05	−.06	.00	+.04	+.04	−.06	−.07
		■	.00	.00	.00	.00	.00	.00	.00	.00	.00	.00	.00	.00	.00	.00	.00	.00	.00	.00	.00
			■	−.15	+.47	+.42	+.90	+.52	+.38	−.18	+.17	−.02	−.20	−.17	+.07	−.02	+.65	+.01	+.05	+.03	+.12
				■	−.02	−.09	−.15	−.20	−.22	+.16	−.15	−.10	+.87	+.14	+.69	−.21	−.16	+.25	+.18	+.07	+.05
					■	+.64	+.61	+.22	+.31	−.13	−.10	−.21	+.53	−.13	+.57	−.23	+.98	+.16	+.20	+.07	+.04
						■	+.74	+.28	+.58	+.11	−.06	−.16	+.33	−.11	+.50	−.09	.00	+.05	+.06	−.12	−.04
							■	+.49	+.58	−.09	+.07	−.11	+.07	−.19	+.31	−.09	+.73	+.05	+.08	−.06	+.04
								■	+.75	−.35	+.80	+.03	−.92	−.08	−.98	+.81	−.71	−.80	−.78	−.04	+.42
									■	−.08	+.47	−.09	−.78	−.04	−.63	+.46	−.79	−.49	−.47	+.06	+.38
										■	−.42	+.12	+.28	−.03	+.48	−.33	−.16	+.38	+.36	+.05	−.11
											■	+.03	−.84	+.06	−.97	+.94	−.64	−.94	−.93	+.03	+.46
												■	.00	−.09	.00	+.17	−.57	+.05	−.16	+.18	−.18
													■	−.22	+.95	−.78	.00	+.80	+.83	.00	−.82
														■	−.51	+.08	−.54	−.07	−.08	+.25	.18
															■	−.94	.00	+.95	+.97	.00	−.92
																■	−.73	−.98	−.99	−.08	+.37
																	■	+.71	+.71	+.90	−.66
																		■	+.99	+.10	−.39
																			■	+.06	−.36
																				■	+.36
																					■

Table 74. *Sample of medical researchers*

Variables	A. Research cluster													
	1	2	3	4	5	6	7	8	9	10	11	12	13	14
A. Research cluster														
1. Family name	■	−.15	−.23	+.09	+.22	+.11	+.10	+.05	−.13	+.03	−.17	+.01	−.25	−.20
2. Age		■	−.09	−.12	−.14	+.03	+.22	−.07	+.25	+.05	+.29	+.26	+.12	+.19
3. Academic performance			■	+.05	+.06	−.05	−.23	+.23	+.07	+.24	+.25	+.12	+.13	+.20
4. University loyalty I				■	+.08	−.01	+.04	+.13	+.12	+.07	−.02	−.04	−.04	+.07
5. University loyalty II					■	.00	+.03	+.12	−.04	+.09	+.08	−.09	+.11	−.06
6. Father's social class						■	−.03	+.03	−.05	−.05	−.10	+.06	+.02	+.12
7. Place of residence							■	+.23	+.33	+.21	−.03	−.06	+.09	+.16
8. Status according to encyclopedias								■	+.22	+.71	+.27	+.10	+.36	+.22
9. Number of lines									■	+.40	+.42	+.01	+.36	+.40
10. Number of reference books										■	+.52	+.13	+.41	+.48
11. Academies etc.											■	+.22	+.29	+.34
12. Swedish honorary doctor's degrees												■	+.08	−.14
13. Government committees													■	+.38
14. Memberships in research councils														■
15. Enumerated international commissions														
16. Foreign guest professorships														
17. Academic positions														
18. Published works														
19. Name of doctor's thesis given in 'Vem är det'														
20. Distinctions														
21. Foreign honorary doctor's degrees														
22. Researcher's status														
23. General status														
24. Academic power														
B. Family cluster														
25. Number of marriages														
26. Number of children														
27. Educational level of the subject's wife														
28. Number of years between first examination and appointment to full professor														
29. Age at doctor's dissertation														
30. Age at appointment to full professor														
31. Income														
32. Income of the subject's wife														
33. Imminence between first marriage and first child														
34. Imminence between first and second child														
C. Social cluster														
35. Number of clubs														
36. Number of hobbies														

										B. Family cluster										C. Social cluster	
15	16	17	18	19	20	21	22	23	24	25	26	27	28	29	30	31	32	33	34	35	36
+.07	+.10	−.07	−.01	−.02	−.05	−.06	−.08	−.12	−.19	−.09	+.10	−.01	−.11	−.18	−.12	+.18	−.26	−.14	−.08	+.08	.00
+.09	+.12	+.14	+.33	−.06	+.49	+.19	+.41	+.17	+.28	−.25	+.01	−.20	+.22	+.31	+.36	−.03	−.02	+.18	−.16	+.10	+.27
−.09	−.08	+.08	+.07	−.08	+.07	+.12	+.15	+.19	+.18	−.03	+.05	+.22	−.47	−.10	−.54	+.06	+.06	+.21	−.13	−.09	−.20
+.04	+.11	−.13	−.04	+.03	−.27	−.08	+.02	+.12	.00	−.08	+.05	+.08	−.14	−.10	−.10	−.11	−.20	−.04	−.06	−.10	−.20
−.10	+.09	−.18	+.10	+.07	−.20	+.09	+.03	+.06	+.01	+.05	−.02	+.15	−.10	−.48	−.13	+.15	.00	−.01	+.01	−.08	+.02
−.01	+.14	+.03	+.07	+.12	+.06	−.05	+.02	−.02	−.03	+.01	+.14	−.15	+.04	+.07	+.04	+.02	−.31	+.11	−.09	−.06	−.08
+.02	+.06	−.07	+.16	+.13	−.01	+.08	+.10	+.33	+.05	−.15	−.12	−.04	−.10	+.05	+.05	−.11	−.02	+.04	+.02	−.12	+.02
+.13	+.08	+.17	−.02	−.04	+.06	+.30	+.26	+.67	+.37	−.22	.00	+.12	−.21	−.23	−.19	+.05	+.14	+.06	−.02	−.07	−.13
+.23	+.08	−.10	+.28	+.02	+.09	+.34	+.53	+.83	+.51	−.31	+.06	+.15	+.02	−.12	−.03	+.13	−.06	+.03	−.02	.00	+.11
+.24	+.10	+.16	+.08	−.01	+.13	+.61	+.55	+.73	+.62	−.29	.00	+.25	−.22	−.32	−.23	+.10	+.08	+.05	−.05	−.03	−.06
+.10	−.03	+.29	+.17	−.06	+.26	+.47	+.70	+.49	+.74	−.24	+.02	+.02	−.23	−.28	−.20	−.09	−.01	+.25	−.18	−.06	+.10
−.10	+.07	+.24	+.36	−.12	+.32	+.19	+.28	+.08	+.08	−.29	+.22	−.03	−.07	−.01	−.11	−.02	.00	+.18	−.04	−.05	−.04
+.18	−.04	−.10	+.02	+.07	+.13	+.41	+.33	+.65	+.65	−.17	−.14	+.11	−.23	−.19	−.15	+.21	+.05	+.21	+.05	+.12	+.09
+.14	+.03	.00	.00	+.12	+.07	+.34	+.43	+.48	+.56	−.08	−.19	+.08	−.02	−.15	−.13	+.01	−.09	−.11	+.04	−.03	−.01
■	+.28	+.05	−.08	+.13	+.02	−.02	+.49	+.26	+.60	−.07	+.10	+.08	+.09	+.08	+.02	+.36	−.10	−.02	−.08	+.54	+.35
	■	−.05	+.28	−.05	−.01	+.19	+.41	+.08	+.10	−.05	+.18	+.05	+.22	−.13	+.11	−.08	−.06	+.10	+.11	−.06	+.13
		■	−.04	−.08	+.38	−.05	+.14	−.01	+.22	−.09	+.10	−.11	−.10	.00	−.11	−.14	−.20	+.06	−.14	+.18	+.14
			■	+.04	+.10	+.22	+.57	+.18	+.05	−.25	+.25	+.12	+.07	−.17	.00	+.05	+.07	+.19	+.03	−.04	+.03
				■	−.04	−.14	+.03	+.01	+.07	+.12	−.01	−.05	+.08	−.03	+.07	+.20	−.28	−.02	−.07	+.06	+.04
					■	+.16	+.22	+.13	+.23	−.21	+.13	−.13	+.14	+.22	+.18	+.06	+.03	−.11	−.04	+.01	+.36
						■	+.52	+.50	+.43	−.28	−.01	+.34	−.15	−.21	−.14	+.05	+.14	−.17	−.06	−.06	+.08
							■	+.58	+.79	−.32	+.16	+.15	−.03	−.24	−.11	+.14	−.04	+.22	−.08	+.16	+.23
								■	+.69	−.34	.00	+.20	−.18	−.24	−.16	+.16	+.05	+.09	−.02	.00	+.04
									■	−.24	−.03	+.09	−.17	−.20	−.18	+.20	−.07	+.18	−.12	+.27	+.25
										■	−.26	−.06	+.15	+.11	+.05	−.14	+.02	−.17	+.06	−.02	+.04
											■	+.06	+.10	+.05	+.07	+.20	−.29	+.21	+.15	+.10	+.04
												■	−.18	−.16	−.20	+.01	+.44	+.01	+.04	−.02	−.09
													■	+.37	+.90	+.02	−.04	−.19	+.09	−.09	−.01
														■	+.48	+.05	+.04	+.03	−.10	+.16	+.07
															■	−.05	+.02	+.01	+.04	−.15	−.02
																■	−.25	+.07	+.06	+.48	+.30
																	■	−.10	+.09	−.18	−.17
																		■	−.17	−.03	−.06
																			■	−.23	+.04
																				■	+.54
																					■

Table 75. *Sample of head physicians*

| | A. Research cluster | | | | | | | | | | | | | |
Variables	1	2	3	4	5	6	7	8	9	10	11	12	13	14
A. Research cluster														
1. Family name	■	−.10	−.06	−.01	−.18	+.09	−.03	−.03	+.10	−.09	.00	+.09	−.03	+.07
2. Age		■	−.43	−.09	−.12	−.16	−.24	−.14	−.01	−.14	−.03	+.15	+.10	−.21
3. Academic performance			■	+.08	−.15	+.04	+.09	+.33	+.28	+.32	+.20	−.17	+.01	+.35
4. University loyalty I				■	+.08	−.22	−.06	−.03	−.18	−.08	−.06	+.09	−.41	+.07
5. University loyalty II					■	−.06	+.19	−.23	−.13	−.19	−.09	.00	−.28	−.15
6. Father's social class						■	+.02	−.11	+.10	−.10	+.04	+.03	+.03	−.27
7. Place of residence							■	+.08	+.17	+.03	+.18	+.05	+.11	+.15
8. Status according to encyclopedias								■	+.42	+.98	+.60	−.03	+.46	+.34
9. Number of lines									■	+.39	+.68	+.37	+.49	+.39
10. Number of reference books										■	+.54	−.03	+.48	+.77
11. Academies etc.											■	+.33	+.41	+.51
12. Swedish honorary doctor's degrees												■	+.09	−.04
13. Government committees													■	+.31
14. Memberships in research councils														■

15. Enumerated international commissions
16. Foreign guest professorships
17. Academic positions
18. Published works
19. Name of doctor's thesis given in 'Vem är det'
20. Distinctions
21. Foreign honorary doctor's degrees
22. Researcher's status
23. General status
24. Academic power

B. Family cluster
25. Number of marriages
26. Number of children
27. Educational level of the subject's wife
28. Number of years between first examination and appointment to full professor
29. Age at doctor's dissertation
30. Age at appointment to full professor
31. Income
32. Income of the subject's wife
33. Imminence between first marriage and first child
34. Imminence between first and second child

C. Social cluster
35. Number of clubs
36. Number of hobbies

										B. Family cluster										C. Social cluster	
15	16	17	18	19	20	21	22	23	24	25	26	27	28	29	30	31	32	33	34	35	36
+.01	-.23	.00	+.07	+.06	+.06	.00	+.02	+.06	.00	+.21	-.02	+.02	.00	.00	.00	+.15	-.05	+.01	+.05	+.07	-.05
-.15	-.05	.00	-.08	-.09	+.42	.00	-.11	.00	-.03	+.18	-.22	-.06	.00	.00	.00	-.36	.00	-.11	+.14	+.13	+.16
+.40	+.22	.00	+.16	+.34	-.09	.00	+.34	+.25	+.24	-.13	+.20	+.17	.00	.00	.00	+.35	+.15	+.05	+.01	+.03	+.11
+.09	+.06	.00	-.18	-.07	-.06	.00	-.03	-.26	-.20	+.07	+.16	-.15	.00	.00	.00	+.06	-.24	+.20	-.09	-.20	-.11
-.01	+.11	.00	-.05	-.21	-.32	.00	-.08	-.21	-.18	-.01	-.03	.00	.00	.00	.00	-.03	+.26	-.13	-.22	-.25	+.11
-.02	+.09	.00	+.04	-.03	+.15	.00	.00	+.07	.00	-.07	+.13	+.03	.00	.00	.00	+.12	-.06	+.03	+.13	+.03	+.24
+.14	+.16	.00	+.10	+.06	-.04	.00	+.22	+.17	+.19	-.01	-.12	-.01	.00	.00	.00	-.07	+.04	-.14	-.15	+.01	-.10
+.43	-.02	.00	+.05	-.06	+.06	.00	+.64	+.60	+.72	-.24	+.05	+.08	.00	.00	.00	+.04	-.03	+.08	-.03	+.11	-.06
+.26	+.13	.00	+.35	+.14	+.19	.00	+.69	+.94	+.68	-.36	+.08	+.15	.00	.00	.00	+.14	+.12	-.05	-.10	+.02	+.10
+.39	-.02	.00	+.06	-.06	+.04	.00	+.58	+.58	+.69	-.26	+.08	+.10	.00	.00	.00	+.03	-.03	+.09	.00	+.09	-.06
+.41	+.21	.00	+.22	+.05	+.20	.00	+.93	+.71	+.86	-.25	-.05	+.11	.00	.00	.00	-.03	+.08	-.12	-.06	+.01	+.01
-.06	-.03	.00	+.09	-.09	+.08	.00	+.30	+.29	+.19	-.04	.00	-.13	.00	.00	.00	-.02	.00	+.03	-.12	-.07	-.04
+.16	+.07	.00	+.16	-.04	+.17	.00	+.41	+.74	+.76	-.14	-.01	+.07	.00	.00	.00	-.05	-.05	-.09	+.02	-.03	-.11
+.37	-.02	.00	+.02	.00	.00	.00	+.58	+.50	+.62	-.14	+.05	+.06	.00	.00	.00	+.06	-.03	+.08	-.13	+.12	-.08
■	+.11	.00	+.06	+.09	+.01	.00	+.62	+.30	+.56	.00	+.01	+.20	.00	.00	.00	+.03	+.05	+.09	-.06	-.02	+.04
	■	.00	+.06	+.06	+.04	.00	+.27	+.12	+.16	+.05	+.08	+.20	.00	.00	.00	-.05	+.27	+.04	.00	-.04	+.04
		■	.00	.00	.00	.00	.00	.00	.00	.00	.00	.00	.00	.00	.00	.00	.00	.00	.00	.00	.00
			■	+.31	-.08	.00	+.40	+.31	+.20	+.01	+.01	+.02	.00	.00	.00	+.09	+.07	-.20	+.02	-.09	-.03
				■	+.17	.00	+.12	+.08	+.02	-.01	-.05	+.09	.00	.00	.00	+.20	+.54	-.10	-.15	+.09	-.03
					■	.00	+.12	+.20	+.19	-.07	+.01	-.04	.00	.00	.00	-.11	+.25	+.08	-.11	+.21	+.23
						■	.00	.00	.00	.00	.00	.00	.00	.00	.00	.00	.00	.00	.00	.00	.00
							■	+.72	+.88	-.17	-.01	+.15	.00	.00	.00	+.01	+.08	-.07	-.08	-.01	.00
								■	+.84	-.34	+.07	+.14	.00	.00	.00	+.09	+.05	-.05	-.07	+.02	+.03
									■	-.21	-.02	+.14	.00	.00	.00	-.03	+.02	-.07	-.05	.00	-.05
										■	-.21	+.08	.00	.00	.00	+.05	-.08	-.08	+.07	+.06	-.03
											■	+.10	.00	.00	.00	+.18	+.02	+.47	+.20	-.09	+.06
												■	.00	.00	.00	+.13	+.54	+.08	+.02	-.18	+.03
													■	.00	.00	.00	.00	.00	.00	.00	.00
														■	.00	.00	.00	.00	.00	.00	.00
															■	+.57	+.03	+.13		+.16	+.28
																■	-.04	-.09		-.17	+.35
																	■	+.08		-.14	-.03
																		■		-.03	+.01
																			■		
																				■	+.37
																					■

Table 76. *Sample of researchers in natural science*

Variables	A. Research cluster													
	1	2	3	4	5	6	7	8	9	10	11	12	13	14
A. Research cluster														
1. Family name	■	−.14	−.07	−.10	−.07	+.10	+.08	−.19	.00	−.17	−.01	+.06	−.11	−.02
2. Age		■	+.03	+.31	−.07	−.05	+.07	+.14	+.47	+.37	+.54	+.25	+.18	+.29
3. Academic performance			■	+.04	−.09	−.10	.00	+.11	+.13	+.15	+.13	.00	+.25	+.14
4. University loyalty I				■	−.03	−.17	−.04	+.15	+.13	+.21	+.17	+.08	+.10	+.11
5. University loyalty II					■	−.01	−.08	+.07	+.07	+.07	+.08	+.06	+.13	+.09
6. Father's social class						■	+.07	−.12	−.06	−.02	−.10	−.15	−.07	−.13
7. Place of residence							■	+.12	+.14	+.08	−.10	.08	−.07	.00
8. Status according to encyclopedias								■	+.23	+.78	+.23	+.13	+.13	+.16
9. Number of lines									■	+.32	+.56	+.29	+.31	+.26
10. Number of reference books										■	+.38	+.13	+.20	+.30
11. Academies etc.											■	+.40	+.41	+.47
12. Swedish honorary doctor's degrees												■	+.17	+.47
13. Government committees													■	+.57
14. Memberships in research councils														■

15. Enumerated international commissions
16. Foreign guest professorships
17. Academic positions
18. Published works
19. Name of doctor's thesis given in 'Vem är det'
20. Distinctions
21. Foreign honorary doctor's degrees
22. Researcher's status
23. General status
24. Academic power

B. Family cluster
25. Number of marriages
26. Number of children
27. Educational level of the subject's wife
28. Number of years between first examination and appointment to full professor
29. Age at doctor's dissertation
30. Age at appointment to full professor
31. Income
32. Income of the subject's wife
33. Imminence between first marriage and first child
34. Imminence between first and second child

C. Social cluster
35. Number of clubs
36. Number of hobbies

										B. Family cluster										C. Social cluster	
15	16	17	18	19	20	21	22	23	24	25	26	27	28	29	30	31	32	33	34	35	36
−.08	+.11	−.05	−.02	+.05	−.03	+.07	−.01	−.06	−.06	+.10	−.09	+.03	−.25	+.02	−.17	+.11	+.13	−.08	+.03	−.04	−.06
+.13	+.01	+.21	+.39	−.06	+.55	+.28	+.58	+.37	+.49	−.28	+.14	−.16	+.51	+.18	+.47	−.15	−.16	.00	−.17	−.06	+.09
+.09	+.04	+.10	−.08	.00	+.09	+.08	+.09	+.20	+.20	−.19	+.04	+.18	−.47	−.19	−.52	−.37	+.41	+.04	−.15	−.09	+.03
+.02	+.06	+.05	+.15	+.11	+.12	+.05	+.18	+.17	+.15	−.04	−.06	+.12	+.15	+.09	+.17	+.10	.00	−.12	−.23	+.05	−.06
+.11	+.05	+.03	+.10	+.15	−.02	+.04	+.12	+.10	+.12	+.09	+.09	+.15	−.17	−.10	−.07	+.10	.00	−.02	−.04	+.04	+.07
−.04	−.16	−.18	−.01	−.03	+.10	+.14	−.07	−.14	−.12	.00	+.03	−.10	−.07	−.10	−.02	+.06	−.06	+.01	+.10	−.28	+.10
+.19	+.34	+.03	+.10	−.13	−.24	−.04	+.04	+.11	−.04	+.05	−.31	−.06	−.04	+.13	−.09	−.10	+.32	.00	−.14	−.14	−.14
+.23	+.16	+.02	−.01	−.03	+.06	+.03	+.21	+.45	+.26	−.12	−.03	+.18	−.02	−.21	−.15	+.03	−.03	.00	+.08	−.02	−.13
+.33	+.18	+.13	+.48	+.12	+.39	+.53	+.72	+.86	+.58	−.24	+.16	+.06	+.05	+.01	+.06	−.02	−.11	+.18	−.06	+.12	+.05
+.19	−.02	+.11	+.15	+.10	+.26	+.11	+.37	+.53	+.40	−.21	−.01	+.07	+.15	−.20	.00	+.04	−.11	+.03	−.03	+.02	−.12
+.23	−.04	+.38	+.29	+.01	+.68	+.63	+.91	+.56	+.92	−.17	+.18	−.13	+.03	−.18	+.02	+.12	−.17	+.04	−.12	+.17	+.10
+.05	+.35	+.14	−.10	−.06	+.24	+.47	+.38	+.27	+.38	−.43	+.26	+.15	−.08	−.19	−.12	+.40	−.03	+.05	+.08	−.05	−.07
+.26	+.01	+.03	+.11	−.10	+.27	+.31	+.43	+.44	+.66	.00	+.15	+.05	−.17	−.11	−.14	+.03	−.11	+.18	−.04	+.08	+.05
+.02	+.03	+.16	+.01	−.04	+.20	+.31	+.43	+.33	+.56	−.09	+.17	+.09	+.01	−.18	−.03	+.14	+.05	+.20	−.13	−.08	−.04
■	+.13	+.15	+.02	−.09	+.17	+.10	+.37	+.33	+.48	+.01	+.07	−.09	−.18	+.07	−.11	−.08	−.27	+.20	−.03	+.36	+.04
	■	−.05	−.06	−.08	−.04	+.08	+.07	+.15	+.01	−.13	+.02	+.20	−.10	−.13	−.09	−.02	−.10	−.01	+.08	−.05	−.10
		■	+.04	+.04	+.14	−.01	+.28	+.11	+.37	+.03	−.05	+.03	+.03	−.13	+.05	−.03	−.19	+.06	−.19	−.03	+.03
			■	+.15	+.24	+.06	+.58	+.35	+.24	+.05	−.09	−.05	+.18	+.11	+.19	−.03	+.02	−.02	−.16	+.10	+.13
				■	+.11	−.10	+.02	+.26	−.04	+.03	−.06	−.10	−.02	−.05	+.04	+.21	−.22	+.07	−.06	−.02	+.07
					■	+.55	+.65	+.35	+.61	−.28	+.23	−.17	+.17	−.01	+.12	−.04	−.37	+.05	−.09	+.06	+.36
						■	+.63	+.45	+.57	−.24	+.18	−.06	−.07	−.18	−.12	+.06	−.20	+.05	+.01	−.04	.00
							■	+.66	+.89	−.15	+.14	−.11	+.04	−.11	+.03	+.08	−.18	+.08	−.14	+.20	+.11
								■	+.62	−.21	+.09	+.06	−.05	−.14	−.09	.00	−.14	+.19	−.04	+.09	−.01
									■	−.12	+.20	−.10	−.06	−.16	−.05	+.08	−.24	+.13	−.12	+.22	.09
										■	−.54	−.02	−.02	+.02	+.01	+.01	+.22	−.13	−.10	+.02	+.08
											■	.00	−.03	−.03	+.03	+.08	−.02	+.36	+.29	+.07	+.24
												■	−.13	+.02	−.04	−.14	+.48	+.13	+.04	−.14	+.03
													■	+.44	+.90	+.01	+.18	−.08	+.01	−.04	+.15
														■	+.51	−.09	+.31	−.04	−.25	−.04	+.09
															■	−.05	+.15	+.02	−.03	.00	+.12
																■	+.07	−.08	+.19	−.01	−.10
																	■	−.10	−.11	−.22	+.09
																		■	+.32	+.10	+.20
																			■	−.09	+.08
																				■	+.12
																					■

Table 77. *Sample of researchers in agriculture and forestry*

Variables	1	2	3	4	5	6	7	8	9	10	11	12	13	14
A. Research cluster														
1. Family name	■	+.02	+.13	+.06	−.11	+.27	+.13	+.11	+.02	+.15	−.06	+.03	−.03	−.18
2. Age		■	−.14	−.22	+.05	+.02	−.29	−.24	+.52	+.07	+.41	+.43	+.03	+.07
3. Academic performance			■	−.06	+.23	+.01	−.05	+.24	+.10	+.20	+.14	−.10	−.06	+.12
4. University loyalty I				■	+.69	+.11	+.11	−.01	−.16	−.10	−.22	−.35	+.07	−.05
5. University loyalty II					■	+.05	+.03	−.12	+.03	−.07	−.05	−.28	+.07	+.14
6. Father's social class						■	+.34	−.03	−.11	.00	−.03	+.05	−.13	+.02
7. Place of residence							■	+.11	−.21	+.09	−.13	−.03	−.04	−.02
8. Status according to encyclopedias								■	+.04	+.69	+.11	−.10	+.15	+.06
9. Number of lines									■	+.34	+.54	+.12	+.40	+.33
10. Number of reference books										■	+.33	+.08	+.28	+.27
11. Academies etc.											■	+.29	+.30	+.23
12. Swedish honorary doctor's degrees												■	.00	+.02
13. Government committees													■	+.50
14. Memberships in research councils														■
15. Enumerated international commissions														
16. Foreign guest professorships														
17. Academic positions														
18. Published works														
19. Name of doctor's thesis given in 'Vem är det'														
20. Distinctions														
21. Foreign honorary doctor's degrees														
22. Researcher's status														
23. General status														
24. Academic power														

B. Family cluster

25. Number of marriages
26. Number of children
27. Educational level of the subject's wife
28. Number of years between first examination and appointment to full professor
29. Age at doctor's dissertation
30. Age at appointment to full professor
31. Income
32. Income of the subject's wife
33. Imminence between first marriage and first child
34. Imminence between first and second child

C. Social cluster

35. Number of clubs
36. Number of hobbies

										B. Family cluster										C. Social cluster	
15	16	17	18	19	20	21	22	23	24	25	26	27	28	29	30	31	32	33	34	35	36

```
+.18 −.14 −.18 +.11 +.31 +.14 −.04 +.07 +.04 −.03    +.02 −.01 +.17 +.25 −.19 +.18 −.24 −.43 +.03 −.17    +.04 −.12
−.04 +.03 +.30 +.31 −.09 +.59 +.34 +.44 +.34 +.27    −.13 −.26 −.30 +.40 +.09 +.34 −.23 +.03 −.29 −.35    +.06 −.05
+.13 +.12 +.16 −.07 +.36 −.15 +.03 +.06 +.13 +.11    −.20 −.05 +.27 −.23  .00 −.21 −.11 −.13 +.07 −.05    −.15 −.23
+.06 −.19 −.15 −.01 −.12 +.11 −.21 −.14 −.12 −.09    +.14 −.08 +.12 +.03 −.27 −.07 −.11 +.16 +.27 −.19    +.08 +.10
+.03 +.08 −.06 −.13 −.06 +.17 −.20 −.11  .00 +.02    −.18 −.15  .00 +.15 −.07 +.12 −.13 +.10 +.46 −.16    +.06 +.07
−.26 −.08 −.07 −.29 +.14 +.07 −.02 −.27 −.12 −.17    +.19 +.02 +.05 +.27 +.06 +.17 −.21 −.56 −.01 +.33    +.05 −.34
−.03 +.06 −.03 −.24 +.07 −.15 −.05 −.23 −.12 −.11    +.06 +.06 +.33 −.15 −.04 −.21 −.28 +.04 +.10 +.24    −.20 −.13
+.31 +.02 +.09 −.05 +.30 +.03 +.02 +.10 +.39 +.24    −.12 +.09 +.10 −.08 +.04 −.05 −.10 −.31 +.06 +.05    −.11 −.02
+.38 +.04 +.20 +.62 +.09 +.43 +.26 +.78 +.90 +.64    −.43 −.07 −.06 +.07 −.20 +.03 +.11 +.20 −.28 −.28    −.01 −.13
+.44 +.07 +.32 +.13 +.32 +.22 +.13 +.38 +.59 +.51    −.06 −.02 +.03 +.05 −.08 +.02 +.14 −.16 −.08 −.08    −.13 −.06
+.11 +.01 +.35 +.15 −.07 +.49 +.28 +.58 +.54 +.72    −.06 +.04 −.25 −.13 −.31 −.17 +.05 +.29 +.06 −.22    −.11 −.17
−.08 +.11 +.27 +.15 −.05 +.12 +.47 +.31 +.57 +.15    +.05 −.18 −.26 −.03 +.06 −.03 −.17  .00 −.22 +.03    +.05 −.16
+.13 −.04 +.23 +.31 +.05 +.18 +.09 +.40 +.63 +.78    −.02 +.13 +.01 −.15 −.23 −.18 +.16 +.37 +.17 +.12    +.04 +.01
+.03 +.08 +.36 −.01 +.09 +.04 +.13 +.20 +.42 +.53    −.14 +.01 +.22 −.12 −.24 −.18 +.23 +.35 +.11 +.09    −.06 −.16
  ■  −.05 +.03 +.43 +.17  .00 +.03 +.59 +.43 +.45    −.32 +.02 +.13 −.02 −.14 +.02 −.03 −.24 −.25 −.61    −.02 +.07
       ■  +.20 −.10 +.09 −.06 +.32 +.04 +.03 +.01    −.14 −.16 +.09 −.13  .00 −.09 −.18 −.32 +.08 −.06    −.05 −.12
            ■  +.03 +.12 +.19 +.22 +.25 +.26 +.46    −.01 −.04 +.01 −.11 −.13 −.14 +.13 +.62 +.15 −.18    −.08 −.12
                 ■  +.02 +.19 +.21 +.84 +.55 +.37    −.30 −.13 −.04 +.02 −.11 −.01 −.03 +.17 −.24 −.53    −.06 +.09
                      ■  +.04 +.11 +.05 +.18 +.08    −.10 −.10 +.16 +.05 +.13 +.05 +.03 −.35 +.09 +.06    −.14 −.10
                           ■  +.32 +.34 +.40 +.35    −.14 −.12 −.18 +.38 −.10 +.28 −.13 +.20 +.05 −.11    −.03 +.10
                                ■  +.40 +.23 +.23    −.11 −.10 −.17 +.01 −.06 −.01 −.29  .00 −.18 −.02    −.06 −.15
                                     ■  +.75 +.72    −.33 −.10 −.09 −.06 −.27 −.09 −.03 +.23 −.22 −.63    −.09 −.04
                                          ■  +.80    −.36 +.01 −.02 −.01 −.21 −.05 +.11 +.15 −.14 −.14    −.04 −.11
                                                     −.16 +.09 −.04 −.17 −.36 −.20 +.15 +.34 −.06 −.24    −.06 −.08

                                                       ■  −.03  .00 −.05 +.06 −.07 +.14 +.10  .00 +.35    +.07 −.03
                                                            ■   .00 +.04 +.03 +.04 +.16 +.36 +.15 +.16    +.11 +.21
                                                                 ■  −.14 −.12 −.09 −.09 +.73 +.17 +.08    −.12 −.08
                                                                      ■  +.45 +.93 +.04 −.19 −.13 +.07    +.31 −.08
                                                                           ■  +.60 −.05 −.29 −.09 +.36    +.15 +.18
                                                                                ■  +.05 −.37 −.14 +.12    +.29 −.01
                                                                                     ■  +.59 −.17 +.13     .00 +.06
                                                                                          ■  +.52 +.07     .00  .00
                                                                                               ■  +.12    +.06 +.09
                                                                                                    ■     +.05 −.22

                                                                                                           ■  −.10
                                                                                                                ■
```

Table 78. *Sample of researchers in commerce, business administration*

	A. Research cluster													
Variables	1	2	3	4	5	6	7	8	9	10	11	12	13	14
A. Research cluster														
1. Family name	■	+.14	−.26	+.08	+.11	+.36	−.26	−.50	−.05	−.19	+.01	+.19	+.08	−.46
2. Age		■	+.21	−.04	+.08	+.13	−.20	−.02	+.49	+.12	+.47	+.14	−.03	−.09
3. Academic performance			■	−.20	−.17	−.09	−.03	+.32	+.32	+.33	+.24	−.25	−.03	+.16
4. University loyalty I				■	+.51	−.23	−.16	+.04	−.46	+.19	−.26	+.14	−.57	−.17
5. University loyalty II					■	+.04	−.13	−.07	−.07	+.09	−.10	+.11	−.11	−.24
6. Father's social class						■	−.16	+.01	+.30	+.10	+.25	+.02	+.34	−.14
7. Place of residence							■	+.13	+.02	+.08	+.07	−.02	+.06	−.06
8. Status according to encyclopedias								■	+.12	+.75	+.26	−.09	+.07	+.49
9. Number of lines									■	+.21	+.76	−.13	+.39	+.14
10. Number of reference books										■	+.40	+.04	+.17	+.24
11. Academies etc.											■	+.09	+.39	+.38
12. Swedish honorary doctor's degrees												■	+.18	+.19
13. Government committees													■	+.04
14. Memberships in research councils														■

15. Enumerated international commissions
16. Foreign guest professorships
17. Academic positions
18. Published works
19. Name of doctor's thesis given in 'Vem är det'
20. Distinctions
21. Foreign honorary doctor's degrees
22. Researcher's status
23. General status
24. Academic power

B. Family cluster
25. Number of marriages
26. Number of children
27. Educational level of the subject's wife
28. Number of years between first examination and appointment to full professor
29. Age at doctor's dissertation
30. Age at appointment to full professor
31. Income
32. Income of the subject's wife
33. Imminence between first marriage and first child
34. Imminence between first and second child

C. Social cluster
35. Number of clubs
36. Number of hobbies

236

										B. Family cluster										C. Social cluster	
15	16	17	18	19	20	21	22	23	24	25	26	27	28	29	30	31	32	33	34	35	36
+.05	−.17	+.15	+.31	−.31	−.15	+.08	+.17	−.16	+.05	−.42	+.12	−.05	−.14	−.13	−.11	−.04	+.76	+.14	+.35	.00	−.02
+.02	+.01	+.26	+.43	−.35	+.42	+.30	+.46	+.37	+.23	−.29	+.13	−.16	−.24	−.26	−.24	−.18	+.04	+.21	−.39	.00	−.09
−.26	−.01	+.12	+.33	+.23	+.20	+.10	+.23	+.35	+.05	−.13	+.02	+.17	+.14	−.13	−.01	+.13	−.59	−.26	+.05	.00	−.22
−.27	−.12	+.22	−.40	.00	−.02	−.44	−.46	−.46	−.47	−.09	+.02	−.27	−.01	+.01	−.14	+.09	+.10	+.32	−.19	.00	+.08
+.22	+.21	+.18	−.14	+.13	+.14	+.09	−.03	−.08	−.04	−.08	+.19	−.13	−.24	−.09	−.44	+.10	+.10	+.34	−.09	.00	+.02
+.28	−.06	+.09	+.31	+.15	+.11	+.12	+.31	+.33	+.36	−.14	+.29	+.03	−.02	+.24	+.21	−.03	+.53	−.19	+.35	.00	+.25
−.01	+.16	−.40	−.03	+.21	+.17	+.07	+.04	+.07	+.01	−.09	+.06	.00	+.09	+.18	+.10	+.15	+.05	+.26	−.05	.00	+.03
−.13	+.17	+.06	−.07	+.24	+.26	+.08	+.06	+.44	+.17	+.09	−.03	+.14	+.05	+.11	+.02	+.35	−.15	−.35	+.14	.00	−.07
+.40	+.53	−.03	+.50	+.11	+.60	+.72	+.81	+.91	+.67	−.21	+.20	+.23	−.16	−.24	−.11	−.15	−.29	+.01	+.21	.00	−.16
+.03	+.42	+.30	+.18	+.12	+.63	−.03	+.33	+.51	+.33	+.03	+.06	+.02	−.06	−.06	−.23	+.60	+.49	−.27	+.07	.00	−.02
+.21	+.31	+.21	+.32	+.07	+.60	+.43	+.69	+.78	+.77	−.41	−.14	+.12	−.09	.00	−.17	+.01	+.19	−.42	+.01	.00	.00
−.05	−.20	+.45	−.03	−.20	−.06	−.09	+.02	−.07	+.18	+.11	−.36	+.18	−.15	−.26	−.33	+.22	+.68	−.16	−.01	.00	+.34
+.62	+.31	−.11	+.28	+.02	+.39	+.32	+.52	+.59	+.85	−.03	+.09	−.03	−.16	+.01	−.16	+.34	+.91	−.28	+.26	.00	+.27
−.19	−.07	+.32	−.31	+.35	−.13	−.08	−.06	+.26	+.25	+.10	−.39	+.22	+.23	+.34	+.08	+.06	−.49	−.69	+.10	.00	−.03
■	+.41	−.11	+.28	−.18	−.36	+.51	+.55	+.44	+.65	+.15	+.17	+.05	−.47	−.03	−.32	+.24	+.91	+.11	+.12	.00	+.12
	■	−.22	+.19	+.25	+.74	+.38	+.50	+.57	+.38	+.14	+.07	−.01	−.08	−.27	−.24	+.20	−.59	+.16	+.14	.00	−.18
		■	+.15	−.15	+.02	−.10	+.12	.00	+.14	+.12	−.08	+.27	−.18	−.13	−.27	+.32	+.40	−.39	−.58	.00	−.04
			■	−.37	+.41	+.46	+.83	+.46	+.37	−.11	+.20	+.14	−.60	−.49	.00	+.24	+.51	+.05	+.05	.00	−.03
				■	.00	−.23	−.21	+.15	.00	.00	+.03	−.04	+.48	+.45	+.36	−.06	−.49	−.13	+.24	.00	+.05
					■	+.31	+.67	+.69	+.57	−.13	+.16	−.17	−.19	−.27	−.30	+.30	+.54	+.09	−.15	.00	−.07
						■	+.70	+.60	+.48	−.08	+.05	+.26	−.31	−.33	−.40	+.05	+.03	+.10	+.20	.00	−.12
							■	+.80	+.74	−.15	+.09	+.19	−.46	−.34	−.22	+.24	+.63	−.07	+.12	.00	−.03
								■	+.80	−.14	+.17	+.20	−.16	−.16	−.15	+.14	+.13	−.17	+.25	.00	−.07
									■	−.15	−.01	+.10	−.24	+.01	−.26	+.28	+.81	−.37	+.13	.00	+.16
										■	−.02	+.17	.00	−.10	−.02	+.24	+.03	−.17	−.10	.00	+.15
											■	−.15	+.03	−.02	+.23	−.21	+.06	+.47	+.15	.00	−.09
												■	−.06	−.22	−.04	−.12	−.13	−.25	+.21	.00	−.27
													■	+.74	+.68	−.29	−.63	−.14	+.20	.00	−.29
														■	+.74	−.20	−.93	−.18	+.17	.00	+.19
															■	−.39	−.33	+.05	+.19	.00	+.06
																■	+.65	−.29	+.02	.00	+.15
																	■	−.37	.00	.00	+.91
																		■	−.16	.00	−.22
																			■	.00	+.13
																				■	.00
																					■

Table 79. *Sample of directors from commerce faculty*

Variables	A. Research cluster													
	1	2	3	4	5	6	7	8	9	10	11	12	13	14
A. Research cluster														
1. Family name	■	+.05	+.05	.00	.00	+.04	+.20	+.18	+.15	+.15	+.01	+.04	+.07	+.05
2. Age		■	+.01	.00	.00	−.15	+.04	−.11	+.23	+.04	+.21	+.17	+.21	+.04
3. Academic performance			■	.00	.00	−.08	−.08	+.02	+.10	+.08	+.29	+.51	+.21	−.03
4. University loyalty I				■	.00	.00	.00	.00	.00	.00	.00	.00	.00	.00
5. University loyalty II					■	.00	.00	.00	.00	.00	.00	.00	.00	.00
6. Father's social class						■	−.12	.00	+.13	−.09	−.02	−.14	−.10	−.08
7. Place of residence							■	+.08	−.04	+.07	−.09	−.03	+.10	−.04
8. Status according to encyclopedias								■	+.44	+.75	+.25	+.14	+.21	+.33
9. Number of lines									■	+.41	+.39	+.09	+.52	+.33
10. Number of reference books										■	+.42	+.34	+.24	+.44
11. Academies etc.											■	+.60	+.07	+.22
12. Swedish honorary doctor's degrees												■	+.16	−.02
13. Government committees													■	+.06
14. Memberships in research councils														■
15. Enumerated international commissions														
16. Foreign guest professorships														
17. Academic positions														
18. Published works														
19. Name of doctor's thesis given in 'Vem är det'														
20. Distinctions														
21. Foreign honorary doctor's degrees														
22. Researcher's status														
23. General status														
24. Academic power														
B. Family cluster														
25. Number of marriages														
26. Number of children														
27. Educational level of the subject's wife														
28. Number of years between first examination and appointment to full professor														
29. Age at doctor's dissertation														
30. Age at appointment to full professor														
31. Income														
32. Income of the subject's wife														
33. Imminence between first marriage and first child														
34. Imminence between first and second child														
C. Social cluster														
35. Number of clubs														
36. Number of hobbies														

										B. Family cluster										C. Social cluster	
15	16	17	18	19	20	21	22	23	24	25	26	27	28	29	30	31	32	33	34	35	36
+.08	.00	.00	+.10	.00	−.02	.00	+.10	+.16	+.08	−.05	−.11	+.05	.00	.00	.00	+.06	+.18	−.19	−.01	+.04	−.08
+.07	.00	.00	+.05	.00	+.41	.00	+.18	+.19	+.25	−.15	+.02	−.12	.00	.00	.00	+.24	−.22	−.03	−.16	+.09	−.04
−.05	.00	.00	+.10	.00	+.03	.00	+.22	+.11	+.23	+.03	+.02	+.17	.00	.00	.00	+.11	.00	+.01	−.06	−.05	+.09
.00	.00	.00	.00	.00	.00	.00	.00	.00	.00	.00	.00	.00	.00	.00	.00	.00	.00	.00	.00	.00	.00
.00	.00	.00	.00	.00	.00	.00	.00	.00	.00	.00	.00	.00	.00	.00	.00	.00	.00	.00	.00	.00	.00
−.11	.00	.00	−.07	.00	−.02	.00	−.12	+.12	−.12	−.11	+.17	−.09	.00	.00	.00	+.04	+.10	−.13	+.27	−.02	+.14
+.16	.00	.00	+.25	.00	+.04	.00	+.16	−.08	+.10	−.01	−.14	+.08	.00	.00	.00	+.03	+.06	+.15	−.18	−.02	−.10
+.17	.00	.00	+.12	.00	+.14	.00	+.30	+.65	+.31	−.05	−.04	+.20	.00	.00	.00	+.28	+.56	+.07	+.09	−.02	+.20
+.32	.00	.00	+.20	.00	+.36	.00	+.46	+.88	+.63	−.16	+.07	.00	.00	.00	.00	+.28	−.03	+.05	+.14	+.03	+.13
+.21	.00	.00	+.36	.00	+.19	.00	+.56	+.53	+.40	−.04	.00	+.31	.00	.00	.00	+.43	+.54	+.12	−.03	−.02	+.66
−.04	.00	.00	+.18	.00	+.45	.00	+.63	+.47	+.37	−.11	+.09	+.08	.00	.00	.00	+.46	+.10	+.16	−.02	+.07	+.34
−.04	.00	.00	+.12	.00	+.15	.00	+.44	+.12	+.30	+.02	+.06	+.13	.00	.00	.00	+.31	.00	+.08	−.08	−.04	+.22
+.46	.00	.00	+.19	.00	+.31	.00	+.36	+.51	+.91	+.05	−.08	−.02	.00	.00	.00	+.04	+.54	+.02	+.04	+.07	−.08
+.10	.00	.00	+.10	.00	+.15	.00	+.28	+.37	+.21	+.03	+.06	−.06	.00	.00	.00	+.20	.00	+.11	−.02	−.05	−.04
■	.00	.00	+.20	.00	+.32	.00	+.53	+.24	+.64	+.16	−.09	.00	.00	.00	.00	−.10	+.26	−.09	−.04	+.10	−.16
	■	.00	.00	.00	.00	.00	.00	.00	.00	.00	.00	.00	.00	.00	.00	.00	.00	.00	.00	.00	.00
		■	.00	.00	.00	.00	.00	.00	.00	.00	.00	.00	.00	.00	.00	.00	.00	.00	.00	.00	.00
			■	.00	+.20	.00	+.74	+.16	+.27	−.21	−.09	+.15	.00	.00	.00	+.05	−.12	−.01	−.02	−.01	−.06
				■	.00	.00	.00	.00	.00	.00	.00	.00	.00	.00	.00	.00	.00	.00	.00	.00	.00
					■	.00	+.48	+.46	+.48	−.15	+.02	+.07	.00	.00	.00	+.35	+.16	+.12	+.01	+.29	+.17
						■	.00	.00	.00	.00	.00	.00	.00	.00	.00	.00	.00	.00	.00	.00	.00
							■	+.45	+.64	−.09	−.01	+.13	.00	.00	.00	+.27	+.11	+.05	−.05	+.07	+.08
								■	+.63	−.15	+.05	+.06	.00	.00	.00	+.41	+.41	+.08	+.98	+.14	+.22
									■	+.05	−.05	.00	.00	.00	.00	+.17	+.43	+.05	+.01	+.10	.00
										■	−.08	+.03	.00	.00	.00	+.01	−.01	−.11	−.06	−.16	−.22
											■	−.08	.00	.00	.00	+.24	−.18	+.29	+.25	+.10	+.18
												■	.00	.00	.00	+.23	+.36	+.03	+.02	+.07	−.06
													■	.00	.00	.00	.00	.00	.00	.00	.00
														■	.00	.00	.00	.00	.00	.00	.00
															■	+.25	+.19	+.04		+.06	+.04
																■	−.25	+.31		+.31	+.18
																	■	.00		−.05	+.13
																		■		−.27	+.08
																			■		
																				■	+.26
																					■

Table 80. *Sample of scientists in engineering*

Variables	A. Research cluster													
	1	2	3	4	5	6	7	8	9	10	11	12	13	14
A. Research cluster														
1. Family name	■	+.15	−.11	+.10	−.11	+.23	−.02	+.11	+.10	+.13	+.09	+.04	−.01	−.08
2. Age		■	−.08	−.05	−.06	.00	+.28	+.13	+.44	+.29	+.50	+.22	+.18	+.04
3. Academic performance			■	−.02	−.15	+.08	+.07	+.19	−.10	+.14	+.02	+.07	−.04	+.06
4. University loyalty I				■	+.41	+.05	−.09	−.14	−.06	−.12	+.17	+.04	+.04	−.06
5. University loyalty II					■	+.12	−.12	−.06	+.13	+.11	+.15	+.03	+.04	−.14
6. Father's social class						■	+.16	+.05	+.03	+.10	−.02	+.09	+.05	−.26
7. Place of residence							■	+.14	+.22	+.08	+.07	+.04	+.06	−.09
8. Status according to encyclopedias								■	+.28	+.72	+.24	+.01	+.18	+.43
9. Number of lines									■	+.41	+.43	+.10	+.52	+.21
10. Number of reference books										■	+.40	+.07	+.34	+.29
11. Academies etc.											■	+.30	+.32	+.08
12. Swedish honorary doctor's degrees												■	+.04	−.03
13. Government committees													■	+.32
14. Memberships in research councils														■

15. Enumerated international commissions
16. Foreign guest professorships
17. Academic positions
18. Published works
19. Name of doctor's thesis given in 'Vem är det'
20. Distinctions
21. Foreign honorary doctor's degrees
22. Researcher's status
23. General status
24. Academic power

B. Family cluster
25. Number of marriages
26. Number of children
27. Educational level of the subject's wife
28. Number of years between first examination and appointment to full professor
29. Age at doctor's dissertation
30. Age at appointment to full professor
31. Income
32. Income of the subject's wife
33. Imminence between first marriage and first child
34. Imminence between first and second child

C. Social cluster
35. Number of clubs
36. Number of hobbies

240

15	16	17	18	19	20	21	22	23	24	B. Family cluster 25	26	27	28	29	30	31	32	33	34	C. Social cluster 35	36
−.11	.00	+.08	+.10	+.02	+.18	+.09	+.14	+.13	+.08	−.04	+.07	.00	−.02	+.12	−.02	−.05	−.08	+.07	+.01	−.18	+.13
+.06	−.05	+.08	+.03	−.10	+.56	+.09	+.31	+.35	+.39	−.24	+.17	−.12	+.63	+.21	+.51	.00	−.10	+.18	−.03	−.10	+.02
−.07	+.11	+.14	+.01	−.03	−.15	−.09	+.03	−.04	−.02	+.08	.00	+.18	−.33	−.11	−.47	−.07	+.17	−.02	.00	−.04	+.06
+.06	−.09	−.05	+.18	+.13	+.18	+.08	+.22	−.04	+.12	+.06	+.03	−.04	−.07	−.05	−.14	+.06	+.07	+.14	+.16	+.08	+.01
+.10	+.07	−.12	+.09	+.05	+.07	+.06	+.19	+.10	+.11	−.39	+.36	+.08	−.21	−.25	−.16	+.21	.00	+.10	+.06	+.06	−.09
+.02	+.07	+.03	+.09	+.13	−.08	−.05	+.05	+.17	+.01	−.08	+.09	+.07	+.05	+.01	+.02	−.06	+.18	−.16	−.15	−.11	+.08
+.09	+.03	+.01	+.11	−.04	+.06	+.08	+.13	+.18	+.09	−.03	−.03	−.11	+.23	+.10	+.25	+.02	+.22	.00	+.03	−.05	+.09
+.13	+.07	+.21	−.07	+.01	+.15	+.15	+.20	+.31	+.32	−.12	+.13	−.11	−.10	−.11	−.11	+.21	+.04	+.03	−.02	−.07	+.23
+.25	+.21	+.09	+.47	+.15	+.42	+.13	+.66	+.75	+.61	−.27	+.23	−.04	+.26	−.01	+.25	+.14	−.12	+.01	−.02	+.11	+.14
+.06	+.17	+.18	+.02	−.02	+.25	+.32	+.34	+.40	+.45	−.24	+.30	−.05	+.09	−.24	−.03	+.24	+.13	+.13	−.03	−.04	+.03
+.14	−.05	+.12	+.04	.00	+.44	+.30	+.63	+.36	+.77	−.24	+.22	−.06	+.25	−.26	+.17	+.14	+.11	+.17	−.02	.00	+.01
−.04	−.02	+.37	−.03	−.05	+.25	−.02	+.16	+.03	+.20	+.02	+.10	−.04	+.07	−.22	+.04	−.11	.00	+.07	+.15	−.02	−.04
+.13	+.08	+.04	+.12	−.03	+.24	−.02	+.33	+.57	+.78	−.21	+.20	−.09	+.06	−.13	+.06	+.29	+.29	+.19	−.24	+.24	+.15
+.06	−.02	+.25	−.08	+.04	+.08	−.06	+.09	+.19	+.33	+.05	+.14	−.08	−.08	−.08	−.05	+.19	+.25	+.13	.00	+.25	+.11
■	+.11	+.09	+.20	+.02	+.11	+.08	+.51	+.10	+.43	−.07	−.01	−.06	+.11	+.14	+.20	+.07	−.15	+.05	+.06	+.09	−.17
	■	−.04	+.15	+.16	+.03	−.04	+.38	+.08	+.05	+.04	+.10	−.05	−.16	−.13	−.18	−.06	−.25	−.15	−.02	−.04	−.03
		■	−.06	−.10	+.06	−.04	+.08	+.05	+.20	+.04	−.02	−.07	−.01	+.01	−.03	−.04	.00	−.02	−.06	−.04	−.08
			■	+.31	+.10	−.11	+.67	+.30	+.13	+.10	+.07	−.05	−.15	+.05	−.09	+.02	−.11	+.10	+.16	−.04	−.05
				■	+.03	−.11	+.22	−.03	−.02	−.03	+.05	+.22	−.14	+.10	−.20	+.11	+.31	−.09	+.17	−.10	+.09
					■	+.28	+.37	+.33	+.41	−.21	+.31	−.25	+.38	−.07	+.29	+.15	+.01	+.12	+.10	+.02	+.08
						■	+.17	+.09	+.17	−.10	+.20	−.08	+.18	−.17	+.10	+.03	.00	+.11	+.13	−.04	−.09
							■	+.44	+.67	−.09	+.21	−.11	+.06	−.14	+.05	+.10	−.07	+.13	+.10	+.01	−.07
								■	+.55	−.30	+.28	−.09	+.21	+.01	+.23	+.21	−.03	+.02	−.14	+.18	+.34
									■	−.26	+.23	−.11	+.19	−.18	+.17	+.27	+.22	+.21	−.13	+.17	+.04
										■	−.27	+.07	−.31	−.01	−.27	−.32	−.45	−.13	+.32	−.07	−.29
											■	−.19	+.14	−.11	+.08	+.26	−.15	+.29	+.17	−.02	+.08
												■	−.02	−.07	−.11	−.01	+.29	+.09	−.03	−.07	+.05
													■	+.63	+.92	+.06	+.04	+.13	−.06	−.01	+.03
														■	+.67	−.02	−.22	−.17	−.10	−.07	+.14
															■	−.05	−.04	+.08	−.02	−.01	+.01
																■	+.48	+.23	−.11	+.39	+.21
																	■	+.33	−.56	+.22	+.09
																		■	+.06	+.19	−.01
																			■	−.21	−.42
																				■	+.20
																					■

Table 81. *Sample of directors from engineering faculty*

Variables	A. Research cluster													
	1	2	3	4	5	6	7	8	9	10	11	12	13	14
A. Research cluster														
1. Family name	■	+.04	−.25	.00	.00	−.12	.00	.00	−.05	−.06	.00	−.19	−.02	−.03
2. Age		■	−.14	.00	.00	−.19	−.06	−.03	+.02	+.09	+.27	+.18	+.15	−.25
3. Academic performance			■	.00	.00	−.19	+.05	+.12	+.16	+.11	+.11	−.04	−.03	+.36
4. University loyalty I				■	.00	.00	.00	.00	.00	.00	.00	.00	.00	.00
5. University loyalty II					■	.00	.00	.00	.00	.00	.00	.00	.00	.00
6. Father's social class						■	−.16	+.02	−.01	−.12	−.10	−.10	−.14	−.03
7. Place of residence							■	+.07	−.03	−.03	+.01	−.07	+.01	−.04
8. Status according to encyclopedias								■	+.33	+.73	+.32	+.21	+.23	+.17
9. Number of lines									■	+.33	+.36	−.08	+.22	+.22
10. Number of reference books										■	+.50	+.50	+.12	+.29
11. Academies etc.											■	+.31	+.27	+.05
12. Swedish honorary doctor's degrees												■	−.09	+.11
13. Government committees													■	+.15
14. Memberships in research councils														■
15. Enumerated international commissions														
16. Foreign guest professorships														
17. Academic positions														
18. Published works														
19. Name of doctor's thesis given in 'Vem är det'														
20. Distinctions														
21. Foreign honorary doctor's degrees														
22. Researcher's status														
23. General status														
24. Academic power														
B. Family cluster														
25. Number of marriages														
26. Number of children														
27. Educational level of the subject's wife														
28. Number of years between first examination and appointment to full professor														
29. Age at doctor's dissertation														
30. Age at appointment to full professor														
31. Income														
32. Income of the subject's wife														
33. Imminence between first marriage and first child														
34. Imminence between first and second child														
C. Social cluster														
35. Number of clubs														
36. Number of hobbies														

										B. Family cluster										C. Social cluster	
15	16	17	18	19	20	21	22	23	24	25	26	27	28	29	30	31	32	33	34	35	36
+.10	+.04	.00	−.01	−.13	−.11	.00	+.02	−.04	+.02	−.01	.00	+.08	.00	.00	.00	−.07	−.23	+.05	+.24	+.05	+.07
+.08	+.05	.00	+.10	−.08	+.56	.00	+.16	+.07	+.19	−.09	−.06	−.16	.00	.00	.00	−.20	.00	−.18	−.23	+.23	+.03
−.07	−.02	.00	+.17	+.41	+.09	.00	+.16	+.07	+.06	+.03	+.03	+.05	.00	.00	.00	+.22	+.77	+.13	+.04	−.10	+.03
.00	.00	.00	.00	.00	.00	.00	.00	.00	.00	.00	.00	.00	.00	.00	.00	.00	.00	.00	.00	.00	.00
.00	.00	.00	.00	.00	.00	.00	.00	.00	.00	.00	.00	.00	.00	.00	.00	.00	.00	.00	.00	.00	.00
+.02	+.07	.00	+.11	−.12	+.02	.00	+.01	+.02	−.13	−.01	+.27	−.08	.00	.00	.00	−.08	−.15	−.02	+.14	+.08	.05
+.11	+.08	.00	−.06	+.08	−.07	.00	+.02	−.06	+.04	+.05	−.10	+.12	.00	.00	.00	+.06	−.07	−.14	+.01	−.13	−.36
+.39	+.34	.00	+.48	−.04	+.13	.00	+.57	+.55	+.43	+.10	+.03	+.05	.00	.00	.00	+.21	−.06	+.19	+.06	−.03	+.12
+.27	+.36	.00	+.60	+.09	+.20	.00	+.66	+.87	+.41	+.02	+.12	+.01	.00	.00	.00	+.28	+.33	+.16	−.08	+.04	+.08
+.28	+.12	.00	+.43	−.04	+.28	.00	+.62	+.54	+.42	+.07	−.03	+.07	.00	.00	.00	+.35	−.10	+.18	+.01	+.05	+.10
+.16	+.31	.00	+.39	−.05	+.32	.00	+.73	+.38	+.63	+.11	+.05	+.07	.00	.00	.00	+.20	−.28	+.13	+.08	+.01	+.05
−.04	−.01	.00	−.06	−.01	+.11	.00	+.17	.00	+.07	+.05	−.05	+.01	.00	.00	.00	−.01	−.18	−.08	−.15	−.07	−.09
+.23	+.22	.00	+.27	−.07	+.17	.00	+.37	+.48	+.83	−.05	+.01	.00	.00	.00	.00	−.09	+.07	+.04	−.07	+.05	+.21
−.10	−.03	.00	+.30	−.03	−.05	.00	+.31	+.28	+.24	+.04	−.01	+.18	.00	.00	.00	+.24	+.03	+.24	−.13	+.07	+.10
■	+.17	.00	+.23	−.03	+.17	.00	+.56	+.30	+.55	+.03	+.04	−.11	.00	.00	.00	+.06	.00	+.03	+.07	−.07	+.28
	■	.00	+.47	−.01	+.08	.00	+.46	+.32	+.32	+.03	+.11	−.04	.00	.00	.00	+.09	.00	+.07	+.05	−.05	+.14
		■	.00	.00	.00	.00	.00	.00	.00	.00	.00	.00	.00	.00	.00	.00	.00	.00	.00	.00	.00
			■	+.05	+.36	.00	+.80	+.65	+.45	−.01	+.07	−.04	.00	.00	.00	+.26	+.05	+.18	−.24	+.19	+.21
				■	+.01	.00	−.02	.00	−.08	+.03	+.11	−.04	.00	.00	.00	.00	.00	−.08	−.02	−.05	−.06
					■	.00	+.38	+.27	+.29	+.04	+.08	−.19	.00	.00	.00	+.03	+.05	−.09	+.01	+.21	+.06
						■	.00	.00	.00	.00	.00	.00	.00	.00	.00	.00	.00	.00	.00	.00	.00
							■	+.65	+.77	+.06	+.08	.00	.00	.00	.00	+.28	−.12	+.19	−.07	+.07	+.25
								■	+.60	+.01	+.09	.00	.00	.00	.00	+.34	+.12	+.12	−.06	+.12	+.16
									■	+.03	+.04	+.02	.00	.00	.00	+.08	−.06	+.13	.00	+.02	+.24
										■	−.02	+.02	.00	.00	.00	+.16	−.42	−.10	+.13	−.18	−.19
											■	−.04	.00	.00	.00	−.03	+.39	+.13	+.36	+.06	+.10
												■	.00	.00	.00	.00	−.30	+.13	+.02	+.11	+.06
													■	.00	.00	.00	.00	.00	.00	.00	.00
														■	.00	.00	.00	.00	.00	.00	.00
															■	.00	.00	.00	.00	.00	.00
																■	−.14	+.16	−.01	.00	+.05
																	■	+.35	−.27	+.10	+.02
																		■	+.18	+.17	−.30
																			■	+.25	−.10
																				■	+.43
																					■

Table 82. *Sample of higher forestry officers*

Variables	A. Research cluster													
	1	2	3	4	5	6	7	8	9	10	11	12	13	14
A. Research cluster														
1. Family name	■	+.01	−.12	.00	.00	+.14	−.04	−.21	−.07	−.20	+.08	−.21	−.06	+.25
2. Age		■	−.22	.00	.00	+.01	−.06	+.01	+.04	+.22	+.15	+.24	+.34	+.02
3. Academic performance			■	.00	.00	−.12	−.17	+.14	+.21	+.10	+.01	−.06	−.16	−.03
4. University loyalty I				■	.00	.00	.00	.00	.00	.00	.00	.00	.00	.00
5. University loyalty II					■	.00	.00	.00	.00	.00	.00	.00	.00	.00
6. Father's social class						■	−.10	+.20	+.07	+.14	−.02	−.16	−.23	+.07
7. Place of residence							■	+.11	+.01	.00	+.02	+.09	+.11	+.18
8. Status according to encyclopedias								■	+.23	+.92	−.10	+.09	−.06	−.06
9. Number of lines									■	+.23	+.26	+.20	+.44	+.12
10. Number of reference books										■	−.03	+.10	+.01	−.04
11. Academies etc.											■	+.50	+.24	+.13
12. Swedish honorary doctor's degrees												■	+.53	−.04
13. Government committees													■	+.09
14. Memberships in research councils														■
15. Enumerated international commissions														
16. Foreign guest professorships														
17. Academic positions														
18. Published works														
19. Name of doctor's thesis given in 'Vem är det'														
20. Distinctions														
21. Foreign honorary doctor's degrees														
22. Researcher's status														
23. General status														
24. Academic power														
B. Family cluster														
25. Number of marriages														
26. Number of children														
27. Educational level of the subject's wife														
28. Number of years between first examination and appointment to full professor														
29. Age at doctor's dissertation														
30. Age at appointment to full professor														
31. Income														
32. Income of the subject's wife														
33. Imminence between first marriage and first child														
34. Imminence between first and second child														
C. Social cluster														
35. Number of clubs														
36. Number of hobbies														

244

										B. Family cluster										C. Social cluster	
15	16	17	18	19	20	21	22	23	24	25	26	27	28	29	30	31	32	33	34	35	36
+.16	.00	.00	−.23	.00	+.26	.00	−.16	−.03	+.04	+.05	+.44	−.26	.00	.00	.00	+.19	−.78	+.15	−.12	−.11	−.18
−.11	.00	.00	+.03	.00	+.44	.00	+.07	+.21	+.29	−.29	+.13	+.01	.00	.00	.00	−.10	+.47	+.34	−.17	+.21	+.22
+.26	.00	.00	+.28	.00	−.12	.00	+.31	+.08	−.05	+.05	−.07	−.06	.00	.00	.00	−.01	−.30	−.17	+.09	−.11	−.14
.00	.00	.00	.00	.00	.00	.00	.00	.00	.00	.00	.00	.00	.00	.00	.00	.00	.00	.00	.00	.00	.00
.00	.00	.00	.00	.00	.00	.00	.00	.00	.00	.00	.00	.00	.00	.00	.00	.00	.00	.00	.00	.00	.00
+.11	.00	.00	+.18	.00	+.08	.00	+.17	−.01	−.15	−.16	−.19	+.12	.00	.00	.00	+.12	.00	+.08	−.10	+.02	+.17
+.15	.00	.00	−.01	.00	−.22	.00	+.04	.00	+.14	−.24	−.16	+.07	.00	.00	.00	−.23	+.18	+.07	+.04	+.09	−.25
+.02	.00	.00	+.66	.00	+.09	.00	+.58	+.24	−.08	−.04	−.05	+.64	.00	.00	.00	−.14	+.76	−.01	+.38	+.03	+.11
+.19	.00	.00	+.51	.00	+.25	.00	+.59	+.92	+.49	−.02	−.07	+.15	.00	.00	.00	+.15	+.31	−.05	−.08	+.15	+.16
−.06	.00	.00	+.61	.00	+.16	.00	+.54	+.27	−.03	−.06	+.08	+.59	.00	.00	.00	−.13	+.74	−.01	+.38	+.06	+.15
+.05	.00	.00	−.08	.00	+.10	.00	+.28	+.34	+.62	−.07	+.19	+.08	.00	.00	.00	+.15	+.70	−.18	+.26	+.32	−.05
−.06	.00	.00	+.11	.00	+.24	.00	+.30	+.42	+.59	−.19	−.16	+.39	.00	.00	.00	−.15	+.70	−.03	+.21	+.43	+.18
.00	.00	.00	−.04	.00	+.51	.00	+.07	+.69	+.85	−.04	+.03	−.10	.00	.00	.00	−.03	+.04	+.06	−.01	+.42	+.32
+.87	.00	.00	−.04	.00	−.08	.00	+.20	+.08	+.40	+.03	−.03	−.04	.00	.00	.00	−.04	.00	−.03	−.27	−.07	+.03
■	.00	.00	+.10	.00	−.17	.00	+.32	+.09	+.33	+.05	−.17	−.06	.00	.00	.00	−.04	−.30	−.03	−.27	−.11	−.04
	■	.00	.00	.00	.00	.00	.00	.00	.00	.00	.00	.00	.00	.00	.00	.00	.00	.00	.00	.00	.00
		■	.00	.00	.00	.00	.00	.00	.00	.00	.00	.00	.00	.00	.00	.00	.00	.00	.00	.00	.00
			■	.00	+.03	.00	+.91	+.40	−.04	−.06	−.16	+.51	.00	.00	.00	−.17	+.50	−.08	+.14	−.05	+.12
				■	.00	.00	.00	.00	.00	.00	.00	.00	.00	.00	.00	.00	.00	.00	.00	.00	.00
					■	.00	+.03	+.47	+.37	+.15	+.16	−.05	.00	.00	.00	+.29	−.08	+.21	+.16	+.32	+.39
						■	.00	.00	.00	.00	.00	.00	.00	.00	.00	.00	.00	.00	.00	.00	.00
							■	+.52	+.27	−.07	−.13	+.50	.00	.00	.00	−.12	+.62	−.14	+.16	+.05	+.10
								■	+.68	−.01	−.02	+.16	.00	.00	.00	+.11	+.41	+.01	.00	+.29	+.25
									■	−.05	+.06	−.06	.00	.00	.00	+.02	+.31	−.05	+.02	+.42	+.21
										■	+.28	−.35	.00	.00	.00	+.17	−.47	−.26	+.27	−.08	+.15
											■	−.23	.00	.00	.00	+.03	−.32	+.22	+.32	+.04	+.08
												■	.00	.00	.00	−.19	.95	−.17	+.21	−.06	−.03
													■	.00	.00	.00	.00	.00	.00	.00	.00
														■	.00	.00	.00	.00	.00	.00	.00
															■	−.67	−.01	+.21		−.02	−.02
																■	−.96	+.42		−.12	−.17
																	■	−.08		.00	−.11
																		■		+.31	+.07
																				■	+.41
																					■

Table 83. *Sample of officers in army, navy and air-force*

Variables	A. Research cluster													
	1	2	3	4	5	6	7	8	9	10	11	12	13	14
A. Research cluster														
1. Family name	■	−.05	.08	.00	.00	.05	.02	−.07	.20	−.10	.04	.00	−.17	−.16
2. Age		■	.29	.00	.00	.05	.15	.01	.33	.04	.34	.00	.14	.07
3. Academic performance			■	.00	.00	.07	−.05	.52	.40	.52	.49	.00	.25	.12
4. University loyalty I				■	.00	.00	.00	.00	.00	.00	.00	.00	.00	.00
5. University loyalty II					■	.00	.00	.00	.00	.00	.00	.00	.00	.00
6. Father's social class						■	.00	.08	.19	.07	.12	.00	.15	.05
7. Place of residence							■	−.04	.10	.00	.10	.00	.08	.08
8. Status according to encyclopedias								■	.21	.97	.18	.00	.19	−.02
9. Number of lines									■	.19	.41	.00	.54	.06
10. Number of reference books										■	.22	.00	.21	−.02
11. Academies etc.											■	.00	.29	.22
12. Swedish honorary doctor's degrees												■	.00	.00
13. Government committees													■	−.06
14. Memberships in research councils														■
15. Enumerated international commissions														
16. Foreign guest professorships														
17. Academic positions														
18. Published works														
19. Name of doctor's thesis given in 'Vem är det'														
20. Distinctions														
21. Foreign honorary doctor's degrees														
22. Researcher's status														
23. General status														
24. Academic power														

B. Family cluster
  25. Number of marriages
  26. Number of children
  27. Educational level of the subject's wife
  28. Number of years between first examination and appointment to full professor
  29. Age at doctor's dissertation
  30. Age at appointment to full professor
  31. Income
  32. Income of the subject's wife
  33. Imminence between first marriage and first child
  34. Imminence between first and second child

C. Social cluster
  35. Number of clubs
  36. Number of hobbies